GOD
OF THE
EMPTY-HANDED

GOD
OF THE
EMPTY-HANDED

*Poverty, Power
and the Kingdom of God*

JAYAKUMAR CHRISTIAN

A division of World Vision
800 West Chestnut Avenue, Monrovia, California 91016-3198 USA

ISBN 1–887983–13–9

MARC books are published by World Vision, 800 W. Chestnut Avenue, Monrovia, California 91016–3198, U.S.A.

Printed in the United States of America. Editor and typesetter: Joan Weber Laflamme. Cover design: J. Nils Lindstrom. Cover photo: Sanjay Sojwal, World Vision.

This book is printed on recycled paper.

Dedicated to my wife and best friend,
Vidhu,
And our loving children and partners,
Jayanth and Vikram

Contents

Foreword

The Bible is packed with numerous injunctions and commands calling the people of God to minister to the foreigner, alien, fatherless, widow and poor in their midst. Such ministry on the part of the church is not optional—it is commanded by our Lord. Much has been written by people from all the various Christian traditions encouraging the church to seriously commit itself to participate in the mission of Jesus: "To preach good news to the poor, . . . proclaim freedom for the prisoners, . . . [seek] recovery of sight for the blind, to release the oppressed, and to proclaim the year of the Lord's favor" (Luke 4:18-19, NIV).

Until now, however, those of us who teach missions have been sorely handicapped by the absence of scholarly, compassionate and readable text that focuses on the poor, powerless, oppressed and marginalized. At long last, Jayakumar Christian has provided us with just such a work.

Christian's writing is no ivory tower theorizing. He draws from his heritage in India and allows his reflection to flow from his more than 30 years of experience ministering among the poor. His teaching, mobilizing and writing have been shaped by his ministry, primarily in India, with World Vision. He knows his topic well, and he demonstrates outstanding depth of wisdom in his vision of mission among, with and through the poor. He shows a profound personal relationship with "the God of the Empty-Handed." And the suggestions he makes for responding to the powerlessness of the poor are practical, contextually appropriate, empowering and transformational. These derive from Christian's wide-ranging familiarity with a broad spectrum of perspectives on the matter of poverty.

Several years ago, it was my joy to sit with Jayakumar Christian over the course of 40 weeks in a doctoral seminar from which flowed a book that Jude Tiersma and I edited, *God So Loves the City* (MARC, 1994). That book includes a chapter by Dr. Christian, "Toward Redefining

Urban Poverty." My life was enriched, my perspective enlarged and my heart challenged through the in-depth interaction of those months.

This book has a unique contribution to make to the field of mission among the poor. Here is a profoundly disturbing, yet refreshingly clear view of reality as seen through the eyes of the poor. And what we see, Christian teaches us, is that poverty is made up of a number of "domains" of powerlessness. Powerlessness at every level of existence is the issue. Christian mission, then, should involve an interdisciplinary search for appropriate responses to the challenge of the powerlessness of the poor.

The book is divided into three parts: "Learning from History," "Learning from the Poor," and "Learning About the Kingdom of God." Part One should some day be published as a book in its own right. It gives a thorough yet concise overview of the Christian response to poverty—one of the best I have ever seen.

In Part Two Christian challenges his readers to look at reality through the eyes of the poor. What we see is a deeply moving picture of powerlessness permeating a number of "domains" of the life of the poor. "Poverty is about power relationships," Christian affirms. Dr. Christian deals with the poor not as objects of our mission, but as fully human subjects who represent a unique challenge, valued and loved persons whose worldview is shaped by power relationships. Here Christian shows how the poor can teach us about their world. In doing so, he breaks new ground in the subject and offers us another step forward beyond the older confines of discussions about evangelism and social action that have plagued evangelical missiology for the past half-century.

Part Three is full of creative and practical suggestions as to how we can allow a "kingdom of God" missiology to guide us toward appropriate responses to the powerlessness of the poor. Here the reader will find a holistic, integral, ecological approach to issues of mission among the poor, a way around the sometimes reductionist, myopic, often paternalistic pitfalls experienced by Christian mission among the poor. Christian calls for approaches that address simultaneously the physical, socioeconomic, relational and spiritual domains of poverty's worldview.

Who should read this book? Insights in this book will be very helpful for pastors of churches all over the world, Christian relief and development workers, short-term and long-term cross-cultural missionaries, Christians involved in mission in the cities of our globe, rural and urban evangelists, and students of missiology. This book should become a basic text in mission courses in Bible schools, seminaries and mission training programs around the world.

Jayakumar Christian has helped me to rethink the way I understand mission among the poor. He has broadened my horizons, challenged my perceptions, and touched my heart. I am deeply grateful for his ministry to me through this work. May we who are the people of the God of the Empty-handed commit ourselves more fully to living out the mission of Jesus Christ in responding to the powerlessness of the poor.

CHARLES VAN ENGEN
ARTHUR F. GLASSER PROFESSOR
OF BIBLICAL THEOLOGY OF MISSION
FULLER THEOLOGICAL SEMINARY
PASADENA, CALIFORNIA

Acknowledgments

This book would have been impossible without the grace and faithfulness of God. The guidance, prayers and care of many enabled me to see the fruits of this investment.

I am grateful to God for the mentor committee at Fuller Theological Seminary that guided me through this endeavor. Their willingness to enter into dialogue with me as I grappled with issues was a special source of encouragement. Edgar J. Elliston helped me time and again in difficult situations. His detailed critique and caring support were great sources of affirmation. I enjoyed rich times of reflection with Charles Van Engen. His thought-provoking dialogue on my research was most encouraging. I am also grateful to Paul E. Pierson for his pastoral care and encouragement, and for sharing lessons from his years of experience and rich insights on mission and movements.

I am indebted to two others with whom I had the privilege of working during the course of my study. Samuel T. Kamaleson, former vice-president at large at World Vision, was a pastor to me during my stay in the United States. I am specially indebted to Charles Kraft for his interest in me even before I began my study and for his prayer support through my years at Fuller Seminary.

Viggo Sogaard's concern for my welfare triggered the whole process of study at Fuller. I am also indebted to Nancy Thomas, research librarian at Fuller's School of World Mission, who patiently read my dissertation and guided me through its final stages.

Apart from these, there were many whose friendship and input made this process of reflection a rich time: Dean Hirsch, president; Watt Santatiwat, vice-president, Asia Region; the late Joan Levett, then vice-president, ministry and partnership support; and Bryant Myers, vice president of ministry (all of World Vision). Apart from financial support, their interest in this work was very encouraging. I am specially grateful to Dean Hirsch and Joan Levett for the caring support they provided for my family and me as we pursued the course set before us. I am indebted to World Vision India for allowing me the time and space to pursue this study. I am indebted to colleagues in the field who were patient with me as they mentored me through their experiences.

I am also grateful to other friends who stood by us as a family during my time at Fuller: Jim Brown, Jan Thornton, John Steward, Steve Commins, John Key, John Robb, Frank Cookingham and George Marhad. I would also like to thank the First Fruit Foundation and World Vision for their financial support.

I could not have done much without the support of my family. I am grateful to God for my late parents. My mother, who has since gone to be with the Lord, stood by us with her constant prayers and love. Our larger family—our brothers and sisters and their families—stood by us and encouraged us throughout this study. Finally, I am grateful to God for my wife and children. My wife and friend, Vidhu, was my companion, my critic and a caring spouse throughout. She was very much a part of—and edited—this study. Our children, Jayanth and Vikram, prayed for me and allowed me to take time that legitimately belonged to them for my study. My family stood with me through various moments of personal powerlessness that were part of this time of study.

My special thanks to Edna Valdez of World Vision Publications, Rebecca Russell and Joan Laflamme, who have very painstakingly gone through this manuscript and invested great effort to convert this academic material into a more readable form. My sincere thanks to them for their patience throughout this process.

It is my sincere trust that this book will be a blessing.

Introduction

Over the years, the issue of poverty has challenged the best minds both at the grassroots level and among academicians. Concerns about poverty have moved back and forth from policy books to manifestos of political parties. Experts have developed many theories to "explain" poverty. Several scales, indices and tools have also been developed to "measure" this complex phenomenon.

However, poverty with all its complexities has remained a major challenge both to the church and to the world. It defies easy solutions and responses. This study is a search for an alternative response to the powerless poor.

In this search I have opted to start with *stories* about the poor and power for three specific reasons and as an intentional part of my methodology. First, stories have a way of capturing the human dimensions of poverty. Poverty is and always will be a human phenomenon. In spite of all the efforts to reduce it to a mere statistic or a concept, its human face can never be wished away. Others have used stories of the poor and the oppressed in their writings, although they do not consciously reflect on the methodological implications of such an approach (see Oscar Lewis's *Five Families;* Peter Berger's *Pyramids of Sacrifice;* and, more recently, Frances O'Gorman's *Charity and Change*). However, there is need to develop the value of story as a valid methodological framework for exegeting the context and theologizing for mission, building on insights gained from narrative theology. To be rigorous in its processing, this should be more than a simple "reading" of the context.

Next, stories serve as windows for larger inquiry into the issue of poverty and powerlessness. "Human beings need story, symbol, image, myth and fiction to disclose to their imaginations some genuinely new possibilities which conceptual analysis, committed as it is to understanding present actualities, cannot adequately provide" (Tracy 1988, 207; also see Walsh 1987, 9–10).

Third, this theological inquiry must be in close interaction with human reality, and stories provide that setting. For "if God is not spoken of in relation to man's experience of himself and his world, then theology withdraws into a ghetto and the reality with which man has to do, is abandoned to godlessness" (Moltmann 1967, 89). Therefore, this study begins with stories of human reality.

Scenarios of Power

Three views of power shape the lives of the poor and the mission of the church among the poor. First, the understanding of power among the powerless, then the perception of the powerful and finally the view from the kingdom of God.[1] The liberation theologians suggest that the "praxis of solidarity" with the oppressed is the starting point of all liberation theology (Gutiérrez 1988, xxx). By starting with the poor, I am not suggesting that the context of mission will shape my biblical reflection or serve as a criterion for interpreting the Bible. However, these stories about the poor serve as a much-needed reminder of the social, cultural, religious and political realities that have compelled me to embark on this search for an alternative response to the poor and their condition. They also raise new questions, as I read and reflect on the Scriptures. In that limited sense this is a theology "from below." However, this study is built on the belief that the Scriptures "have primacy over practice [or pathos of poverty situation] and determine what correct practice [or what should be done to correct the poverty situation] is . . . in order to make the man of God 'equipped for every good work' (2 Tim. 3:17)" (Volf 1983, 11–19; also see Van Engen 1993, 29–35).

Therefore, I have opted to begin my process of inquiry at the very doorstep of poverty with a story about a community of the powerless.

A View from Among the Poor

The Harijans of Mogalliwakkam live 12 miles from Madras, the fourth-largest metropolitan region in India. In a semi-urban village tucked away from the main road, as are most lower castes, the Harijans have been a community of landless agricultural laborers since time immemorial. "God has willed that we should be agricultural coolies and live on the income we get through our hard labor," explained a Harijan.

Harijan literally means the "children of God." However, over the years, the term has come to mean the lower caste and the outcastes.

Although these Harijans did not own the land, it had always been their sacred workplace.[2] Mogalliwakkam has 400 families. Traditionally, this village has been an agriculture-based community. Agricultural land in the area was owned mostly by the higher-caste Mudaliars. Although the Harijans did not own the agricultural land on which they worked, they "belonged" to it. But over the years Mogalliwakkam has undergone changes that have shaken the very foundation of community life. With agricultural land being sold at very high prices for housing construction, the economic base and employment profile of the village slid drastically. The landless do not have a say in the sale of their land, even though it is their work at stake.

The Madras Metropolitan Development Authority, in its effort to relieve congestion in nearby Madras, permitted the elite from Madras to buy agricultural land in Mogalliwakkam for housing.

> Now there is not much of an agricultural operation. . . . We do not produce paddy anymore; we are forced to buy rice from the market and it is expensive (Selvam, a community leader from Mogalliwakkam).[3]

Madras is taking over this small agricultural community. The factory owners bring in skilled laborers from other states. Once the people of Mogalliwakkam were called skilled laborers, but now they are considered unskilled laborers and have to wait by the highway to be picked up and hired for daily wages. "Our workplace, the agricultural land, has been taken over by the new factories. We are not wanted in these factories," stated a community leader in Mogalliwakkam. Even when they are hired, they are paid low wages. These former agricultural laborers are now helping skilled masons. They are gradually being alienated from the land they belonged to. Today, their agricultural tools lie silent in the dark corners of their houses, reminding them that they have become tools in the hands of the urban elite.

What does poverty mean in this context? Is poverty merely the sum of low per capita income, a state of being below the poverty line, lack of basic needs, backwardness, lack of access and control, increased environmental degradation, and large family size? What poverty theories and mission paradigms help us fully understand the experiences of the poor in Mogalliwakkam? Could "power" serve as an integrating motif[4] to explain the relationship between these forces and poverty? What does power and powerlessness mean for the poor in Mogalliwakkam? How should the church respond to the powerlessness of the landless in Mogalliwakkam?

A View from Among the Non-Poor

Josiprasda is a typical village in the Gatapar area,[5] Raipur district. It is a heterogeneous community of Brahmins, Purnis, Chandrakars, Chamars, Satnamis, fisher folk, and the Tellis or Sahu (names of different castes in Josiprasda village.) The Satnamis in the area worship Saint Kasidas, an untouchable who demonstrated the power of truth. They believe that Kasidas unites them and that their beliefs are not as divisive as those of other religions.

The nearest primary health center for this community is 17 kilometers away. There is a middle school in the village (up to grade eight). The children have to travel far to reach the nearest high school. For this and other reasons, the girls from this village do not attend high school. Only two individuals from Josiprasda attend college. The village is cut off from other villages and towns during the monsoon season.

The "non-poor"[6] in Josiprasda have been successful in excluding the poor from the mainstream of society. The major political parties of the state have a strong presence in the area, but as one of the villagers pointed out, "Because of the corrupt politics we are unable to sit along with our brothers. . . . The leaders are rich . . . and we do not have honest leaders to represent us." The Sahus are the landless laborers of this village. They are paid 10 to 12 rupees (the equivalent of 30 to 40 cents) as wages for a day. A villager in nearby Belvetta village explaining this remarked, "We work every day just to earn some money for food. . . . We cannot save. If we start any business the higher castes will boycott us and we will fail."

In Josiprasda a few landlords and landless farmers like Asha Ram and Toli Ram wanted to farm on the government wasteland (common property resource). However, the landlords, with the help of the local police, evicted these landless laborers and took them to court. The case was only against these landless laborers. Their appeals for justice were always denied by the officials with a comment, "You do not even have money to buy a copy of the constitution. . . . How can you get justice?" Describing their plight, one of the villagers from Belvetta commented, "We do not even have the money to garland *Murthy* (a Hindu deity)— how can we garland the ministers and the MLAs (local elected politicians)?"

What does "power" mean for the rich and the powerful in Josiprasda? What is the relationship between power and intergenerational poverty here? These and other such experiences have caused the poor in Josiprasda and the Belvetta area to conclude that God is on the side of the rich. What does it mean to "be the church" among the powerless poor who perceive that God is involved in perpetuating their powerlessness? This study is built on the premise advanced by David Bosch that "the contemporary world challenges us to practice a 'transformational hermeneutics' . . . a theological response which transforms us first before we involve ourselves in mission to the world" (Bosch 1991, 189).

A View from the Throne

The perception of power that the local church among the poor often grapples with is the expression of power seen at the throne in the hereafter, as narrated in passages such as Revelation 5.

The hereafter (the vision of the future) is a key and determining point of reference in this inquiry into the relationship between the kingdom of God and power. It is the hereafter that represents the "already—not yet" nature of the kingdom of God.

The kingdom of God and the vision of the future as shaped by the kingdom of God "molds and determines the content of our mission" (Samuel 1987, 148). As Jacques Ellul points out, "All facts acquire their value in the light of the coming Kingdom of God" (Ellul 1989, 37). There are three specific reasons for focusing on the future model (the hereafter):

1. An examination of the hereafter and a missional response to the powerless based on a vision of the future will surely enable missions to move away from mere reactionism. Very often facts and figures about the poor are so compelling that we are urged to react or pursue empty pragmatism. Ultimately we end up "formulat[ing] our theories and imperatives of development on our assumptions about the future . . . [without checking] against God's plan for the future" (Sinclair 1987, 161).

2. By beginning with the future, we affirm the fact that the future of God has already invaded the present. In the Old Testament understanding of time, there was no cleavage between present history and the eschatological future. Wolfhart Pannenberg rejects the idea that the futurity of God's kingdom implies that God is developing. Instead, Pannenberg affirms that "the notion of the futurity of God and His Kingdom most emphatically does not 'remove' God and the future. . . . Quite to the contrary, as the power of the future he dominates the remotest past" (Pannenberg 1968, 62) and the present. Tomorrow's kingdom has invaded the today.

3. Beginning with the future brings the faith dimension to the process of reflection and action. When we mold an alternative paradigm for responding to the powerless based on the kingdom of God, we are not merely making a mechanical logical choice. We go beyond. We make a faith claim. We believe the future as perceived in Scripture is of such determining value that we allow that future to shape our present responses to the powerless poor. Only by faith can we please God (Heb. 11:6). "Faith does not wait for God's sovereignty to be established on earth; it behaves as if the sovereignty already holds full sway" (Wink 1992, 323). For these reasons this study surveys the future vision of the throne—the shape of things to come.

This portrayal of the throne is one of the many descriptions contained in the book of Revelation. Indeed, Revelation is "preoccupied with the problems of power" (Prior 1987, 172).[7]

Power and the Slain Lamb

The view from the throne in Revelation 5 provides several clues for understanding power in the kingdom of God. Following are some brief reflections on power as seen from the throne in this passage.

First, power as understood in the kingdom of God will reverse the so-called natural order and the popular understanding of power. In Revelation 5:5 the elder announces that the Lion of Judah is entering to open the scroll. The curtain is drawn and in walks the "little lamb" (v. 6).

The Greek word for lamb—*arnion*—will appear twenty-nine times in Revelation; strictly translated, *arnion* should be given as "*little lamb*" because the Greek here is diminutive (Palmer 1982, 166).

Reflecting on this, Leon Morris observes,

> When earth-bound men want symbols of power they conjure up mighty beasts and birds of prey. Russia elevates the bear, Britain the lion, France the tiger, the United States the spread of the eagle—all of them ravenous (1987, 94).

In India the symbol of power is the tiger. However, in the kingdom of God the symbol of power is this "little lamb," a slain lamb. Power as expressed from the throne is not just different, it reverses the popular understanding of power.

> The lordship of Christ is not grounded on military might, but on sacrificial love. It is not oppressive and emasculating, but creative and liberating. It is not totalitarian, but communal and fraternal. It facilitates the formation of a new community on the basis of love and service (Costas 1982, 9).

This pattern of reversal is evident throughout Scripture. For example, the very idea of the Lamb on the throne is a reversal. In Revelation 7:17 we see the Lamb at the center of the throne; later, the Lamb "will be their shepherd, and he will guide them to springs of the water of life." We see this description of the throne and its power arrangement as contradictory to "normal" images. We see a Lamb in the center, a Lamb becoming the shepherd, and finally a Lamb leading God's people to the springs of the water of life. "The verb *poimanei* (lead) is normally associated with a shepherd, and it is an unusual word to use for a lamb. It makes for a complete reversal of roles" (Morris 1969, 118). After all, this same lamb earlier in salvation history was the One that was "led to the slaughter, and like a sheep that before its shearers is silent" (Isa. 53:7). Therefore, this view from the throne suggests that in the hereafter, when the kingdom of God comes in its final glory, there will be reversals in the natural order and the popular understanding of power.

Second, in the kingdom of God the slain Lamb is the paradigm of power. The passage in Revelation also presents the Lamb as the "slain One." The slain One is found worthy (5:9, 12) and is described as the One who has conquered (5:5). "His worthiness is now not reckoned in terms of his power or the majesty of His Person, but of His death for us" (Morris 1969, 97). The slain Lamb is a worthy expression of power. The slain Lamb reverses the world's understanding of power to make it look like powerlessness.

Third, power in the kingdom will include all. Earlier, Jesus said, "Blessed are you who are poor, for yours is the kingdom of God" (Luke 6:20). However, when the kingdom of God is finally fulfilled we see that the kingdom will comprise "every tribe and language and people and nation." This is John's way of saying *all* people (Rev. 5:9).

> The universal scope of redemption is brought out by piling up expressions to show that the redeemed come from no restricted group but from all over the world (Morris 1987, 97).

This kingdom of God, which Jesus said belongs to the poor, will, at the end of time, include all. How could this happen? The poor and powerless, who are excluded from the kingdoms of today, will have the unique joy of seeing every tribe and language and people and nation included in the kingdom of God. Following through this insight from the throne, we have a third clue about the kingdom's understanding of power. The kingdom of God affirms that power should always be relational and inclusive.

Finally, in the kingdom of God all expressions of power will affirm the theocentric nature of the kingdom. The slain Lamb in Revelation 5 will purchase and make us into priests and a kingdom so that we may serve God. In the kingdom economy, "Redemption is not aimless; [people] are bought so that they may belong to God" (Cf. 1 Corinthians 6:19–20)" (Morris 1987, 97). Again, we are redeemed to be a kingdom and priests for "serving our God" (Rev. 5:10). In the kingdom of God, serving precedes reigning. Here then is the fourth clue from the throne. All power, according to the kingdom of God, will be directed toward God. All power will belong to God (Ps. 62:11).

Therefore, in the kingdom of God power will reverse the natural order, reverse the world's understanding of power, be relational and always affirm that power belongs to God. Power expressed here at the throne is transformational (Rev. 5:9, 10), is worthy of a new song (Rev. 5:9, 12),[8] and is the final understanding of power (Rev. 11:17).

Overview

These three scenarios—from the perspectives of the poor, the non-poor and the throne of God—suggest at least three conflicting views of power evident in poverty situations. One is the deep-seated powerlessness of the poor, as in Mogalliwakkam. Second is the different expressions of power among the non-poor in communities like Josiprasda. Finally, for the church in mission among the poor, there is also the determining understanding of power as seen in the kingdom of God.

These three scenarios of power raise a number of questions. How will the understanding of power as seen from the throne critique the other two views of power? How will it transform the understanding and experience of powerlessness of the poor? How will the kingdom of God transform the very nature of power that keeps the poor powerless?

Any inquiry into poverty must involve a study of many disciplines (Max-Neef 1989, 18ff.). Therefore, we will seek here to apply insights from the fields of anthropology, sociology, politics, as well as Hinduism and Christian theology to inform and shape the inquiry into the meaning of powerlessness. However, this study intentionally avoids developing the alternative paradigm merely on the basis of insights from history or from the context of powerlessness. Neither history nor powerlessness nor culture nor an understanding of the role of principalities and powers can provide the basis for developing an alternative response to powerlessness. Only an understanding of the view of power from the throne (kingdom of God) can provide the foundation for adequate response to the powerless.

In the context of these three scenarios of power, Part One of this book examines different paradigms of poverty that governed historical reflections and responses. It explores reflections of secular development theorists; liberation, Dalit and evangelical theologians; and responses of several historical and contemporary ministries. Part Two, based on insights from history, inquires into the meaning of powerlessness. Part Three is a search for an alternative response, specifically exploring the understanding of power in theology of the kingdom of God to construct this alternative response to the powerlessness of the poor.

In concluding, I examine key themes for constructing a kingdom of God-based paradigm and guidelines for reequipping local practitioners and the local church for responding to the powerlessness of the poor.

The Study

Sifting through the stories of communities like Mogalliwakkam and Josiprasda, one is struck by the fact that powerlessness has become synonymous with poverty.

Consequently, power has become an inescapable part of the context of mission. David Bosch comments:

> Even more important was the entire area of *power*. It became clear that, deep down, this was the real issue, and that authentic development could not take place without the transfer of power (1991, 357).

Issues of power have become primary in all poverty situations, and the church among the poor is called to respond in a new and a more effective way.

The Alternative Paradigm

How do we equip the poor to become agents of transformation instead of being mere recipients of transformation? Underlying our commitment to do so is the belief that missional involvement among the poor must equip the church to trigger movements with the poor as the key agents of transformation.

Reflections on the alternative paradigm presented in this book are based on the fundamental belief that the grassroots practitioners among the poor are the "hermeneutical community." This community of grassroots practitioners is a network of persons with strong commitments, shared examples and shared values. They possess wisdom critical for the task of responding to the powerless poor. They own the primary responsibility to construct the paradigm for their own response. In this sense, the present study can only serve as the "directions for map making" (Kuhn 1970, 109); it cannot provide a map.

Reflections in the concluding chapter on an alternative paradigm raise questions for the grassroots practitioners about how to construct maps relevant to their part in God's mission. The chapter specifically raises questions about their perception of the reality of poverty and powerlessness. It enables the community of practitioners to reevaluate the facts that have shaped past missional involvement.

Apart from raising questions, reflections in the concluding chapter also offer alternative operational definitions for concepts common among grassroots practitioners among the poor: sustainability, empowerment and transformation. It also proposes key themes for analyzing poverty situations.

Finally, the alternative paradigm also contributes to the self-definition (reequipping) of grassroots practitioners as they respond to the powerlessness of the poor. Transformation of the church and the grassroots practitioners must take place even as we seek to transform the lives of others. We, too, must be reequipped even as we respond to the powerless poor.

Some Definitions

I have used a few terms that need defining at the outset.

Hindu refers to practitioners of popular Hinduism. While examining the role of worldview in poverty situations, it was necessary to focus on a particular group of people. Hence, the study examined popular Hinduism as a case in point rather than philosophical Hinduism.

Power is defined as the capacity of some persons within a social relationship to be in a position to carry out their own will toward creating intended and foreseen effects on others despite resistance.

Poverty relationships is used in the study to mean the various relationships within poverty situations that affect the poor, their households and their communities. However, the term *poverty relationships* does not suggest an evaluation of the quality of relationships. It is only a description of the many socioeconomic, political, bureaucratic and religious relationships in poverty situations.

Worldview is understood to be the set of assumptions, values and commitments/allegiances that have shaped the perceptions and responses of the poor and non-poor involved in poverty relationships.

Principalities and powers is used to mean the fallen forces of the kingdom of Satan who are personal cosmic powers. They challenge God's purposes for God's creation by exercising dominating influences on persons and structures.

Scope and Limitations

While gathering data on contemporary approaches to the poor, the study focuses on the assumptions about poverty that governed the church's response to the poor. Field study was not designed to gather data about the poor or the whole theology of mission of the church. The focus was specifically on understanding the church's assumptions about poverty or the church's theology of poverty.

Finally, this study recognizes that there is more than one kingdom theology; there are ecumenical, Roman Catholic, Eastern Orthodox, and evangelical theologies of the kingdom. However, due to my understanding of Christian faith, the nature of ministry that I am involved in and the kinds of groups that I interact with in the various ministries among the poor in India, this inquiry confines itself to foundations of evangelical theology on the kingdom of God without examining the richness that is available in other Christian traditions.

Notes

[1] This study is the summary of a process of interaction among three interlocking aspects of mission: the context of poverty; biblical and theological reflections; and, finally, historical reflections of the church (the faith community) on issues related to poverty and missional response among the poor (see Van Engen 1993, 30).

[2] About 12 of the Harijans in this village are Christians, while the rest are Hindus. The village has one temple each for Mariamman and Venkatesaperumal. There is a Church of South India within the village and an Evangelical Church of India outside the community that serves the Christians in this village. The agricultural laborers earned 15 to 20 rupees (approx. US 50–60 cents) a day. The higher-caste Mudaliars live in the village adjacent to Mogalliwakkam colony. Mogalliwakkam has a government grade school where 600 children study. The nearest high school is three miles away, which only 25 to 30 children from Mogallliwakkam attend; only 12 children from Mogalliwakkam make it to the college located in Madras.

[3] The interviews and the data on the Mogalliwakkam community were gathered during my field study in July 1992.

[4] Throughout this book, I have used the idea of *integrating motif* as a way of inquiring into the whole, without being reductionistic or fragmentary. The concept of integrating motif affirms that powerlessness is only a part of the larger phenomenon called poverty. It also avoids the danger of reducing all of poverty to this single theme of powerlessness and keeps the whole process and the conclusions integrative.

[5] AWAZ, a Christian organization, is working in Josiprasda and 20 other villages in the area.

[6] I use the term *non-poor* to refer to the rich and the middle class. This term does not assume any oppressive relationship, unless specified.

[7] There are different perceptions of power in the Bible. The Exodus event presents power as God's liberating power. The royal tradition saw power as the ability to change the course of history. The sages saw power as stewardship of earthly power here and now, and the priests saw power as the root of all uncleanness and sin (Weber 1989, 167). The life of Jesus Christ, Pauline teaching on power and a detailed word study on power, authority and dominion are also required for understanding scriptural teaching on power.

Within the book of Revelation there are several images of power. Jesus is described as the coming judge, the rider on the white horse and so on. However, all through the book of Revelation the author consistently points to the "Lamb on the throne" as the defining image to refer to Jesus Christ. Further, the Lamb does not contradict the image of the judge or the other images referred to in the book of Revelation.

[8] The word *new* is a predominant theme in the New Testament. Charles Van Engen in his survey of the "covenant theme" suggests that the more popular concept is the term *kainos*. Van Engen suggests that *kainos* refers to *new* as being continuous with the past but an enrichment of the past understanding. Van Engen then proposes that understanding *new* as the "continuous but enriched" idea also implies that there is contextualization (Van Engen 1989, 86–88).

New is also a common theme in the Book of Revelation. It applies to the new name (2:17; 3:12), to the new Jerusalem (3:12; 21:2), to the new heaven and the new earth (21:1), and finally there is the resounding declaration that God makes all things new (21:5). "In so far as the Greek term *Kainos* can be differentiated from the other word new, *neos* (which does not occur in Revelation), it signifies 'fresh' as against 'recent.' It is concerned with quality rather than date" (Morris 1987, 96).

PART ONE

LEARNING FROM HISTORY

Poverty is a complex human phenomenon. It is a value-loaded concept involving evaluative judgments regarding minimum standards, basic needs and desired levels of living.

Development theorists and missiologists have sought to better understand poverty by classifying it using different criteria. *Poverty situation* has been classified as that which "afflicts the few or in any case the minority in some societies . . . [and] . . . that afflicts all but a few in other societies" (Galbraith 1979, 1). There is the concept of relative poverty over against the notion of absolute poverty.

The 1980 report of the World Bank defines "absolute poverty" as "a condition of life so characterized by malnutrition, illiteracy and disease as to be beneath any reasonable definition of human decency." Relative poverty on the other hand involves maldistribution of assets, income and power (World Bank 1980, 32).

Peter Townsend has suggested that the community—local, national or international—be the reference point for defining relative poverty (S. P. Gupta 1987, 11). Moralists have divided poverty into two types: the deserving type and the non-deserving (ibid., 23ff.).

Biblical scholars, based on different descriptives used in the Bible, classify the poor as follows:

1. The poor who lack basics for living—mostly bread, water (Hebrew *chaser*);
2. The poor who have been dispossessed through acts of injustice or lack of diligence (Hebrew *yarash*);
3. The poor who are frail and weak (Hebrew *Dal* or *dallah*);
4. The poor who are needy and dependent (Hebrew *ebyon*);
5. The poor who have been oppressed or afflicted (Hebrew *Ani* and *anau*). Sometimes *ani* is also used to mean the humble (Perkins 1987, 34–35; also see LCWE 1980).

Part One is divided into three groups of global reflections on poverty:

1. reflections of various development theorists (chapter 1),
2. reflections of liberation and Dalit theologians (chapter 2), and
3. reflections of evangelical theologians as reflected in the journey from Wheaton '66 to the Oxford Conference on Faith and Economics '90 (chapter 3).

1

Development Theories
and Poverty Assumptions

A large number of poverty debates in the past have been based on a single-variable analysis of poverty. The focus has either been on resources and income, calorie intake, literacy, structure or other such variables. Further, poverty was considered essentially a matter for measurement and analysis. It was assumed that by reducing the complex phenomenon of poverty to numbers, the policy-makers, managers of development and politicians could "compare, reduce and control" poverty.[1] The following are brief descriptions and analyses of major assumptions about poverty that shaped these different efforts to measure and explain poverty.

The Poor Lack Resources

A logical starting point for any analysis of poverty is that poverty essentially is "lack of resources." This assumption guided policy formulations of governments and development interventions for years. As V. B. Dandekar and Nilankath Rath suggest, in the "rural areas, an important cause of poverty is lack of land resources" (1971, 14). This would include lack of capital equipment, low investments and landlessness (Bajaj 1985, 87). The "poor are poor, because they lack capital" (Galbraith 1979, 10).

Based on this assumption about poverty, per capita income became a key variable for measuring poverty. Consequently, progress and development became synonymous with economic growth.[2] Early models of development emphasized per capita income, progress, transfer of resources and increase in the level of income. Development was measured based on its ability to

1. sustain rapid economic growth,
2. modify the pattern of economic growth so as to raise the productivity and income of the poor,
3. improve access of the poor to essential public services, and
4. maintain an international environment supportive of development (World Bank 1978, 65).

At macro and international levels, nations were categorized as poor if their capital, income and production were low. The Bretton Wood conference convened in New Hampshire (USA) by the International Monetary and Financial Conference of the United and Associated Nations responded by giving birth to the Bretton Wood "twins": the International Monetary Fund (IMF), and the International Bank for Reconstruction and Development (IBRD) or the World Bank (World Bank 1985, 15). Large lending and structural adjustments followed.

The United Nations Development Decades then followed suit to define development as economic development and poverty as lack of resources. The First UN Development Decade (1960s) focused on "accelerating progress toward self-sustaining growth."[3]

This emphasis on lack of resources, however, did not imply ignoring other needs of the poor. Lack of access to public services and the need for supportive services were also recognized. However, these were considered secondary to pursuit of the goal of economic growth.

Analysis

Defining poverty as lack of resources ignored other aspects of poverty. Let me briefly reflect on some of them.

First, economic growth resulted in increased inequalities. In communities and countries that reflected increase in income and growth, traditional inequalities of income, assets and power were reinforced (Bajaj 1985, 76). As Gunnar Myrdal points out:

Economic inequality—the unequal distribution of income and wealth, and consequently of economic power—raises some issues that are apt to be more controversial. It is commonly observed even by those who are supporters in principle of the idea of leveling, that historically economic development has often led to a greater concentration of wealth and power; sometimes the inference is drawn that this result is inevitable (Myrdal 1968, 766).

However, proponents of this view respond by pointing out that normally economic development strategies do not benefit the poor in the first few years (Berger 1974, 141; also see Berger's discussion on the capitalism that emerged from the Brazilian revolutions of 1964). They argue that there are long-term benefits for the poor in these economic development programs (World Bank 1985, 59). Active proponents of this view also suggest that wealth has to be created before it can be distributed equally (Berger 1974, 141). The wealth thus created, according to this view, would "trickle down" to those in the lower levels of society.[4] Another underlying assumption of this view about economic growth by "trickle down" was the belief that those who had the ability to develop would do well and progress. This variation of Darwin's theory of survival of the fittest was called Social Darwinism.[5]

Second, this view of poverty tended to exclude the landless and the "hidden poor" (Remenyi 1991, 1). Levels of production and per capita income levels were vital for applying this view of poverty. At the micro level, this meant that laborers in the unorganized sector[6] and the "hidden poor"—including women, the frail and children—were normally neglected.

Third, structural factors like market influence were not given adequate consideration. The market marginalized small farmers (whom I would include as the virtual landless) and especially those who owned small pieces of dry land with no irrigational facilities. The market was designed to exclude small producers. Their products were priced low, because of institutional bottlenecks (Bajaj 1985, 89). Consequently, these small farmers were compelled to sell their meager produce at a very low price (distress sale) and in the process move further down the steep path of poverty.

To summarize, early debates on the economics of being poor suggested that poverty is lack of adequate income, wealth, capital investment and the means to contribute to national income. However, growing inequalities, the exclusion of a large number of poor, the neglect of structural factors and other negative implications gave way to the theory of neocolonialism and dependence. On the other hand, this debate on economics of poverty set the stage for inquiry into the so-called poverty line and the subsequent emphasis on modernization.

The Poor Below the Poverty Line

Arthur Young was the first to use the concept of the poverty line. However, it was Charles Booth (1889) who first defined the term in his door-to-door surveys.[7]

Booth defined the poverty line as "an income level where 'means may be sufficient but are barely sufficient for independent life'" (see Jain 1987, 21). In India debates on the poverty line in the 1970s defined the poverty line primarily in economic terms.[8]

Gradually the definition moved from per capita income to include expenditure patterns and food intake (in calories). Discussion on expenditure patterns was based on what was needed to lead a full and fruitful life in society.

Analysis

At least four issues tend to be neglected by defining poverty using the poverty-line framework.

First, fixing the poverty line based on average national per capita income ignores the seasonal nature of income in rural areas, a serious problem (Bajaj 1985, 89). Seasonality also affects other aspects of the life of the poor. Exploitative relationships become stronger in the time between harvests.

> It is when the poorer people are driven to sell or mortgage land, livestock, jewelry, their future crop, or their future labor; they beg from patrons; they become indebted to money lenders (Chambers et al. 1984, 123).

Montek Ahluwalia concludes that there is "a pattern of fluctuation, with the incidence of poverty falling in periods of good agricultural performance and rising in periods of poor performance" (1977, 39).

However, debates on the poverty line appear to have paid scant attention to this issue.

Next, discussion on the poverty line tends to overemphasize measurability. It is, as Robert Chambers suggests, an expression of professionals' need to count (1988, i). In spite of this emphasis on measurability, it is not always easy to get data for analysis: (1) information for knowing the population's per capita income or expenditure is very difficult to obtain, (2) living standards vary from population to population, (3) different living standards lead to different conclusions, (4) there is a variance when income level is used and when expenditure pattern is considered, and finally, (5) there is fluctuation in financial resources through the year (Vyas and Samadani 1987, 10).

Third, use of calorie intake to calculate average expenditure level for a population ignores other non-food expenses. It also ignores variations in food habits in different regions. For example, the poor tend to focus on a narrow range of food grains and types (Vyas and Samadani 1987, 20).

Finally, the professional obsession with numbers and the tendency to reduce poverty to a single variant also reduces the poor to mere statistics. This then allows proponents of the poverty line to shift their attention to whether those statistics are on the rise or diminishing. As Malcolm Adiseshiah, an Indian economist, points out,

> We are fighting each other over the precise numbers of the poor living with us. The numbers involved will vary with the norm used . . . and the percentage could move a few points either way depending on the methodology used. But these definitional and methodological problems do not change the stark fact of the shocking magnitude of the poor . . . and the more human dimensions of genuine development (Desrochers and Joseph 1988, 84).

Basics for Living

Policy makers and development practitioners began to see that the different models of economic growth were not producing satisfactory results. Growth benefits were not trickling down to the poor. Frustrations with this revived special concern for the needs of the neediest.

In the late 1970s the policy-makers determined that the purpose of various national development strategies, international negotiations and global aid was

> to meet the human requirement of people, and especially the minimum needs of the neediest. . . . The appearance of "basic needs" at the center stage begins a new act in the continuing drama of World Development (McHale and McHale 1977, 3).

But questions arose about survival of the neediest. Many of the neediest were not economically productive, because they were struggling with survival issues. As Shamsuddin, a young farmer from Bangladesh whose land was ravaged by the 1991 cyclone, stated, "Right now it is an effort for me even to talk to you. How can I dig and shovel earth without food in my belly?" (Pratap 1991, 39). How can the poor raise income and contribute to the GNP, when they do not have food for survival and are unable to keep their life together? Hence, the question of basic needs was raised as a logical next step in the debate as well as a moral question (Doyal and Gough 1991, 153).

The concept of basic needs was first articulated by the International Labor Organization during the World Employment Conference in Geneva (1976). The World Bank also shifted its focus to basic needs but maintained an economic emphasis (Welsh 1990, 99). However, the basic needs concept served to bring theoretical explanation, moral persuasion and practical recommendations together and began with an effort to determine the desired level of living for the neediest.[9]

The UN Declaration of Human Rights was eventually used as a framework to define basic needs. Subsequently, desired levels of living included social security, education and other such rights. The International Definition and Measurement of Standards and Levels of Living (1954) prepared by the UN included in its list of basic needs health, food and nutrition, education and literacy, conditions of work, employment, consumption and savings, transportation, housing, clothing, recreation, social security and human freedoms (McHale and McHale 1977, 13). In 1957 the Indian Labor Conference laid down some standards while fixing the minimum wage. In its definition of "the minimum," the conference included food intake of calories for an average adult of moderate activity, clothing (18 yards per annum per head), rent for a minimum space prescribed by the government and fuel (ibid. 1977, 13). In these sorts of attempts the definition of human needs became broader and more clumsy.

To cope with these never-ending lists of basic needs, proponents of this view further categorized basic needs as "first-floor human needs" and "second-floor human needs." First-floor human needs include food, health and education, to which all who are born are entitled. The second level include those needs each nation-state can decide for its own people, within the context of the interdependence of all societies.

John McHale and Magda Cordell McHale categorized basic needs differently. They proposed that basic needs could be of three types: (1) deficiency needs, (2) sufficiency needs, and (3) growth needs. They defined deficiency needs as threshold needs that are mainly biophysical and necessary for survival. Those needs beyond a marginal level of survival they called sufficiency level needs. Growth needs, according to the McHales, were those beyond the sufficiency level and included enjoyment of nonmaterial ends and aspirations (1977, 30–31). However, according to John Friedmann, these basic needs were only a subset within the larger category called human needs (1984, 210).

On the whole, the debates on basic needs broadened the discussion on poverty into a multidisciplinary dialogue. Unfortunately, at the international level the timing for pushing this basic-needs agenda proved difficult: "It was the eve of the world debt crisis and the wave of neoliberalism which swept the world during the 1980s under which many basic human needs programs had to be cut in order to service the debt" (Hadjor 1992, 47).

Analysis

Critiques of basic needs point to several "gaps" in this theory of poverty.

First, if earlier discussions on lack of resources and the poverty line tended to reduce the complexity of poverty, this discussion of basic needs complicated the matter with its multiplicity of variants. No attempt is evident in the debate to aggregate the various pieces of the puzzle called basic needs.

Second, the basic needs model lacked analytical rigor. However, as Ralph van der Hoeven pointed out, the basic-needs model at least addressed distributional aspects and focused on the poor (1988, 17).

Third, the basic-needs model involved a high level of subjectivity. The question inevitably asked of the basic-needs approach is, Who decides what is basic? The question gradually led to emphasis on felt needs and people's participation in need identification. An effort arose to differentiate between the subjective (contextual needs) and the objective (universal needs). Len Doyal and Ian Gough suggested that human autonomy and health are the two most important objective or universal human needs (1991, 53, 59).[10]

Fourth, proponents of the economic-growth model pointed out that the basic-needs model took the focus off growth and therefore would subsequently retard growth.

Fifth, the basic-needs approach ignored class analysis and the structural causes of needs. The weaknesses of this understanding of poverty caused critics to look at the questions of structure and poverty and also of technology and poverty more carefully. Proponents of the New Economic Order (NEO) suggested that the basic-needs approach

- was a pragmatic approach to world poverty and lacked the depth that the NEO suggests,
- diverted attention from inequities within the world economic system, and
- ignored corruption, political instability and other structural defects that are inherent in the system (Welsh 1990, 99).

The Poor Are Backward

The next major assumption that shaped development response was that the poor are backward in their social and economic practices. Poverty is the result of using traditional techniques. Poor nations and communities lack "trained, educated or experienced technical and administrative talent" (Galbraith 1979, 10).

This assumption about poverty shaped the modernization of development. Rustow's *Stages of Economic Growth*[11] was based on a concern for the backwardness of the poor and poor nations. Rustow envisaged a take-off from a stationary state of development to an advanced state.[12] According to Rustow's theory, the poor need to move from their traditional state to the age of high mass consumption. By the end of the

1960s, modernization[13] was a "collection of rather different perspectives, in which neo-evolutionism, structural functionalism and diffusionism were all to be found" (Harrison 1988, 61).

At the micro level, this assumption about poverty implied that the poor were recipients of massive technology transfers and modern approaches. Modern-day neoliberals are a classic example of this view.[14] Transfer of modernization approaches involved preaching the ideals of planning and modernization. "It also represents, however, a rationalization by those who are much better off about how people living in utter poverty and deprivation should feel" (Myrdal 1968, 730). Proponents of this view preached that traditional poor communities need to have the right kind of policies and the right attitude in order to move toward an advanced society. Therefore, modernization and development were perceived to be results of the right "mindset"[15] that marked modernity.

However, modernization theorists focused on the nation-state relationship. Modernists believed there are dual societies. Consequently, modernization was defined as the influence of the modern sector or "growth pole" (industrial modernized enclaves), gradually radiating until rural, traditional environments (traditional underdeveloped communities) are transformed, economically, politically and socially (Harrison 1988, 59–60).

These assumptions about poverty shaped the development theories of the sixties.[16] Development theorists looked to the West to provide clues for the development of the poor.

Analysis

However, the "backwardness" frame did not answer many questions grassroots practitioners encountered among the poor.

First, the modernization approach was on the whole an ethnocentric reading of poverty. Engineers and economists were the high priests of modernity (Giri 1992, 286). At the micro level, development workers became the priests who administered this concept of modernity. Development communication strategies reflected these assumptions.[17] Consequently, the backwardness paradigm ignored the wisdom of the poor, often rural wisdom, and their history as a people. Even following Rustow's prescription for the undeveloped, this ethnocentric approach ignores the fact that each society may be at a different stage in development.

Second, by unlinking development from underdevelopment, this view also disregards structural causes of poverty, creating regional imbalances. K. C. Alexander, former director of the National Institute of Rural Development in India, points out that although government poverty-alleviation programs like the Intensive Agricultural Development Program[18] increased agricultural production, they also

> widened social disparity between the wealthier sections of society who could use the necessary inputs for agricultural production, and the poorer sections who could not (Alexander 1989, 73).

Third, the backwardness framework for explaining rural poverty disregards the "opportunity factor." Lack of technical knowledge and skills raises a prior question that must be considered before branding the poor as backward; namely, did the poor have the opportunity to acquire the skills and knowledge?

These assumptions about poverty do not pay adequate attention to the *context* of the "wrong choices" that the poor are accused of making. They overlook the fact that these choices are influenced by choices the non-poor make and are also shaped by the life experience and exposures of the poor.

Finally, the backwardness paradigm and the modernity prescription tend to prefer early innovators and risk-takers, over against the landless, who do not have the wherewithal to take a risk. Apart from benefiting the rich, focus on technology and improved methods tends to favor the few (Giri 1992, 289).

Structural Factors that Maintain Poverty

The growth that did not develop, the "trickle down" that did not happen, and the wealth that constantly moved toward the non-poor but was derailed by a skewed distribution system—all these caused much concern among development theoreticians and policy-makers.[19] Concern was expressed about poor distribution and regional disparities that resulted due to existing structural inadequacies and increasing absolute numbers of the poor, even while food production increased. A large part of the world was also being systematically excluded from access to what was produced. In the midst of all the increase in food buffer stocks, inadequate nutrition and hunger also grew. Similarly, as the production of clothes was on the rise, many of the poor were still ill clad. Furthermore, land disparities continued to increase.[20] On one hand, society saw increased production and growth, while, on the other, the world watched the poor struggle with issues of survival. It was recognized that wealth *and* poverty emerged from the ferment called economic growth and development.

Out of this concern about the role of structures, systems and policies rose theories like the dependency theory (the theory of *dependistas*).[21] This theory critiqued the modernization assumptions about underdevelopment and poverty. The Marxist theory of class encounters and its tools for social analysis provided an alternate reading of poverty and underdevelopment.

In general, the theory of dependency divided society into two conflicting groups; the stronger oppressors and the weaker class. *The Communist Manifesto* (quoted from "the preface by Friedrich Engels to the English edition of 1888" in *The Fundamental Proposition of Marxism*) suggests that

> the history of all hitherto existing society is the history of class struggles. Free man and slave, patrician and plebeian, lord and serf, guild master and journeyman, *in a word, oppressor and oppressed, stood in constant opposition* to one another, carried on an uninterrupted, now hidden, fight, a fight that each time ended either in a revolutionary reconstitution of society at large or in the common ruin of the contending classes (Curtis 1981, 158–59, emphasis added).

Having divided society into two rather neat categories, the poverty of several millions of workers was then defined as the inequality between the two classes.[22] C. T. Kurien proposed that poverty is "the socio-economic phenomenon whereby the resources available to a society are used to satisfy the wants of the few while the many do not even have their basic needs met" (1978, 8).

Second, the dependency theory assumed that underdevelopment of the poor had its roots in history and in worldwide systems. Subsequently, it focused heavily on international relationships. Andre Gunder Frank, of the *dependistas* (dependency) school, in his analysis of world systems, proposed that relationships within a country and poor societies were a reflection of worldwide systems.[23]

In his political-economic analysis Paul Baran did not ignore the internal structures within a poor society. He pointed out that the "potential" surplus within poor societies went to four groups: (1) the *lumpenbourgeoisie*, an indeterminate category (that includes moneylenders, merchants, real estate agents, and such others); (2) industrial producers, who tend to be monopolistic in their operation; (3) foreign entrepreneurs; and (4) the state (Harrison 1988, 71–73).

The dependency theory highlights the causal role government policies and priorities play in poverty. It challenges the unhealthy tie between the non-poor and local government. It stresses the negative influence of government policies on the poor, especially implications of the present trend in two-thirds-world economies moving rapidly toward the free-market system.[24] It identified policies on labor (Gupta 1987, 345), wage structure (World Bank 1980, 41), and the legal system (Chambers 1983, 152) as contributing to the underdevelopment of a people.

Analysis

Although this view of poverty received wide acclaim for placing its finger on some sensitive issues, some concerns need to be considered.

First, the structural view places blame solely on the outside "other." Internal flaws within poverty situations are perceived merely as reflections of flaws in the world system. This ignores internal political structure and oppression among the poor. This tendency to focus on the outside, without a commensurate critique of internal factors, can cause the poor to take on a victim posture.

Second, structural analysis of poverty often tends to be at a macro level, ignoring micro-level causes.

Third, emphasis on structural dimensions ignores economic dimensions of poverty. It fails to emphasize adequately the fact that poverty is an economic phenomenon and that no development occurs without wealth creation.

Fourth, those who share the structural view of poverty are strong in analysis; however, an overemphasis on cause analysis can result in postponement of action. Often focus on present needs appears to be the necessary fuel for igniting the anger of the poor against structural and systemic causes of poverty (issues of tomorrow).

Finally, structural analysis of the causes of poverty can at times be too direct and insensitive. It ignores the social and economic cost the poor will have to incur if rapid, emotionally charged response occurs without considering implications. "Outsiders" have other options, but the poor pay with their lives for challenging structures and systems.

According to this analysis poverty is the result of structural inadequacies and flawed systems at the village, macro and global levels; the unhealthy alliance between governments and the rich, and the wrong policies of the government.

However, neglect of structural and systemic inadequacies at the micro level and the tendency to postpone action to a distant future has caused concern among grassroots practitioners and development theoreticians.

The Poor Lack Access to Resources

With the growing emphasis on social learning and empowerment, the debate on poverty shifted its focus toward issues such as access and control, participation and ownership.

In the 1980s appreciation grew of the potential of the poor to contribute to their own development. This emphasis directly conflicted with the "poor are backward" theme. Emphasis was now on people-centered development, with a focus on

the creative initiative of the people as the primary development resource and to their material and spiritual well-being as the end that the development process serves (Korten and Klaus 1984, 201).

Central concerns underlying these assumptions about poverty included human growth and well-being, equity and sustainability. It entailed a new approach to planning that emphasized mutual learning alongside the poor. David C. Korten (in his proposal for fourth-generation voluntary action) calls for efforts to "energize a critical mass of independent, decentralized initiative in support of a social vision" (1990, 127). Hence, the new debate called upon the development community to reconsider its assumptions about poverty and the poor.

A key question raised among development experts from this school of thought was who controls the resources, decisions and other factors that shape the lives of the poor. This question was "central to current policy debates, but not as the question has been defined by traditional socialists and capitalists" (David C. Korten 1990, 174). The question of control and access was a political issue.

Responding to the "control" question, development strategists initiated people's participation and social mobilization programs. For Korten, control and access presumed the need for "true economic democracy," one in which there is meaningful participation in ownership and control of productive assets. Other agencies at international and national levels called for redistribution of political power[25] and participation.[26]

Ranjit Gupta in his analysis of tribal poverty points out that

> so long as the tribals have no mechanism for taking strong political and instrumental action on their own behalf, their prospects for breaking out of the poverty trap remain almost totally dependent on externally initiated action (1983, 119).

Participation was the "internally initiated action" that helped, according to Frances Korten, in organizing and uniting the poor for their development (1983, 189).

The emphasis on participation was also an attestation that poverty is about motivation and knowledge. Participation and organizing the poor is an assertion that development,

> contrary to what many believe, is not a condition or a state defined by what people have. . . . It is more a matter of motivation and knowledge than it is of wealth (Ackoff 1984, 195).

Analysis

Emphasis on people's participation, social learning and people-centered development brought a necessary corrective to the backwardness assumption. However, this new emphasis also sidestepped several crucial dimensions of poverty.

First, emphasis on people's potential and participation often results in neglecting macro causes of poverty. At the grassroots level, participation approaches tend to focus exclusively on micro causes of poverty.

One reason could be that the participation process presupposes a community. Such a community is real primarily at the micro level. Therefore, David C. Korten proposes a corrective by calling on voluntary organizations to initiate people's movements with a global agenda as a corrective (1990).

Second, emphasis on people's resources can be construed as ignoring the needs for wealth creation and for external resources. As mentioned earlier, without wealth creation there can never be any real development of the poor.

Third, experience with people's participation indicates that structural issues can be neglected. People's participation should normally lead to grappling with issues of structural inadequacies. In fact, participation can become an inward-looking exercise and miss issues of structure. One reason for this could be that the poor rarely consider challenging structures as being within their jurisdiction. The participation process must intentionally address structural causes of poverty. Without such intentional focusing on causes of poverty in their entirety, people's participation can become a mere project-planning exercise.

The Poor Have a Large Number of Dependents

The issue of population has always informed various debates on poverty. It has been the canvas on which profiles of poverty often have been painted.

Malthus (1766–1834)[27] reasoned that

> while population tends to grow geometrically (at a constant rate), the means of subsistence only increase arithmetically (by a constant amount). Hence poverty and want are virtually inevitable and . . . are due to fast breeding of the *lower classes* (quoted in Hadjor 1992, 187, emphasis added).

Concern among development experts was primarily that the majority of the world's population increase would happen in households that are already poor.[28] Commenting on living standards of the poor, Lewis T. Preston, president of the World Bank, concluded, "We are making progress, but it is not fast enough. The overall level of poverty remains totally unacceptable" (World Bank 1994, 1). Large family size, therefore, was perceived to be a significant cause of poverty. In relation to the household, studies showed that size of a family affected the size of family landholding and family income, thus perpetuating poverty (Ahmed 1987, 168).

At the end of the 1970s the World Bank concluded that "growth alone is not enough. This is partly because rising population is tending to swell the numbers in absolute poverty" (World Bank 1980, 40). Galbraith points out that "to this day, emphasis on population pressure as a cause of poverty is somewhat muted. This is partly because any resulting improvement is long delayed" (1979, 38).

The population question also led development thinkers to be concerned about depletion of the world's resources.

According to the Malthusian or neo-Malthusian view:

> unrestrained population growth eventually leads to falling wages and rising food prices because, as the labor force expands, a rising ratio of labor to land leads to smaller and smaller increments in output per worker. Population growth is ultimately checked by rising mortality (World Bank 1980, 80).

Some experts believe that certain resources such as land, forests, and fisheries, though fixed, are renewable. However, sustainable yields are limited. Defenders of this view point out that "a population whose needs (subsistence and commercial) exceed sustainable yields will have lower per capita incomes in the long run" (ibid.).

Finally, others propose that there are "no real natural resource limits, because population growth itself brings the adjustments that continually puts off the doomsday" (ibid.). They quote Julian Simon's *The Ultimate Resource* to support their claims:

> The ultimate resource is people—skilled, spirited, hopeful people— who will exert their wills and imaginations for their own benefit and so inevitably, for the benefit of us all (see ibid.).

The optimism of Simon's view, while admirable, has short-term difficulties. According to Simon, it takes thirty to eighty years before a turn-around will take place. By then, two to four generations of the poor will have gone through life having suffered poverty and powerlessness. Simon also reckoned that in that period even moderate population growth could be detrimental to the world's resource base.

Analysis

These assumptions about worsening poverty are not without their problems.

First, for the poor, a large family is an economic necessity. For the landless whose labor is their only marketable commodity, the number of hands, especially male hands, represents an asset. Hence, large family size is a resource base.

Closely related is the preference for a male child. In India, where dowry (although legally abolished) is a "nurtured evil," the birth of a girl child goes to the debit side of family accounts, while a male child is considered on the credit side.

Third, for the poor, numbers are their only political resource. During elections, these numbers earn them some privileges. For a community whose power base is narrow, numbers are an important source of power, at least when it comes to political bargaining.

Finally, in some communities large family size is tied to socioreligious practices. In some poor communities the child is the focus of curses during inter-family and inter-village hostilities. Consequently, families safeguard their future against possible loss by having more children.

History and Environment in Poverty Scenarios

Poverty, like the rest of life, is affected by forces that have influenced life situations over time. Analysis of intergenerational poverty, especially, will never be adequate if we do not consider the time variable. Poverty is a real life experience in both space and time.

Marxist analysis of class relations brought the question of history to the fore. Marx proposed a materialistic reading of history. He suggested that economy is a key determinant of all historical processes and that the mode of production is the primary form of economic relationship.[29] Marx proposed that exploitation was the hallmark of these class relationships. Consequently, for Marx, history was perceived as a history of class struggles.[30] Hence for those who pursued a Marxist reading of reality and poverty situations, history, specifically the history of class struggles, was consequential data.[31]

Until recently it was assumed that environmental issues concerned only the rich and the rich nations. However, more recent debates have focused on the relationship between poverty and environmental degradation. The report of the Club of Rome, *Our Common Future*, pointed out that the "environment ought to be a part of the forethought and not the afterthought of every development initiative" (Welsh 1990, 312). Development and economic growth without concern for the environment was recognized to be an "imperfect proxy for progress" (World Bank 1992, 34); thus the World Bank (1992) focused specifically on "development and environment." Experts constantly reminded development workers that earth is a spaceship with limited renewable resources (David C. Korten 1990, 135ff.).

This debate suggests that poverty both results from the exploitation of the environment and places considerable pressure on the environmental resources of the world.

Multi-Variant Analysis of Poverty

Most current efforts to understand poverty have recognized that

any attempt to analyze the problem in terms of one or two variables such as low capital formation or absence of policy measures to ensure adequate distribution of income must be viewed with suspicion (Galbraith 1979, 44).

This realization caused policy-makers and development experts to explore the multifaceted nature of mass poverty.

J. K. Galbraith proposed that rural poverty is the result of the "circular causation" of several forces:

Since life is near the bare levels of subsistence, there is no saving. Without saving and the resulting capital investment, there can be . . . no investment in improved agricultural technology. . . . Without such investment there can be no improvement in income that allows savings and further investment (ibid., 52).

The World Bank suggested that this circle of causes and symptoms of poverty is intergenerational. If human development is a "virtuous circle," poverty is a "vicious circle that sentences the children of the deprived parents to deprivation themselves" (World Bank 1980, 70).

The World Bank in its 1980 report proposed a multifaceted model—'the seamless web'—to explain the relationship between poverty and policies. Differentiating between core concerns and the environment in poverty-related issues, this report suggested that income, nutrition, health, education and fertility are influenced by shapers of the environment (religion, culture, natural resources, climate and political realities, including administrative constraints and the world economy).

In its 1993 *Human Development Report* the UN brought together life expectancy, educational standards and individual buying power (Lewis 1993, 6) to construct the "Human Development Index." However, like most other indices and measurements, this scale also depends heavily on information that is difficult to gather and on averages.

The debate on causes of poverty was particularly enriched by the contributions of Robert Chambers. Chambers was probably the first to differentiate between poverty and powerlessness. He made two crucial contributions. First, Chambers understood the urgency of reexamining the causes of poverty from the perspective of the poor. Second, his reflections on the "deprivation trap"—poverty, isolation, powerlessness, vulnerability and physical weakness—provided a helpful tool for understanding the multifaceted nature of the causes of poverty (1983, 112ff.).

John Friedmann also explored the theoretical foundation for an alternative approach to development, proposing the (dis)empowerment model. In his model Friedmann defined poverty "as lack of access to bases of social power." Using the household as the basic political and economic unit, he identified eight bases of social power, "the principal means available to a household economy in the production of its life and livelihood": financial resources, social networks, appropriate information, surplus time over subsistence requirement, instruments of work and livelihood, social organization, knowledge and skills, and defensible life space (Friedmann 1992, 67).

In this model empowerment is defined as the movement of the poor from abject poverty—lack of access to these bases of social power—to complete access to all eight bases of power.

Notes

[1] More recently, development approaches have been reviewed by Robert Chambers, John Friedmann and others. Robert Chambers in his analysis of views on poverty categorized these views into two "cultures." The first Chambers called the "political economists" of the "negative social science pole," who explain poverty from a social, economic and political perspective. The second is the "physical ecologists" of the "positive practitioners pole," who explain poverty using physical and ecological terms (1983, 35ff.). John Friedmann classifies the views on poverty into three groups: those who consider themselves as social superiors over the poor, social reformers and state bureaucrats (1992, 55). Len Doyal and Ian Gough classify the views on poverty into six broad categories: the Orthodox economic view, New Right, Marxist, Cultural Imperialist, Radical Democrats and the Phenomenological view of the sociologists (1991, 22ff.).

[2] "The success of the Marshall Plan in the 1940s and 1950s led many to believe that a similar transfer of capital to developing countries would, despite their physical, human and institutional limitations, achieve similar results" (World Bank 1985, 97).

[3] Comparison of the objectives of the three UN Development Decades provides some helpful insights into the views of policy makers about poverty. The First Development Decade (1960s) set for itself the goal "to accelerate progress towards self-sustaining growth of the economy of the individual nations and their social advancement so as to obtain in each underdeveloped country a substantial increase in the rate of growth, with each country setting its own target, taking as the objective a minimum rate of growth of aggregate national income of 5 percent at the end of the Decade" (ibid. 1990, 426). The Second Development Decade (1970s) moved slightly away from focus on economic development by stating that the "ultimate objective of development . . . must be to bring about sustained improvement in the well-being of the individual and bestow benefits on all. If undue privileges, extremes of wealth, and social inequalities persist, then development fails in essential purpose. This calls for a global centered action by developing and developed countries in all spheres of economic and social life: in industry and agriculture, in trade and finance, in employment and education, in health and housing, in science and technology" (Welsh 1990, 876). The Third Development Decade (1980s) covered the whole package of trade, aid, monetary reform, energy and industrial issues. Controversy over aid from rich countries and the issue of two-thirds-world debt became a major deterrent during the Third Development Decade. Therefore, over these three decades the UN shifted its emphasis from an economic view of poverty to include a structural understanding.

[4] A classic example of this approach at the national level has been the budget of the Indian government. The Indian finance minister Manmohan Singh

pointed out that "with sufficient growth, say 6% annually, India can abolish 'extreme poverty' by the year 2000" (*Los Angeles Times*, 5 March 1994, 2).

[5] The active proponents of Social Darwinism theory were Herbert Spencer (1820–1903) and William Graham Sumner. They were nonconformist individualists who believed that the state should not place too many restrictions on free enterprise. Social Darwinists believed that "if the unworthy are helped to increase, by shielding them from that mortality which their unworthiness would naturally entail is to produce generation after generation, a greater unworthiness" (Curtis 1981, 254, 263).

[6] Adam Smith in *The Wealth of Nations* (1894) in describing the agricultural system refers to the "unproductive class"—those who live out of the wages given by the proprietors and the cultivators. The labor of the unproductive class adds nothing to the value of the sum total of the crude produce of the land.

[7] Charles Booth (1840–1916) was a British businessman whose mammoth surveys of poverty, industry and religion were published as *Life and Labor of the People in London (1889–1891)* (Abercrombie 1988, 20).

[8] In India the national per capita income served as a useful index to define the poverty line. The per capita income in the Indian Union in 1960–61 (the base year used for poverty line calculations) was the total national (excluding Portuguese and French territories) income (Rs. 13, 308 crores or US$4436m at the 1994 exchange rate) divided by the total population (43.4 crores or 434m people on 1 October 1960); it was reckoned to be Rs. 306.7 or US$12 at the 1994 exchange rate. The 1994 exchange rate used for conversion here is Rs. 30 to US$1 (Dandekar 1971, 1).

[9] The debate on what constitutes basic human life is not a new one. Plato and Aristotle extolled the virtue of reason. Descartes restructured this idea further and saw humans as material body and non-material mind. Kant suggested that to be human, a person must have a body that is alive and the mental capacity to deliberate and choose. Gunnar Myrdal uses a list of what he calls "pertinent aspects of levels of living." His list includes food and nutrition, clothing, housing, educational facilities, information media, energy consumption and transportation (Myrdal 1968, 538). S. R. Gupta defined the desired level of living as the "level of satisfaction of [a nation's] needs attained in a unit of time as a result of flow of goods and services the population enjoys in that unit of time" (1987, 16).

[10] Len Doyal and Ian Gough suggest that by emphasizing that basic needs can be universal and objective, three political functions can be achieved: "First it illustrates the common bond between oppressed groups. . . . Second, such commonality suggests the extent to which their different experiences are similar and holds open the door for a great deal of mutual understanding and sympathy. And third, this in turn makes possible joint action with a common aim" (1991, 74,75). I do not think that to have a universal and objective understanding of basic needs is a prerequisite for common action. There is something

about the experience of being poor that will provide the fuel for such action. It is not necessarily a common understanding of a specific human need, specially the kind that Doyal and Gough are trying to suggest in their book.

[11] Subtitled "A Non-communist Manifesto," *Stages* was an invitation to the Third World to follow the West in its economic growth. Rustow's stages for economic growth for all societies included traditional society, preconditions for take-off, the drive to maturity and the age of high mass consumption (Hadjor 1992, 276–78).

[12] "The Cambridge model of the 1940s and 1950s assumed that output would grow in proportion to reproducible inputs, or capital. Rosenstein-Rodan (1943) postulated the big push by which an economy propels itself into self-sustaining industrialization and rapid growth." Rustow's take-off theory and the consequent formulation of the stages to development was based on this neoclassical view about growth (World Bank 1989, 35).

[13] Harrison, tracing key dimensions of a sociology of modernization in the context of development, proposed that there was no single theory of modernization. Like Marxism and other theories of development, modernization also had several versions (1988).

[14] Amy Sherman presents a case for a neoliberal response to the poor of Latin America. She recommends that nongovernment organizations (NGOs) consider the neoliberal option seriously, now that the socialist economic model has collapsed. She provides a helpful definition of the neoliberal view and suggests that it is rooted in six basic propositions: (1) economic decisions about production, consumption, distribution and investment are best determined by market mechanisms; (2) political and economic power should be separated as much as possible; (3) development practitioners and policy-makers should place greater emphasis on wealth creation than on wealth redistribution; (4) free trade and a free labor market are superior to protectionist policies and excessive government regulation; (5) private property rights are legitimate and should be protected, and (6) the government's role in the economy, generally speaking, is to perform certain "core" tasks (Sherman 1991, 6).

[15] The following is the mindset the modernists prescribe for the "backward" poor and nations: (1) readiness for new experience and openness to innovation; (2) interest in things other than those of immediate relevance; (3) a more "democratic" attitude toward the opinions of others; (4) orientation to the future rather than the past; (5) readiness to plan one's own life; (6) belief that we can dominate our environment and achieve our goals; (7) acceptance that the world is "calculable" and therefore controllable; (8) awareness of the dignity of others, for example, women and children; (9) faith in the achievements of science and technology; and (10) belief in "distributive" justice (Harrison 1988, 20–21).

[16] The following were key themes in orthodox development theories: (1) development does not involve irreconcilable interests between the developed and the underdeveloped to the different social groups; (2) there is no structural or causal linkage between development and underdevelopment; (3) what is

modern is good and what is traditional is bad; (4) development means becoming modern, like the West (Crocker 1991, 464).

[17] *Communication of Innovations: A Cross-Cultural Approach* (Rogers and Shoemaker 1971, 6ff.) is a classic example of this assumption. The emphasis on adoption and early innovators and other such concepts was built on the assumption that innovations were the key to development and had to taken in from outside.

[18] Intensive Agricultural Development Program (IADP) was one of the many poverty-alleviation programs the government of India introduced. The program focused on increasing agricultural production in areas with a higher potential for good results. When the government realized some of these programs were causing regional imbalances, programs with a specific area focus were initiated, including Small Farmer Development Agency, Drought Prone Area Program, the Tribal Area Development Program, the Minimum Needs Program, the Integrated Rural Development Program and the National Rural Employment Program (Alexander 1989, 73).

[19] According to the World Bank, the following seven general pitfalls of development must be avoided: (1) lack of ownership undercuts a program; there is need for internal consensus; (2) "flip-flops" in reform hurt credibility; (3) institutional demands must not be glossed over; institutional capacity must be developed; (4) attention must be given to macro-economic instability; (5) vulnerable people must not be forgotten; (6) partial attempts always fail; and (7) it pays to be realistic (World Bank 1991, 152).

[20] "Over 72% of the people (owning less than two hectares of land) own 23.5% of the land, 24.4% (owning 2–10 hectares) owned 50.25% of the land while the rich 3% (owning over ten hectares of land) own 26.35% of the land" (Desrochers 1988, 130).

[21] Birth of the dependency theory of underdevelopment was greatly aided by Andre Gunder Frank's popularization of the work of Paul Baran, especially *Political Economy of Growth* (first published in 1957, reprinted in 1973).

[22] Marxist critique of the capitalist system included a strong reaction to negative implications of the division of labor. The Marxist response to such a "dehumanizing" system is the ideal communist state. Marx and Engels described the communist state as a society "where nobody has one exclusive sphere of activity but each can become accomplished in any branch he wishes . . . (and it will be a place where it will be possible) . . . for me to do one thing today and another tomorrow, to hunt in the morning, fish in the afternoon, rear cattle in the evening, criticize after dinner, just as I have a mind, without ever becoming hunter, fisherman, shepherd, or critic" (see Nisbet 1980, 261). However, the fall of the socialist system suggests that the road to that ideal state is not as smooth as was originally thought, or that the Marxist strategy for reaching that communist state was far from adequate.

[23] According to Andre Gunder Frank, the following are critical for understanding the poverty of (some) nations: (1) there cannot be any theory of underdevelopment without taking into account the actual history of

underdeveloped societies; (2) a chain of metropolitan/satellite relations in the structure of this worldwide system transcends national boundaries; (3) it is incorrect to suggest that only countries closely tied to the West develop and industrialize; (4) internal class structures are a reflection, in the final analysis, of the worldwide system; and (5) the history of underdeveloped societies has not been and cannot be a mere duplication of the history of the capitalist West (Harrison 1988, 81–84).

[24] Sahoo 1992, 64–67. Sahoo points out that the government's nondevelopmental expenditure increased from 56 percent of total expenditure in 1984–85 to 65 percent in 1990–91. This "increase has been at the cost of the developmental expenditure which declined by 7.3%" (66). Sahoo concludes by pointing out that "today drastic changes in the fiscal approach have been fixed upon not by the needs of the poor, but by the disaster of our economy in the external sector" (67).

[25] In response to these concerns agencies including the UN and the World Bank prescribed some essentials for good development. UNICEF's list of "seven deadly sins" or "don'ts'" in development include the following: (1) development without infrastructure; (2) development without participation; (3) development without women; (4) development without environment; (5) development without the poor; (6) development without the achievable (there is a need for implementing research and development that has gone into development strategies and theory); and (7) development without mobilization (Welsh 1990, 311–13).

[26] Demand for participation, mobilization and people-centered development came from different sources. USAID and other aid agencies began to look seriously at the question of investing in humans and emphasizing people's involvement. They realized that "the real goal of development is not building impressive factories, dams and highways but ensuring that individuals lead fuller lives and enjoy more choices" (Paul Lewis, "New UN Index Measures Wealth as Quality of Life," *The New York Times International*, 23 May 1993, 6). UNICEF, based on its review of past involvement, concluded that participation and mobilization were critical for any good development. FAO, based on the World Conference on Agrarian Reform and Rural Development, called for a redistribution of economic and political power, with "expanded opportunities of employment and income for rural people, and development of farmers' associations, cooperatives" (Welsh 1990, 854).

[27] See Malthus's theory of population in his *Essay on the Principles of Population* (1798). The neo-Malthusian theory is based on a common-sense derivative of Malthus's theory; that is, if there are more people, less food is available. This concern has led countries, including India, into massive birth-control programs.

[28] World Bank officials point out that more than 1.1 billion people live on the equivalent of less than a dollar a day. The rate of poverty reduced faster in the 1970s than in the 1980s (World Bank 1994, 1).

[29] Corbridge 1990, 623–39. Corbridge suggests that "Marxism has been charged not just with economism, but with reducing the several circuits of the economy to a narrow productionism based on the logic of capital accumulation" (629).

[30] Marx's idea of dialectical materialism informed his view of the process involved in historical class struggles. He believed that the real world "developed according to the dialectical sequences" (Abercrombie 1984, 70). The dialectical logic involved three moments—thesis, antithesis and then synthesis.

[31] Poverty and oppression do not appear to be limited only to class relationships. The Marxist "class" framework to define poverty situations tends to neglect several other forms of oppression.

2

Liberation Theologies
and Poverty Assumptions

In the mid-1960s *liberation* moved from being a technical political term to a theological motif. The word became attached to a major peoples' movement and theological reflection within the Catholic tradition. The Medellín Conference (Second General Conference of Latin American Bishops, 1968) provided a stimulus for initiating the theologies of liberation.

Historical Background

Liberation theologies in Latin America were born in the midst of revolutionary ferment. Conditions of poverty and oppression in Latin America provided the context for the emergence of a radical shift within the Catholic church. Frustration with various models of development and growth of the dependency theory compelled the church to look for a more radical alternative for responding to Latin American poverty.

Past attempts to deal with poverty were considered totally inadequate. Underdevelopment was no longer assumed to be the result of economic, social and political backwardness but of capitalism. Aid and reformism were rejected as perpetuating oppression and dependence in Latin America. Aid was seen as a "Band-Aid" approach, and reformism was seen as impotent in dealing with structural causes of poverty.

Developmentalism, according to Gustavo Gutiérrez, was considered "synonymous with reformism and modernization . . . and counterproductive to achieving a real transformation" (1988, 17, see also 49–51). The prevailing model of development in Latin America was described as "dependent capitalism characterized by rapid industrialization and urbanization" (Boff 1988, 8). In this sense the liberation theologies were a reaction to the dominant development theories and an embrace of the dependency theory. However, the dependency theory was also reckoned inadequate to deal with particular challenges in Latin America (see McGovern 1989, 273; Gutiérrez 1988, 53–57). The liberation theologies were also a reaction to many dichotomies within classical Christianity, namely, between evangelism and involvement in the temporal sphere, and between clergy and laity (Gutiérrez 1988, 37,39). Out of this milieu liberation theologies began their search for an alternative reading of the context.

However, liberation theologies were not confined to the Latin American context. Similar theologies emerged elsewhere, including Minjung theology in Korea, Peoples Theology of Struggle in the Philippines, Dalit[1] theology in India, and black theology and feminist theology in North America.

In the Indian context in which I work, there are two distinct tracks within liberation thinking.[2] First is the extension of Latin American liberation theologies, led primarily by Catholic theologians. These theologians, apart from applying liberation theologies to the Indian context, also grappled with challenges of the pluralistic Indian context. The other track, led primarily by Protestant theologians, gave rise to Dalit theology.

The Dalit movement has its roots in the nineteenth century. Theological reflections *about* Dalits moved to theological reflections *for* Dalits and then to theologizing *by* Dalits (Webster 1992, 191).

In the early 1930s Wascom Pickett's study *Christian Mass Movements in India* was challenged for its paternalistic reflections on Dalits in the study and exploitation of the numbers. However, for V. S. Azariah and Pickett, evangelizing Dalits with the Christian gospel provided the only real solution to "the Dalit problem" (Webster 1992, 216).

Then John Subhan, in "The Good News of Christ for Depressed Classes," called for a transformation of individuals and restructuring of society in general and of the depressed classes in particular (ibid., 212). An intentional Dalit theology, however, developed only in the mid-1980s.

Today Dalit theology is represented by the works of Arvind P. Nirmal, M. E. Prabhakar and others.

Framework for Theologizing

Both liberation and Dalit theologies offer a rich array of theological motifs in relation to the poor:

1. The concept of "starting point" in theologizing.
2. Preferential option for the poor.
3. Theology as a "second act" in the process of theologizing.
4. The hermeneutics of suspicion.
5. The Marxist connection.

The Starting Point

Traditionally, the "scandal" of poverty and oppression is the only "starting point . . . [from] which the flag of liberation can be raised" (Boff and Boff 1990, 2,8). James Cone argues that "any other starting point is a contradiction of the social *a priori* of the Scripture" (1975, 97). For liberation theologians this is the "pre-theological" step in theologizing (Boff 1990, 22).

Specifically, liberation theologies suggest that the actual practice of liberation among the oppressed of the world ought to be the starting point of theologizing. Leonardo Boff identifies three levels of action that challenge structures and systems: the pastoral level, the church's involvement in political action, and political activity (1988, 13, 14). "The discussion of praxis constitutes one of liberation theology's most far-reaching and controversial contributions to theology" (Dyrness 1990, 90). Miroslav Volf, agreeing that theology must always be oriented toward practice, points out that the term *praxis* as used by liberation theologians generally refers to "practical political involvement for liberating the poor and the oppressed" (1983, 15). There cannot be a neutral stand, as Leonardo Boff points out: "We all take stances; it happens that some people have not been conscious of their positions" (1981, 27). According to liberation theologians, only through such a stance can there be a true reading of the Scripture. Therefore, the liberation theologies start with the church's sensitivity and involvement in response to the poor.

Dalit theologians approach the question of starting point from a different perspective. In Dalit theology "pathos is prior to praxis." It begins with "the story of their *pathos* and their protest against the socio-economic injustices." Dalit theology is built on the assumption that *pathos* must give birth to the protest, a protest that will be "so loud that the walls of Brahminism [will] come tumbling down" (Nirmal 1991, 141, 58, 62).

Preferential Option for the Poor

In liberation theologies the crucial question is not whether God is alive but whose side the living God is on (Bosch 1991, 439). Reckoning that this living God is on the side of the poor, liberation and Dalit theologies begin with a preferential option for the poor. As Gustavo Gutiérrez points out, the historical womb from which the liberation theologies emerged was the life of the poor (1988, xxxiii). For liberation theologians,

> God is the God of the cry of the victim of injustice. God hears the cry. A theology deaf to the poor weeping for their innocent suffering is also dumb before God and before society (Boff 1989, 41).

This option is a recognition that God loves the poor not because they are better but because they are poor (Gutiérrez 1988, 140). It is a recognition that we will encounter the Lord through encounters with the poor (Gutiérrez 1983, 33).

This preferential option for the poor is expressed in many different ways. But the primary thrust is that it is not a mere dialogue with the poor but actually "adopting the place of the poor" (Boff 1988, ix). This preference calls for a political engagement in the issues of the poor. Dalit Theology describes this as being conscious of the Dalitness. of recognizing that "Dalit humanity is constituted by their *Dalitness*" (Nirmal 1991, 48). For Dyanchand Carr, a Dalit theologian, this option is a recognition that Jesus represents the oppressed of all history. Jesus "[forgave] sins on their [the poor's] behalf and claimed he would one day judge the world on behalf of the oppressed of all history" (Carr 1991, 36). In black theology this option implies that the "gospel, by the very definition of its liberating character, *excludes* those who stand outside the social existence of the poor" (Cone 1975, 79).

Theology as the "Second Act"

Arising out of a commitment to begin with praxis and the pathos of the poor, both liberation and Dalit theologies recognize that theology is the "second act"; it follows the "silence of action" and listening to the cry of the poor. It is "derived from the first stage, which is contemplation and action as a response to the oppression of the poor" (Boff 1978, 41).

This second-act status assigned to theology does not imply that theology is secondary in importance. It is, rather, a call for theologians themselves to be converted, abandoning their ways and entering into the life of their neighbors, particularly the poor. Theology is the second act in the sense that this context provides the theological criteria for the reading of Scripture. It provides new questions for our biblical reflection and challenges in a new way our former ways of reading Scripture. It shifts the focus from emphasizing cognitive content to searching for the "liberative impulse" (Volf 1983, 15). For Dalit theologians this means affirming the "Dalitness of Jesus and His Father"—a Dalit God and a servant God (Nirmal 1991, 63).

The Hermeneutics of Suspicion

Closely related to the issue of theology as a second act is the affirmation that the liberation theologies are a new way of doing theology. Within this way of doing theology, a central piece is its "hermeneutics of suspicion." As Harvie M. Conn points out:

> Hermeneutical suspicion as a tool seeks to uproot from our selective viewing of Scripture those unnamed, transplanted ideologies with which we rationalize self-interest, those ideals that support the oppressive status quo and resist change (1976, 403).

James Cone suggests that hermeneutical suspicion does not simply ask the question of relevance. Instead, it asks, "In the absence of the theme of freedom or the liberation of the slave, did the Church lose the very essence of the gospel of Jesus Christ?" (1975, 114). It involves a critical suspicion of all ideologies that have meant oppression for the poor. It involves a necessary break from the conventional attitude and activity of society and church alike. Therefore, hermeneutical suspicion is a tool and a stance. It is a necessary prerequisite for reflection, according to liberation theologians.

Dalit theologians go further, adopting what they call "methodological exclusivism." Arvind Nirmal, describing Dalit theology as a counter-theology, suggests that it adopts exclusivism in order to prevent the theology of the dominant class from overpowering the Dalit reflection process. He insists that the "Christianness" of Dalit theology is in its being exclusively Dalit (Nirmal 1991, 59).

Marxist Connections

At the heart of liberation theologies is commitment to context. Liberation theologies call for close interaction with reality and a close interpretation of reality. Leonardo Boff, recommending "dialectical structuralism" as an appropriate tool for understanding reality, suggests that "it is the play of these [owners of capital and owners of working power] that explains the genesis, development and continuance of the type of society we experience" (1991, 418). Gutiérrez points out that poverty is a complex situation: "There is no question of choosing among the tools to be used. . . . The point is getting at the deepest causes of the situation" (1988, xxv).

Liberation theologies have been committed to analyzing the deepest causes of poverty and oppression. Marxism enabled liberation theologians to identify those root causes of poverty. Leonardo Boff and Clodovis Boff point out that liberation theologies borrowed from Marxism certain "methodological pointers" (1990, 28).[3] Jose Miranda acknowledges that liberation theologians owe much more to Marx than is usually acknowledged. Miranda develops, through massive exegetical work, several parallels between the Christian reflection on liberation and Marx (1974). Marxism appears to have provided liberation theologies in particular (not as much for Dalit theology) the instruments for applying a dialectical structuralist analysis of society.

Assumptions About Poverty

Liberation and Dalit theologies are an expression of a commitment that "it is not enough to describe the situation [of poverty]; its *causes* must also be determined" (Gutiérrez 1988, xxii). Having set the context, let us look at eight assumptions about poverty reflected in liberation and Dalit theologies.[4]

1. Poverty is a structural issue.
2. Poverty is a collective phenomenon.
3. Poverty is the result of institutional violence.
4. Poverty is sin.
5. Poverty is death.
6. Poverty is the result of a sociohistorical process.
7. Poverty is the poor becoming non-persons.
8. Poverty does not, however, mar the potential of the poor to be agents of transformation.

Let us begin with a theme that is probably most obvious to any in-quirer into the liberation and Dalit theologies—the structural causes of poverty.

Poverty Is Structural

Poverty is about the "'wretched of the earth' . . . whom the system cannot clothe, cannot house, or give . . . health or freedom" (Dussel 1989, 245).

In their analysis of society the liberationists trace the roots of pov-erty to "the rich and the powerful in this world . . . [and] the social and economic structure" (Cone 1975, 38). Jose Comblin claims that the powers abuse their "cultural, social, political or economic superiority. . . . They crush [the poor] without even noticing them" (1989, 94).

Liberation theologians also suggest that poverty has its roots in both international and national political and economic systems. At this point liberation theologians very often look to the dependency school to ex-plain the international causes of poverty at the grassroots level. They suggest that the rich and the poor nations, the center (metropolitan or the imperial centers) and periphery are locked into dependent relation-ships, where structures in all these situations serve the powerful.

Liberation theologians then go further to suggest that within these dependency relationships several forces are at play: culture, religion, education systems, laws and others.

National security law, for example, is commonly used within these dependency relationships to exploit the weak and poor. Leonardo Boff suggests that the term *national security* "masks international capitalism's strategic concern to defend itself through the coercive power of the state" (1988, 22). Jose Miranda goes even further, suggesting that the "cosmos" in Paul's teaching is equivalent to Marx's treatment of the capitalist system (1974, 250). Within the capitalist economic system, liberation theologians argue, wages and prices are "the two valves or channels through which . . . pass the distribution of income and therefore the distribution of ownership" (Boff 1981, 55).

Religion is another tool used to exploit the poor. Jose Comblin suggests that the powerful elite tends to spiritualize life's issues that affect the poor. On this issue of religion as a tool for oppression, Dalit theologians point out that religion "sanctions and sanctifies both the caste system and untouchability" (Nirmal 1991, 21; see also Puthanangady 1985, 10).

Both liberation and Dalit theologians also cite the role of the institutional church as an example of oppressive structures that exercise power to exploit and whose practices of power generate marginalization. Dalit theologians suggest that the most difficult form of oppression for Dalit Christians is the "oppression they face by a hierarchical church and by the Caste Christian community" (National Seminar on Dalit Theology 1989, 131). C. B. Webster, in his survey of the history of Dalit Christians, faults the kind of gospel Christians of the dominant classes have preached all these generations. He comments about the Christian concept of sin and salvation:

> Like the "traditional Hindu social dharma," it locates the roots of the Dalit predicament within the Dalits themselves from birth and not in the oppressive institutions of society (in Webster 1992, 225).

Based on these reflections on structure and poverty, both liberation and Dalit theologians call for a structural analysis of poverty. Since a preferential option for the poor is an "option for one social class against another" (Gutiérrez 1983, 45), liberation theologians call for assuming a conflict posture through social analysis. Contained within the pages of liberation and Dalit theologies is a demand for dismantling oppressive structures. These oppressive structures are the "sin of the world" that contradict the will of God and wrong our brothers and sisters. Miranda goes so far as to suggest that the state has to be dismantled

(1974, 30). And Indian theologian Geevarghese Mar Osthathios claims that

> the powerless must be aided by those who stand for a classless society to consolidate their power in such a way that they can exert power on the powerful through collective bargaining, strikes, and so on (1986, 343).

Therefore mission, according to liberation theologians, breaks down the walls of class. For Dalit theologians, "untouchability will not truly disappear until the purity of Brahmin . . . is itself radically devalued" (Nirmal 1991, 21).

In this context liberation theologians point out that the cross "demonstrates the conflict-ridden nature of every process of liberation undertaken when structures of injustice have gained the upper hand" (Boff 1978, 290; also see Nirmal 1991, 68). And the kingdom of God is "a total, global, structural revolution of the old order, brought about by God and only by God" (Boff 1978, 65).

Poverty Is a Collective Concept

Both liberation and Dalit theologies are a reaction to the individualism within post-Renaissance Christianity. Liberation theologians go so far as to claim that poverty is a result of individualism within a capitalistic society.

Liberation and Dalit theologians suggest that poverty is a phenomenon which describes the experience of a people. *The poor* is a collective concept that is broader than the proletariat of Marxism. *The poor* includes the exploited workers, the under-employed who are pushed aside, the reserve army, the laborers and the migrant workers (Boff and Boff 1990, 4). *The poor* is a people before it is individuals. Black theology expresses this understanding of the poor being a people through its consistent emphasis on narratives of the people as an integral part of black theologizing. In black religion

> story is thought of in two ways. First, it is the story of a people as a whole. It is the story of a people's struggle to survive the ordeal of servitude and to retain a sense of togetherness in their struggle (Cone 1975, 105).

In Dalit theology the starting point for theologizing is the pathos of a people who in their suffering have lost their humanity.

Liberation is also defined as a collective concept. Dalit theology is essentially a search for

> community-identity, community-roots and community consciousness. The vision of a Dalit theology therefore, ought to be a unitive vision—or rather a "community" vision (Nirmal 1991, 60).

Becoming a community restores the humanity of a people. Gutiérrez sees the journey from the "dark night of injustice" as a passage "of an *entire people* toward its liberation through the desert of structural and organized injustice" (1984b, 129, emphasis added).

The spirituality of liberation is the experience of a whole people. It is not the practice of individualistic piety. "Walking with the spirit" is the walk of an entire people (Gutiérrez 1984, 3, 4). Spirituality within the liberation movement, according to liberation theologians, always seeks to avoid "privatizing" the faith of a people.

To sum up, according to liberation and Dalit theologians poverty, liberation and even the spirituality of liberation are collective concepts. Poverty is the experience of a people, and liberation is the journey of a people toward becoming a community.

Poverty Is the Result of Institutional Violence

A major contribution of the Medellín conference was its definition of the concept of institutional violence (Latin American Episcopal Council 1986, 8). In Gutiérrez's opinion institutionalized violence is

> responsible for the deaths of thousands of innocent victims. . . . [It] takes no account of the dignity of the human beings, or their most elemental needs. [It] does not provide for their biological survival, or their basic right to be free and autonomous (Gutiérrez 1983, 63, 28).

In the Bible (referring to words like *ashaq*) oppression is seen as violent robbery or despoilation (Tamez 1982, 24). Wealth accumulated for its own sake is stolen treasure, and the kingdom of God that liberation theologians seek to establish calls for sharing resources. "Hoarding excess wealth in this world does not profit a person, but by sharing the same with those who are in need one becomes *eligible to enter* the King-dom" (Robinson 1990, 107, emphasis added).

Jose Miranda describes poverty and oppressive situations as involv-ing "violence that is institutional, legal, juridical, pseudo-moral, cul-tural" (1974, 11). Dalit theologians point out that in India Dalits have been targets of frequent attacks "of retribution and violence in the hands of upper castes" (National Seminar on Dalit Theology 1989, 127).

> Within a framework of inbuilt structural violence the Dalits have been pressured to respond with violence and this has led to brutal repression of Dalits by the state and by private armies of the rich upper castes (ibid.).

Both liberation and Dalit theologians call for a fresh look at the use of counterviolence in missional response to poverty situations.

> This view allows for a study of the complex problems of counterviolence without falling into the pitfalls of a double stan-dard which assumes that violence is acceptable when the oppres-sor uses it to maintain "order" and is bad when the oppressed invoke it to change this "order" (Gutiérrez 1988, 63–64).

Poverty Is Sin

Most Christian reflections on poverty recognize that poverty is the result of the Fall. However, the link between poverty and sin is probably closest in the liberation theologies.

First, poverty is the result of sin. Sin in liberation theologies is not just an impediment to be bridged in the afterlife but also "a breach of the communion of persons with each other . . . a multifaceted with-drawal from others" (Gutiérrez 1988, 85). "Sin is always the harbinger of divisions. Sin is the sense of being rejected by God which expresses itself by hating one's own brother" (Osthathios 1980, 30). "Sin makes the powerful selfish, oppressive, and exploitative" (Osthathios 1986, 343). Selfishness and greed in poverty situations are sin and ultimately the result of sin (Gutiérrez 1983, 147).

Next, poverty itself is sin. "Poverty that results from injustice and exploitation is the most visible and striking sign of the sin of the world"

(Elizondo 1983, 93). The emphasis here, however, is not on the fall of the individual, which then causes poverty, but on the evil of social structures that sustain poverty. Sin is always connected with injustice and oppression. Poverty is as sin in that it is a rebellion against God's will for creation.

Having thus defined poverty as sin, liberation theologians take the next step of redefining salvation as liberation and holiness as conversion of enemies to neighbors. Gustavo Gutiérrez points out that "our conversion to the Lord implies this conversion to the neighbor" (1988, 118). And according to Dalit theologian Dyanchand Carr,

> belief in Jesus then cannot be separated from a turning (in repentance) towards the oppressed. This then is the true meaning of having faith in Christ (1991, 8).

Apart from redefining salvation, liberation and Dalit theologians also redefine holiness.

> Holiness of the church consists in its participation in the world after the manner of the Spirit, who brings the future world—free, equal, comradely—forward into this world (Comblin 1989, 101).

The liberation event is also defined as the salvific act of the kingdom of God. Gutiérrez suggests that "the historical, political liberating event is the growth of the Kingdom and *is* a salvific event" (1988, 104).[5] Philip LeMasters, commenting on Gutiérrez's *The God of Life*, claims that liberation theologies establish a strong continuity between liberation from sin and historical and political liberation (1993, 237). Dalit theologians conclude that a liberating act of any persons—and indeed any liberating act—is a salvific event (ibid., 239).

Poverty Is Death

Complementing the definition of poverty as sin, liberation theologies affirm that poverty spells death to the poor. With liberation theologies the issue is not the so-called death of God but the death of the people. Poverty destroys people, families and individuals. It is death brought through hunger and sickness.

Poverty is also the poor being held captive in a death-dealing system. Structures and systems in poverty situations all seek to "do away with everything that gives unity and strength to the dispossessed of the world" (Gutiérrez 1984, 10). Gutiérrez describes this type of death as "cultural death."

Finally, poverty situations are full of symbols of death. Black theologian James Cone, analyzing poverty in black communities, writes that "the most visible symbol of death's power was found in the everyday presence of white people who violated black dignity at every level of black existence" (1975, 122).

Liberation theologians suggest that "misery and oppression [in poverty situations] lead to a cruel, inhuman death and are therefore contrary to the will of the God of Christian revelation who wants us to live" (Gutiérrez 1988, xxii).

Poverty Is the Result of a Sociohistorical Process

For liberation and Dalit theologies, poverty is the result of a historical process. Dalit theologians point out that the Dalits were a "no people" in history. Poverty is the product of a long process of social marginalization.

Poverty is the distortion of the cultural history of a people. It is the capturing of power by oppressors and the higher castes or classes. For Dalit theologians, poverty is the result of the Brahmins' "capturing the apex of the feudal pyramid and dictat[ing] the pattern of socio-cultural developments" (Devasahayam 1991, 5).

Poverty is also seen as a historical process wherein the poor are gradually excluded from the social mainstream of life. This process is an inevitable part of any human society. Elizondo speaks of "anthropological laws of human behavior" that consist of three tendencies in human behavior: to include and exclude, to create and maintain social distance, and to eliminate those who threaten or destroy those barriers that exclude and maintain social distance (1983, 17–18).

History is central to understanding poverty in liberation reflections.[6] Liberation is also defined as the subversion of history from the perspective of the poor (Gutiérrez 1983, 20). It involves a rereading of history that would result in

> remaking history. It means repairing it from the bottom up. And so it will be a subversive history. History must be turned upside-down from the bottom, not from the top (ibid., 21).

History is also seen as the arena within which God's salvation history is enacted. Jose Comblin goes further to suggest that the work of the Holy Spirit is confined within history.

> The Spirit was given in history and will be active in history till the end of history. There *will be no* reign of the Spirit outside history or beyond the history of this world (1989, 57, emphasis added).

Therefore, for both liberation and Dalit theologies, history provides crucial clues to understand poverty.

Poverty Is the Poor Becoming Non-persons

Both in liberation and Dalit theologies the poor are described in their present state as "non-persons" (Gutiérrez 1988, xxix) or as "no people" (Azariah 1991, 90). Poverty is the state of becoming "no people" in their own land and becoming non-persons in at least five ways (see Gutiérrez 1984).

First, poverty causes the poor to get lost in anonymity (Boff and Boff 1990, 31). Second, poverty disfigures the image of God in the poor. Considering poverty from a "Christian view," Leonardo Boff and Clodovis Boff suggest that poverty is the "disfigured image of God" (ibid., 31). Third, poverty is servitude (Cone 1975, 77). For Dalits, this servitude means being compelled to do "polluting jobs" (Devasahayam 1991, 10), and liberation implies challenging concepts of purity and pollution that have resulted in the Dalits being reduced to "no people" (Robinson 1990, 116). Fourth, the poor becoming non-persons also implied, according to Latin American liberation thinkers, stunting their ability to think and reflect (Gutiérrez 1983, 90). Following clues given by Paulo Freire's *Pedagogy of the Oppressed,* liberation thinkers defined liberation as a problem-solving exercise in which the ability of the poor to reflect and decide is developed. Liberation theologians then called the church to restore to the poor the right to participate in the sociopolitical life of society (Gutiérrez 1983, 137). Finally, becoming non-persons also implied denial of basic dignity to the poor (National Seminar of Dalit Theology 1989, 128), where oppressors were the real "definers of the humanity" of the poor (Cone 1975, 193).

Poverty Does Not Mar the Potential of the Poor to Be Agents of Transformation

In spite of all the harshness of poverty, liberation and Dalit theologians recognized that the poor still retain a stamina that should not be missed in social analysis. The poor have the ability to work out their own liberation.

> Liberation is emerging as the strategy of the poor themselves, confident in themselves and in their instruments of struggle: free trade unions, peasant organizations, local associations, action groups and study groups, popular political parties, base Christian communities (Boff and Boff 1990, 6).

Second, the poor can be agents of transformation of society. According to C. Rene Padilla, liberation theologians identify three levels where the poor are agents of transformation: historical praxis resulting in a new society; renewal of the church resulting in a new way of being the church; and, finally, theological reflection where the poor become privileged mediators of the Lord's presence (1987, 158).

However, some liberation theologians go further. They suggest that a natural corollary to the preferential option for the poor is recognition that the poor have a privileged position in making God's presence known to the church and the world. "Only the poor and the weak have the axiological grid necessary for the hearing and the doing of the divine will disclosed in their midst" (Cone 1975, 94).

Summary

Liberation theologians have significantly shaped global thinking about poverty and the response of the church to the poor. These theologies have gone beyond the boundaries of Latin America to several other countries. In India, they have emerged in the form of Dalit theology.

Reflection on liberation and Dalit theologies provides several important clues to understand how analyses of poverty have developed. We have examined eight major themes, each with several implications for the mission of the church among the poor. None of these assumptions has gone unchallenged.

The greatest challenge the liberation theologies have faced in Latin America, however, has been the explosion of Protestantism, especially the Pentecostals, among the masses (Martin 1990). In many ways the explosion has been aided by the grassroots work of the Pentecostal movement. These shifts away from the liberation theologies indicate that "while the language of Pentecostalism is 'odd' and many of its practices initially unattractive, the language of liberationism can easily remain remote" (ibid., 290).

In spite of these challenges, the process of reflection that liberation and Dalit theologians have begun has been rich. Most valuable has been the attempt to view poverty from among those who experience it, namely, the poor themselves.

Notes

[1] The term *Dalit* refers to the Harijans and outcastes within Indian society.

[2] There are commonalities as well as variations between liberation and Dalit theologies. However, the focus here is not on comparing the two theologies but is rather on understanding their assumptions of poverty.

[3] There are others who challenge the possibility of borrowing Marxist tools without buying into Marxist assumptions about society and class conflicts. See Conn 1976, 416; Dyrness 1990, 95; McGovern 1989, 283.

[4] These themes emerged from a survey of selected writings including Hugo Assman, Leonardo Boff, James Cone, Jose Comblin, Enrique Dussel, Virgilio Elizondo, Gustavo Gutiérrez and Jose Miranda; Dalit theologians Abraham Ayrookuzhiel, M. Azariah, Dyanchand Carr, Arvind Nirmal and Gnana Robinson; and Indian liberation theologians Gevarghese Mar Osthathios and Paul Puthanangady,

[5] Gutiérrez goes on to point out that this understanding is "not *the* coming of the Kingdom, not *all* of salvation" (104).

[6] Samuel Escobar, in his critique of this reading of history, points out that the outcome of such a reading has been "that the mission of the Church and her self-understanding have come to be formulated in categories that owe more to sociological analysis, ideological choice and political preference than to traditional theological, biblical and historical categories" (1992, 3).

3

Evangelical Reflections
and Poverty Assumptions

While the church in some parts of the world was grappling with issues related to poverty, evangelicals were also making great strides in their recovery from the "great reversal." Evangelicals were coming out of their reactive stance and were no longer defining their identity or mission in separatist categories (Van Engen 1990, 207). Instead, they embarked on a search for a new theology of mission.

A key element in this recovery was the long journey of theologizing that evangelicals undertook from Wheaton '66 to the Oxford Conference on Faith and Economics '90. These congresses and conferences accelerated the process of evangelical awakening and also expressed the evangelical mind on issues related to the mission of the church. In the 24 years between Wheaton and Oxford, prime emphasis through the process of theologizing was on finding that "balance" or "relationship" or "middle ground" between evangelism and social action.[1] This journey reflected crucial theological shifts that evangelicals were making. Linda Smith, in her survey of evangelical shifts during the last few decades, described four specific shifts in values:

1. Reacknowledgment of the humanity of Christ;
2. Rejoining of Word and deed, body and spirit;
3. Renewed, but significantly different emphasis on the kingdom of God; and

4. Resulting theological paradigm shift in view of the relationship of Christ to culture (1989, 377).

The evangelical shift was phenomenal. From a cursory reference to racial discrimination at the Wheaton '66 conference to a detailed discussion of causes of poverty in the Oxford Conference on Christian Faith and Economics,

> Evangelicals have come a long way, both practically and theologically, in their affirmation of a *whole* gospel ministry. To this extent they have re-appropriated their evangelical heritage (Shenk 1993, 73).

On the whole, the direction of evangelical theologizing has been affirmed in various surveys of these events.[2] Charles Van Engen, in his review of 40 years of evangelical theology, comments, "The relationship of evangelism to social action as the goal of holistic mission has not yet been resolved" (1990, 232). Wilbert Shenk points out that evangelical theologizing has been from a "flawed paradigm," where focus has been on the "parts rather than on the whole, which is God's *new order*" (1993, 74). David Bosch, while critical of the "cause-effect thinking" that guided most evangelical theologizing, affirmed the general direction and quality of the shifts in evangelical thinking (1991, 407–8).

Even as evangelicals were grappling with the issue of evangelism and social action,[3] they were also formulating interpretations of social reality, particularly poverty situations, oppression and such issues. They were formulating their theology of poverty.

This chapter focuses on key themes within the evangelical theology of poverty as reflected in the journey from Wheaton '66 to Oxford '90.

Historical Background

The Sixties

Late in the 1960s the Wheaton Congress on the Church's Worldwide Mission (April 9–16, 1966) heralded a fresh initiative on the part of evangelicals to actively consider theology of mission. It introduced a "tremendous burst of dynamism . . . from within the evangelical wing of the church" (Van Engen 1990, 211). The "Wheaton '66 Declaration" condemned racial inequality and all forms of injustice throughout the world. It called for applying "scriptural principles to such problems as racism, war, population explosion, poverty, family disintegration, social revolution and communism" (Evangelical Foreign Mission Association 1966, 3).

At the World Congress on Evangelism (Berlin, 1966), Billy Graham called evangelicals to go back to proclaiming the gospel. The congress described the context of mission as the "world on fire, [in which] man without God cannot control the flames" (Mooneyham 1967, 23). During the conference itself concerns were expressed regarding population explosion; racial tensions; and social, psychological and moral needs. The closing statement from Berlin '66—"One Race, One Gospel, One Task"—also affirmed the need for the church to respond to the inadequacies in the human race. It rejected the notion that "men are unequal because of distinction of race or color . . . [and described the world as] mankind in spiritual revolt and moral chaos" (Mooneyham 1967, 5). Apart from this final statement from the congress, Paul Rees's paper "Evangelism and Social Concern" also expressed evangelicals' reading of the context of the "one task" of the church. Rees suggested that race relations was not the only area of social concern. He described the other challenge:

> [It is] a terrifying thought that, in a presumably free society, abject poverty, family disorder and disintegration, job insecurity and joblessness, can erect psychological barriers to the reception of the Gospel that are as real as the suppression of free speech (in Mooneyham 1967, 307).

Rees called on evangelicals to join him in prayer saying, "Lord, I want no part in the cult of the complacent" (ibid.). But C. René Padilla in his later review commented that the Berlin Congress did not establish any theological basis for social action (see Padilla and Sugden 1985, 7; Nicholls 1985, 221).

The Seventies

The 1970s began with the Thanksgiving Workshop on Evangelicals and Social Concern in Chicago (November 23–25, 1970). "The Chicago Declaration" called on evangelicals in the West to express their

Christian discipleship by confronting social and political injustice in the world (Padilla and Sugden 1985, 9). The Lausanne Congress (1974) then came as

> the birth of a covenant [that] demonstrated to the world the developing unity, growing confidence, increased enthusiasm, and broadened vision of evangelicals in mission in the world (Van Engen 1990, 224).

"The Lausanne Covenant" described the context of poverty as marked by injustice, oppression, marring of human dignity, exploitation and evil. The covenant called the task of responding to these sociopolitical challenges as "spreading the righteousness of the gospel in the midst of an unrighteous world" (Douglas 1975, covenant 4). On the question of wealth and lifestyle, "The Lausanne Covenant," while affirming the mandate for a simple life (covenant 9), tied it too closely to the call to contribute generously to both relief and mission. This suggested that a simple lifestyle was primarily a fund-raising strategy. Recognition of the link between a simple life and poverty had to wait until the Hoddesdon (UK) Consultation on Simple Life Style (1980). At the Lausanne Congress, a group of participants called attention to more radical dimensions of evangelical commitment. This statement, "Radical Discipleship" (1974), described the context of mission as full of injustice; where demonic forces keep humans less than human; and there is neglect of creation, resources and the powerless. It described the good news as "Good News of liberation, restoration, of wholeness, and of salvation that is personal, social, global and cosmic" (Sugden 1981, 174). It called the churches' attention to the world's contrary value system, totalitarianism and violence, social and institutional sin, and the struggles for freedom and justice.

The Lausanne Congress triggered a series of consultations at the regional level in India and on specific aspects of mission. The Devlali Congress (1977) in India was one such conference. In "The Devlali Letter," the final declaration from this congress, church leaders called on fellow Christians to focus on the vast numbers of the unreached. In their hermeneutics of the context, descriptives like "body-soul" unity; the whole man; personal, corporate and institutional sin and injustice; dignity and value of persons, the poor, hungry and the homeless were included (All India Congress on Missions and Evangelism 1977, 1). Although descriptions of social reality at Devlali were too general, the congress set the tone for the next move among evangelicals in India, namely, the All India Conference on Evangelical Social Action (October 1979).

On a global level, after the Gospel and Culture Conference (January 1978), "The Willowbank Report" (the final statement from the conference) showed evangelicals following the cue given by "The Lausanne Covenant" (Douglas 1975, covenant 10), specifically addressing the relationship between culture and the gospel. Evangelicals affirmed the "interconnectedness of systemic evil," especially when applied to poverty and exploitation.

The All India Conference on Evangelical Social Action focused on evangelical hermeneutics in the context of poverty and resulted in "The Madras Declaration," as it is popularly known, which highlighted the "critical situation" in the country and the large "percentage of the population living below the poverty line" (Sugden 1981, 184). It described the increasing oppression of the underprivileged classes, entrenchment of casteism and communal violence, the high percentage of people (40–60 percent) below the poverty line, violation of human rights, and structural and systemic injustice as the context for evangelical social action. It challenged evangelicals committed to the lordship of Christ and to the authority of the Bible to obey God through involvement among the poor (ibid.). "The Madras Declaration" also pointed out that

> the gains of development are mainly benefiting the top ten per cent of our society who control the Indian economy, while masses of people are shackled by abject poverty (Sugden 1981, 185).

Evangelicals at the All India Conference on Evangelical Social Action also renounced the false god of mere economic growth that devalues human rights. With "The Madras Declaration" analysis of society gained greater attention as an integral part of evangelical theologizing.

The Eighties

The 1980s began with the Consultation on Theology of Development (March 10–14, 1980, Hoddesdon, England). The consultation contributed to widening the scope of social analysis. In its statement of intent, the consultation linked issues of justice with the role of government, living standards of the rich with those of the poor, issues of poverty and arms trade and injustice with sociopolitical structures (Sider 1981, 15). It asserted that the "dignity and worth" of the poor were at stake in poverty situations.

The Consultation on Simple Lifestyle (March 17–21, 1980, Hoddesdon, England) in its statement, "An Evangelical Commitment on Simple Lifestyle" affirmed the link among lifestyle, injustice and poverty in the context of mission. At this consultation evangelicals denounced "environmental destruction, wastefulness and hoarding" (ibid., 18). They traced the roots of the misery and powerlessness of the poor to destruction of the environment, stewardship of God's resources, wealth and consumption patterns of the rich, state authority, and the arms race at the international level (ibid., 13–19).

In June 1980 evangelicals met at Pattaya, Thailand, affirmed "The Lausanne Covenant" and denounced injustice toward the suffering millions (Consultation on World Evangelization 1981, 29–31). However, "in some ways Pattaya was a step backward from Lausanne and a restatement of the Student Volunteer Movement 'watchword'" (Van Engen 1990, 227). At Pattaya, evangelicals defined the "people group" concept rather narrowly and thus excluded specific references to the poor and oppressed. Consequently a group consisting of two-thirds-world theologians issued "A Statement of Concerns on the Future of the Lausanne Committee for World Evangelization." The statement chided the Lausanne Committee for not being "seriously concerned with the social, political and economic issues in many parts of the world that are a stumbling block to the proclamation of the gospel" (Padilla and Sugden 1985, 14).

At the Consultation on the Relationship Between Evangelism and Social Responsibility (CRESR) in Grand Rapids, Michigan, USA, June 16–23, 1982, evangelicals focused on the causes of poverty rather than the many symptoms of poverty. Social action was differentiated from social service. CRESR participants focused on the 800 million "oppressed by the gross economic inequality from which they suffer and the diverse economic systems which cause and perpetuate it" (LCWE 1982, 16). They identified the oppressive global system, the exploitation of nonrenewable sources of energy, the spoiling of the environment, community violence and war as challenges before the church of Christ. Later, Edward Dayton in an article commenting on the framework developed at

CRESR, pointed out that "we are faced with the fact that non-Christian cultures often live out the very holism we preach" (c1982, 4, 5).

Deliberations at CRESR led to the next major event on evangelical social action, Wheaton '83. There evangelicals expressed deep concern about the secular margins of Christian development. The final declaration, "Transformation: A Church in Response to Human Need," proposed that transformation be considered as the Christian alternative to development. Participants at Wheaton '83 highlighted the economics and politics of poverty (Samuel 1987, 254–265). They identified clearly the causal role of culture in perpetuating poverty. The Wheaton '83 Statement pointed out that cultures "bear the marks of God's common grace, demonic influences, and mechanisms of human exploitation (ibid., 259).

The issue of culture also came up for discussion at a smaller consultation among Indian evangelicals (Church and Caste, February 1983). "The Declaration on Caste and the Church" condemned the caste system as "man made and totally unjust. . . . [It] has directly or indirectly permeated the total fabric of our nation" (Asia Theological Association 1985, 1).

Pentecostal/charismatic renewal leaders and evangelical social action leaders came together at Fuller Theological Seminary from January 12 to January 15, 1988. In July 1989 the Manila Congress in its manifesto again affirmed the relationship between evangelism and social action, and described the poor as those deprived of justice, dignity, food and shelter. "The Manila Manifesto" challenged injustice and oppression both at personal and structural levels (LCWE 1989, agendas 8, 9). In detailed notes the Manila Congress described the human predicament as "God's image being corrupted in human beings" (ibid., agenda 3). Defining the marginalized, "The Manila Manifesto" included the handicapped along with the sick, the hungry, prisoners, the disadvantaged and the oppressed (ibid., agenda 5). However, in its description of the "whole world," the manifesto did not recognize the presence of the poor as a significant bloc in the world.

The Nineties

The 1990s began with an important conference on faith and economics (Oxford, UK, January 1990). "The Oxford Declaration," for the first time in evangelical theologizing for the last 24 years, devoted a significant portion of its time to understanding the causes of poverty (*Transformation* 1990a, 2).

Discussion of the economics of poverty moved into the realm of political economics. Describing the "many and complex" causes of poverty, "The Oxford Declaration" specified cultural attitudes, micro- and macro-level causes, natural disasters, and creation and distribution of wealth as some aspects for social inquiry.

These milestones in evangelical theologizing reflect a gradual shift from merely describing missional response to a bold analysis of the context of mission.

Assumptions About Poverty

Even as evangelicals journeyed from Wheaton '66 to Oxford '90, they consistently affirmed certain foundational commitments.

- They affirmed that God was involved in history. "It is significant that a paragraph which relates entirely to 'Christian social responsibility' should open with an affirmation about God. This is right. . . . *We affirm that God is both the Creator and the Judge of all men*" (Stott 1975, 26).
- They ministered to the hurting world as "a Kingdom community where we all live under the cross, rejoicing in the Savior's unmerited forgiveness and knowing Him as our life" (*Transformation* 1988, 1). Evangelicals saw themselves as those saved by the grace of God and, as evangelists, called to minister to the poor.
- They were involved among the poor as learners. The movement from Wheaton '66 to Oxford '90 reflected the desire of the church "to know the poor and oppressed people, to learn issues of injustice from them, to seek to relieve their suffering and to include them regularly in our prayers" (Sider 1980, 15).

A review of final declarations from these congresses, conferences and consultations suggests ten key elements in the evangelical reading of the context of poverty.

Poverty: Marring the Image of God in the Poor

Evangelicals have consistently affirmed that "it is the divine image in man which gives him *an intrinsic dignity* or worth, a worth which belongs to all human beings" (Stott 1975, 27). Even as early as the Berlin

Congress in 1966 the issue of race relations was addressed, based on the understanding that all men were made in the image of God.

Through the years, a key element developed in the evangelical response to poverty involving healing the marred image of God in the poor. "The Madras Declaration," affirming this foundational commitment, commits evangelicals to "define and defend [the image of God in the poor and] . . . identify violations of human rights and assist the victims in obtaining their legitimate rights" (Sugden 1981, 186).

Poverty: Perpetuated by Flawed Structures

An important assumption in evangelical reflections through the years has been that poverty and oppression are closely tied with the corporate and institutional dimensions of sin. Evangelical theology strongly has affirmed

> that poverty is not necessarily evil but often the result of social, economic, political and religious systems marked by injustice, exploitation and oppression. . . . [The poor's] plight is often maintained by the rich and the powerful (Samuel and Sugden 1987, 260).

"Radical Discipleship" points out that societal and institutionalized sin needs to be condemned (Sugden 1981, 175). In a paper presented at Devlali '77, Bruce Nicholls argued that "the political, economic and social institutions of our complex society also have to be 'converted'" (Nicholls 1977, 3).

The Wheaton '83 statement is even more outspoken, suggesting that "either we challenge the evil structures of society or we support them" (Samuel and Sugden 1987, 256). "The Manila Manifesto" (1990) and "The Oxford Declaration" (1990) were both marked by a clear recognition of structural and systemic causes of poverty.

Evangelical theology of poverty affirmed that confronting poverty must involve "action to encourage institutional and structural changes which would foster these [Christian] values in our communities" (*Transformation* 1990, 8). These affirmations and conclusions reflect a clear paradigmatic shift. Evangelicals moved away from the withdrawn stance of the 1920s to a stage where they now define evangelical mission in terms of confronting structures and systems.

Poverty: Distorting the Truth

Participants at the Indian Devlali Congress proposed a crucial link among poverty, caring for the poor and taking a stand for truth and righteousness (All India Congress on Missions and Evangelism 1977, 2; also see "The Madras Declaration" in Sugden 1981, 185–86). Participants confessed that the church in India

> failed to become personally involved in caring for the poor and the oppressed, leaving it to institutions, and that we have remained indifferent or neutral when we should have taken a stand for truth and righteousness (All India Congress on Missions and Evangelism 1977, 2).

In the same document Indian leaders also identified falsehood along with injustice at personal and social levels as issues needing to be dealt with (ibid., 3).

Careful review of these statements and assumptions suggests that evangelicals now acknowledge poverty as in many ways an expression of falsehood in society. Evangelical theology suggests that involvement with the poor must invariably mean taking a stand for truth and righteousness.

Poverty: Result of Lack of Compassion and Love

Along with growing understanding of the complex nature of poverty, evangelicals also consistently recognized emotional, soul and heart dimensions of poverty. The recent "Manila Manifesto" calls evangelicals to "demonstrate God's love visibly by caring for those who are deprived of justice, dignity, food and shelter" (LCWE 1989, agenda 2). Wheaton '83 affirmed, "It is clear that justice and mercy belong together" (Samuel and Sugden 1987, 261).

This assumption within the evangelical paradigm suggests that poverty by its very nature is a state of deprivation of compassion and love. This is an arena often neglected in studies of mass poverty and impersonal structural and systemic analysis of poverty situations.

Poverty: Micro and Macro Dimensions

The process of evangelical theologizing recognized very early the impact of macro issues on the lot of the poor. Apart from institutional

and systemic causes, "The Willowbank Report" highlighted the inter-
relatedness of the global system and its role in exploitation and oppression (Stott 1978, 454). The report affirmed that the world is

> an interrelated global system of economic, political, technological
> and ideological macro-structures, which undoubtedly results in
> much exploitation and oppression (Stott and Coote 1978, 454).

Questions about the international arms race, environmental destruction, wastefulness and the whole question of lifestyle of the non-poor
have consistently arisen. The Consultation on Simple Lifestyle held in
the UK (March 1980) specifically affirmed the relationship between
poverty and wealth. The document "An Evangelical Commitment to
Simple Lifestyle" recognizes clearly a

> connection between resources, income and consumption; people
> often starve because they cannot afford to buy food, because they
> have no income, because they have no opportunity to produce,
> and because they have no access to power (Sider 1980, 17).

These affirmations among evangelicals were a challenge to popular
modernization and neoliberal assertions denying a relationship between
wealth and poverty.

At the Oxford Conference on Faith and Economics (1990) participants discussed the world economic scene in relation to poverty. Third-
world debt, work ethics, economic systems, political systems and
bureaucratic systems all came under the purview of evangelical reflection.

The shift from Wheaton '66 reflections on population and race relations to Oxford '90's grappling with issues related to the world economic system marks a critical shift for evangelicals. The presence of a
larger system of oppression has become an important part of the evangelical hermeneutic.

Poverty: Rooted in the Fallenness of Cultures

Evangelical reflections over the years have also inquired into cultural
aspects in relation to poverty situations. Wheaton '83 participants, de-
liberating on culture and transformation, affirmed that culture is God's

gift to human beings but also bears the marks of the fallenness of humanity.

However, there is need for more work here. Apart from discerning the impact of human fallenness on the culture of the poor, it is important to identify how various elements of culture are used by the non-poor to perpetuate poverty. Further, it is also necessary to inquire into elements of the culture of poverty that cause the poor to "settle down" in their state of powerlessness.

Poverty: Perpetuated by Principalities and Powers

"The Willowbank Report" (1978) challenged the mechanistic myth of the Western worldview, emphasizing the "reality of demonic intelligences which are concerned by all means, overt and covert, to discredit Jesus Christ and keep people from coming to him" (Stott and Coote 1978, 449). "Radical Discipleship" (Lausanne 1974) goes further to state that demonic forces not only seek to prevent the work of the church but also "deny the Lordship of Christ and keep men less than fully human" (Sugden 1981, 173). Growing recognition of the direct role of principalities and powers in perpetuating poverty caused evangelicals to look beyond the role of demonic forces in frustrating church programs to find these forces marring the very image of God in humans. The question of how the principalities and powers affect the poor and the non-poor as persons needs further study.

Economics of Poverty: Political Ramifications

The Consultation on Simple Lifestyle (1980) emphasized "the unjust distribution of capital, land and resources" (Sider 1980, 17). Its document went on to label these as issues of power and powerlessness and to suggest that without "a shift of power through structural changes these problems cannot be solved" (ibid., 17).

The Oxford Conference on Faith and Economics (1990), declared, "Justice is basic to a Christian perspective on economic life" (*Transformation* 1990, 1). Evangelicals at the Oxford event affirmed that the evangelical framework cannot divorce the question of economics from the issue of wealth creation and distribution. They pointed out that evangelicals' essential Christian perspective requires them to emphasize the political ramifications of economics. This is a crucial aspect of evangelical theology that must be further considered.

Evangelicals in the last two decades have moved from confessing their unscriptural isolation to affirming that working with the oppressed is a mark of Christian discipleship and then to beginning to shape social analysis with their faith.

Poverty: An Issue of Power

As early as the Berlin Congress in 1966 the question of power surfaced in relation to the poor and the deprived. Paul Rees called attention to "power—the moral management of power and structures of power in society" (Mooneyham 1967, 307).

"The Oxford Declaration" (1990), in discussing the work ethic, suggested that "justice requires special attention to the weak members of the community because of their greater vulnerability" (*Transformation* 1990, 5).

The Consultation on Simple Lifestyle went further than merely seeking preferred treatment for the vulnerable and the powerless. At this event evangelicals described the powerless poor as those who cannot protect themselves. They called on governments and the church to obey God and defend and take a stand alongside the powerless (Sider 1980, 14).

However, power as a key issue has not received the same attention among evangelicals as among secular development theorists and liberation theologians. While descriptives like *oppression* and *exploitation* do indicate recognition of power issues, discussion of power as a critical theme in the evangelical paradigm of mission has not been frequent.

Poverty: The Result of Humanity's Fall

Evangelical reflections through the 24 years from 1966 to 1990 have always been under the general rubric of the Fall. However, since key debates focused on "bridging" the gap, much time was spent on differentiating between evangelism and social concern and discussing the question of primacy.

Evangelicals always emphasized that restoration of relationship with God is the motivation for Christian involvement with the poor and issues of oppression. The Fall was recognized as the cause of all poverty. Evangelical theology further affirmed that poverty and the powers, structures, systems, cultures and people all, in some form or other, expressed the fallenness of creation. Evangelical theology recognized that the

doctrine of the fall highlights the innate tendency of human beings to serve their own interests, with the consequences of greed,
insecurity, violence and the lust for power (Samuel and Sugden
1987, 257).

It affirmed that "authentic human development depends on right relationship to God" (Sider 1980, 18). In the final analysis, evangelicals
recognized that their theology of mission rested on the belief that

> human beings, though created in the image of God, are sinful and
> guilty, lost without Christ, and that this truth is a necessary pre-
> liminary to the gospel (LCWE 1989, agenda 4).

Summary

At the Chicago Workshop (1970), and ever since, evangelicals have
confessed the church's failure to be disciples in its mission among the
poor and the oppressed. Then, at Oxford '90, in the midst of crumbling
economics and super powers, evangelical Christians called for their faith
to shape their analysis and hermeneutics of the context.

To sum up, according to evangelical theologians and missiologists,
poverty

1. involves a "marring" of the image of God among the poor,
2. is perpetuated by flawed structures,
3. is the result of many distortions of truth,
4. is a result of lack of love and compassion,
5. involves both micro and macro dimensions,
6. is a result of fallenness of the culture,
7. is perpetuated by principalities and powers,
8. involves political ramifications of economic issues,
9. includes issues of power distribution, and
10. is the result of the Fall of humanity.

These reflections of secular development theorists, of liberation and
Dalit theologians and of evangelical theologians provide important pointers to inquiry into the nature of the powerlessness of the poor and the
search for a kingdom-based response. The next two chapters examine
responses of the church to the poor.

Notes

[1] Another feature of the evangelical journey thus far has been the role of two-thirds-world theologians. As Shenk points out, the emergence of leadership from the non-Western churches has been one of three motivating forces in the journey (Shenk 1993, 72; see also Van Engen 1990, 218). Padilla, in his survey of events since Wheaton '66, concludes, "Wheaton '83 completed the process of shaping an evangelical social conscience, a process in which people from the Two-Thirds World played a decisive role" (Padilla and Sugden 1985, 17).

[2] See Padilla and Sugden 1985; Nicholls 1985; Van Engen 1990, 203–32; Shenk 1993; Chester 1993.

[3] The author recognizes that the evangelical journey from Wheaton '66 to Oxford '90 was filled with tensions and conflicts like any other debates on issues such as these. A survey of the various reviews on the evangelical theologizing indicates that there already has been extensive coverage to the conflicts and debates.

4

Historical Responses

In his analysis of the church's role in development, Tom Sine concluded that the church has, on the whole, followed Western models of development (1981, 72). He challenged the church to examine the extent to which evangelicals have borrowed secular Western values in Christian development. David Korten, in his analysis, used a time line to classify different voluntary actions and identified them as four "generations." The first generation focused on relief and welfare, the second on community development, the third on sustainable systems development and the fourth on people's movement with a global agenda (Korten 1990).

In her analysis of voluntary action, Frances O'Gorman used five metaphors to analyze responses to the poor. They were the Band-Aid (handouts and relief), the Ladder (providing information and skills), the Patchwork (self-help projects), the Beehive (grassroots movements) and the Beacon (confronting society and constructive action) (O'Gorman 1992).

Each of the above classifications highlights different aspects of secular and Christian responses to poverty.

This chapter describes seven historical approaches toward the poor. While this review of historical models could be imposing modern-day categories on history, it does not seek to evaluate these models. Instead, we will look for clues to understanding popular assumptions about poverty reflected in these models. The seven approaches are:

1. Conversion resulting in social change;
2. Social service as pre-mission work;
3. Love in action;
4. Rural reconstruction;
5. Modernization;
6. Ministering to victims (rescue missions); and
7. Social service along with public policy initiatives.

Conversion Resulting in Social Change

One of the most common approaches adopted by the church historically was to affirm and pursue social improvements that resulted from conversions. This approach was most evident in the early part of the twentieth century, when conversions to Christ were popularly categorized as mass movements.

In India, several people's movements were reported among the Chuhras in Punjab, and the Angami, Ao, Sema and the Lothas in the northeast (Grist 1979). Various studies of people's movements also affirmed the socioeconomic needs that motivated conversions in these people's movements.

One such study, by Wascom Pickett and commissioned by the National Christian Council of India in 1928, highlighted several beneficial social changes in the lives of converts. Pickett suggested that these changes

> appear to have taken place most generally where Christian worship has been most firmly established as in Nagercoil, Vidyanagar, Ranchi and Guntur. . . . They have acquired concepts of God and of themselves in relation to him that have powerfully affected their social standards, their conduct and in course of time their status in their villages (1933, 128).

Moral changes and better personal habits were reported. Improvements in education and health standards, combined with giving up of wasteful habits, brought economic gains to families and communities (ibid., 141). Communities that came to Christ also experienced increased security. The Chuhra community members in Punjab found in Christianity the acceptance and the security which they needed. They saw in Christian community the strength to throw off the oppression of the landlords who took advantage of their inferior status (Grist 1979, 52).

"The name 'Christian' gave a new dignity" (ibid., 105) to many lower-caste participants in these mass movements. New leadership emerged among several northeast Indian communities (ibid., 55). The poor from these mass movements also learned that evil spirits did not control their lives anymore. It was evident to the church that social, economic and even political relationships were transformed as a result of conversion, and this approach was also a source of witness. These transformations among the poor caused other high-caste Hindus "to consider the claims of Jesus Christ" (ibid., 98). The poor were becoming agents of transformation even as they were being transformed from their poverty.

This approach, in the words of John R. Mott, offered

proof positive that the living loving Heavenly Father is brooding over these most abjectly needy and neglected of His children, creating in them hopes and aspirations for longer life and liberty and by His Spirit moving them to will and to do (in Pickett 1933, 7).

As social transformation resulting from conversion became a model of ministry, assumptions also developed that

social action and social improvement are valuable only where the new birth has preceded and prepared society to accept and sustain them. . . . The call to become fishers of men precedes the call to wash one another's feet (Adeyemo 1985, 52).

Corollary to this assumption, poverty may be seen as the result of the personal sins of the poor themselves. The poor who are hurting from poverty bear the major portion of blame for their condition. Hence, ministries focused primarily on the personal conversion of the individual. However, as David Moberg points out, it is necessary to recognize that "some of these problems have natural causes over which man has no control. . . . Only a portion are the direct effect of the victims' personal sin" (Moberg 1977, 68).

Second, this approach adopts a simple, moralistic interpretation of causes of social problems. Pickett, sharing this understanding of the causes of poverty, asserts that

> abject dependence, lack of ambition and initiative, carelessness, deceitfulness, extravagance, drunkenness, insolence and harshness in dealing with others are character weakness which many observers have found to be especially common among the untouchables: they probably all enter into the common understanding of depressed class mentality. Their exceptional prevalence may, we think, be traced to distorted reactions to oppression (Pickett 1933, 83–84).

Consequently, ministries such as these aggressively pursued efforts to erase the depressed class mentality and distorted reactions of the oppressed toward oppression.

This approach ignores the fact that poverty is a web of relationships within which the poor are captives. It also excludes the non-poor from the scope of analysis. Further, structural causes of poverty and systemic evils are not dealt with adequately. A ministry with a distinct people-group approach to conversions is individualistic in its analysis of social problems and poverty.

Additionally, this approach suggests that large-scale social action is possible only in communities and countries where the majority of the population are Christians, or that many people need to be converted before any substantial changes can be initiated. Donald McGavran states this flatly, "The only place large social action is possible is in countries where the majority of the population are members of Christ's Church" (1965, 3).

Finally, almost unintentionally, this approach to the poor affirms that personal conversion and social transformation of a community are related. Although the approach itself does not intentionally pursue socioeconomic change, results of conversion include socioeconomic and political changes. This suggests, to borrow Mott's words, "that the living loving Heavenly Father is brooding over" the affairs of the poor and that sociopolitical transformation is within the purview of the work of the Holy Spirit.

Social transformation resulting from conversion is still a dominant paradigm in missional involvement among the poor in India and elsewhere in the world. Its moralistic reading of reality neglects socio-structural dimensions and the role of the non-poor in analyzing poverty.

Social Service as Pre-mission Work

Closely related to the earlier approach is belief that social service serves as an effective pre-evangelism tool, preparing people to receive the gospel. Even today, ministries are established on this premise. Many schools, hospitals and leprosariums are funded based on this belief. Advocates "win the winnable" and seek those who are "adjudged prepared by God" (McGavran 1973, 109).

Mission involvement in education is a case in point. "The mission schools were started primarily to care for small groups of Christian children in various villages and partly to bring in converts" (Pickett 1933, 43). Such schools played a key role in evangelism. These schools had

the task of raising the intellectual understanding of the people so that they could for example read the scriptures or the hymnal and develop a set of concepts that could contain the key elements of Christian revelation. . . . In many Victorian minds, literacy and religion were regarded as inseparable (Elliott 1987, 18).

Schools sought "to change, to civilize and to Christianize"—the three Cs (Nicholls 1985, 52). However, church schools gradually turned their focus to providing excellent education and in the process moved away from serving the poor. The elite in post-independent India were drawn from these high-quality church schools (Elliott 1987, 18), where "occasionally education and excellence took priority over evangelism" (Grist 1979, 88). Pickett's study on mass movements in 1928 pointed out that the "primary schools for non-Christians have not won large groups of men to Christ; instead, they have actually hardened their pupils" (1933, 89).

Church involvement in medical work was another expression of this approach. Petty Orville points out that 57 of 64 leprosy asylums in India in 1927 were part of Christian mission work (1933, 38). In 1910, medical work in Mizoram created a positive response to the gospel in at least 80 villages (Grist 1979, 91). Effective medicine liberated the poor from the fear of evil spirits. This suggested that the gospel had power over the spirit realm as well. Medical missionary work also reflected Christian compassion and love among the poor.

Christian involvement in humanitarian relief and social-welfare programs served as pre-evangelistic tools in several parts of the world. "Evangelistic motivations are very strong in social welfare programs for American Indians, Puerto Ricans, Cubans and other minority ethnic groups as well aş in church programs for migrant workers and in gospel missions" (Moberg 1977, 108). John Clough's mission work during the crippling famine (1876–79) in Andhra Pradesh was an example of social service with a pre-evangelistic intent. Evangelism in India was perceived as the positive results of social service.

All these ministries enabled the church to pioneer in the fields of education and medicine. The lives of the poor were touched. The poor heard and understood the gospel.

However, this social-action model had its critics. Ken Gnanakkan of the Asia Theological Association points out that this approach "makes our social response a dubious decoy for some unutterable intention" (in Nicholls 1985, 51). John Stott describes this approach to the poor as "the sugar on the pill and the bait on the hook" (in ibid., 51).

This approach recognized that poverty was about basic needs. The church responded to the education and health needs of the poor. However, little evidence shows that this concern for the non-Christian poor continued to show up on the church's agenda beyond conversion. Some contemporary ministries adopting this approach have tended to neglect the poor as the ministries gradually institutionalized. Focus shifts toward reaching out to serve other potential converts.

Again, the wealth of the non-poor is not related to poverty situations in this model. These ministries also seek to "win the winnable," and as converts move up the social ladder, leaving the rest of the community behind, a new group of elite emerges through the process of redemption and lift.

Because of this individualistic understanding of society and problems, such ministries also tend to neglect sociopolitical and cultural dimensions of poverty. Very often, neglect of these aspects results in lack of sustainability of impact. When converts find that they are not improving socioeconomically, they lose motivation to participate in further missional activity.

Love in Action

Traditionally, love has been a key motivation for Christian mission among the poor. In this particular approach, the whole mission is seen as a concrete expression of love. One example of this model is the life and ministry of Ida Scudder.

Ida Scudder's involvement in medical work in Tamilnadu, India, began with a sad encounter with a 14-year-old girl who needed medical attention. Her husband, a well-known Brahmin of the town, refused to let his wife be treated by Ida's father. The girl's husband took his wife back, saying "It is better that she should die . . . than that another man should look on her face." The girl did die. This motivated Ida, in 1900, to pursue the study of medicine and return to India as a medical missionary (Wilson 1959, 32–33). Ida Scudder was moved by the helplessness of the poor. Her typical response to the sick was, "*Ayoh Pavvum* what a pity, but why *amma*, why did you not bring him to me before? He must have been suffering" (ibid., 105).

Scudder's work was based on the strong relationships she developed with the poor. Two years after she opened her tiny clinic, she had treated 5,000 patients. Ida Scudder's approach to the poor very often took her out of her office. She was known far and wide for her "under the tree clinic" and also for her involvement in the 1903 plague in North Arcot district. In many towns, people fled their homes primarily out of fear of health officers and their strange inoculations.

> The Black Death, despite its horrors, was familiar. Like smallpox and cholera they knew it as the visitation of Mari Ammal, incarnation of Kali and goddess of death, to be accepted with outward reverence but inward terror and to be averted only by flocking to her shrines with prayers and gifts (Wilson 1959, 98).

But Ida's relationships helped her find acceptance for her treatments among the poor.

> Disease was frequently the least powerful enemy. . . . [She] had to combat ancient superstitions, and quack remedies took their toll again and again. There were certain feast days she discovered, when not a drop of medicine could be given (ibid., 82).

Ida's ministry addressed these forces, and thus confronted the very heart of the powerlessness of the poor to the gods and goddesses. Such love in action also ministered to the emotional needs of the poor. The poor, in turn, responded to Ida's mission of love with gratitude. They came to the mission hospital for that love. As one villager said to Ida, "Madam . . . we go the government hospital for many things but when we want sympathy we come to the missionaries" (Jefferey 1945, 76).

Ida's love in action confronted injustices within the society. A story is told of Ida's relationship with Lakshmi, a 13-year-old girl dedicated in childhood by her devout parents to temple dancing. Lakshmi was brought to Ida for medical care at age 15, and she accepted Christianity. Ida's appeal to the court in Madras to free Lakshmi from the temple failed. Very soon Lakshmi was taken away by the temple authorities. Ida pleaded with them. After some time Ida received a message, "The girl bade everybody good-bye and hoped to meet them in God's house. That very night she threw herself into a well" (Wilson 1959, 112, 113).

Ida Scudder and her team in Tamilnadu sought to build the kingdom of God. As Ida herself pointed out (referring to the medical school she was then establishing):

> What you are building is not a medical school later. It is the Kingdom of God. Don't err on the side of being too small (Wilson 1959, 275).

Love in action, as reflected through the ministry of Ida Scudder, recognized the cultural and religious dimensions of poverty. Early in her stay in India, Ida realized the dominant role religion and culture played in the lives of the Hindu poor. The Black Plague and other epidemics brought to the surface the determining role of religion.

Scudder's approach recognized that the gods and goddesses influenced the condition of the poor. Ida encountered the evil within the system, which showed itself in superstition as well as in fear of the evil one.

This approach to the poor also assumed that poverty was related to ignorance. The poor were poor because they were not aware of "right practices." Such approaches to the poor, therefore, have tended to emphasize education and social awareness. These ministries were active in literacy and awareness-building programs.

This approach was most sensitive to emotional needs of the poor as those who lack love and compassion.

Finally, this approach, too, assumed that one can respond to poverty without addressing structural forces or political realities of the day.

Ida was little concerned with politics, either British or Indian. She was too busy creating healthier citizens to implement the fundamental freedoms which Gandhi considered of supreme importance (Wilson 1959, 189).

Rural Reconstruction

About the time of India's independence and in the face of rural disaffection, the British Raj initiated a series of rural development programs.

[The] rural movement, a true child of colonial paternalism, resembled Victorian philanthropy, which also blamed the poor for their poverty and offered self-help as a panacea (Khan 1978, 11).

The church in India, recognizing that rural reconstruction would provide an opportunity to serve the poor, joined hands with the government.

In the words of the chief architect of the Rural Reconstruction Program, the underlying philosophy of this approach to the poor was "reform yourself, help yourself and follow the official leader." This paralleled the "ethical policy" in Indonesia introduced to rehabilitate rural areas (Khan 1978, 10). *Cooperation* was the key word in the program, and cooperative societies were patterned on the German approach (ibid., 11). Hence, this was part of a larger movement and emphasis.

The reconstruction included schools, health education, various forms of agricultural education, general education, and cooperative effort. However, Indian national leaders, including Gandhi, were critical of the Rural Reconstruction Program.

In a number of regions the church itself led rural reconstruction. Its efforts included religious education and evangelization, apart from government programs. Working alongside the government, the churches tried to "make the enterprise thoroughly Christian in spirit" (Orville 1933, 111).

The Rural Reconstruction Program assumed that ignorance and habits of the poor were the major causes of their poverty. According to program leadership, the "misery of the Indian villages was due mainly to their own ignorance and bad habits, their folly and vices; they are their own enemies" (Khan 1978, 10). The poor were described both by foreign and Indian leaders as "India's dumb millions who need to be roused from their pathetic contentment" (Adishesiah 1992, 26). However, for Gandhi and other critics of the rural reconstruction paradigm, imperialism was the key issue, and "the misery of the villages was mainly caused by the selfishness and greed of the ruler, the rich and of themselves as well" (Khan 1978, 11).

The reconstruction paradigm also assumed that poverty resulted from backwardness. The poor were to follow the "official leader," dependent on this outsider. Reconstructionists did not see any potential in the poor, except as good followers. In Gandhi's approach to rural development, on the other hand, the center of the program was the Ashram community; the missionary was to be only a guide, philosopher and friend (Khan 1978, 11).

Poverty was seen as a moral issue, and agencies like the church were to provide much-needed emphasis on moral education. However, this emphasis on moral and spiritual dimensions was not integral to program design. On the other hand, rural reconstruction and

> economics [were] the outflow of spirituality and all his [Gandhi's] economic thought, action, teaching, his economic precepts and practice were based on this moral foundation (Adishesiah 1992, 31).

Over time, officials realized that the reconstruction, despite being more community-oriented than earlier approaches to poverty, resulted in very little participation by the poor. Its programs merely confirmed the paternalism of the elite and did not solve the national food crisis (Khan 1978, 18). Consequently, emphasis shifted to modernizing agriculture, land reforms and improving technology.

Modernization

Modernization became popular in the church's missional efforts among the poor in the early 1960s, and it is still a dominant approach in the Two-Thirds World among the poor.

After independence, the Indian government focused primarily on modernization. Growth, progress, industrialization, state intervention, nationalization and trickle-down were some key characteristics of the idea of modernization. Further, Westernization and secularization became synonymous with modernization. In Tom Sine's words,

> Western development is a child of the European and American Enlightenment. It is based on the implicit belief that human society is inevitably progressing towards the attainment of a temporal, materialistic Kingdom. . . . The good life became synonymous with self seeking and the ability to produce and consume ever increasing quantities of goods and services (Sine 1981, 3).

In India, the community development program initiated in 1952 gave this growth-oriented approach an impetus. Agricultural extension and transfer of technology, adult literacy, health, and community organization were strategic components of this program. Commenting on the Indian approach to development, Akhter Khan suggested that the

> Indian model . . . can be fairly described as a shabby, genteel, rural capitalism—disparate anarchical and unstable, full of rewards and profits for the rich and strong, but also full of distress and despair for the weak and poor (1978, 41).

On the international scene, the birth of new nations in the 1940s raised awareness of deprivation in these nations. In the 1960s the UN began its development decades. Development projects in the Two-Thirds World involved large-scale funding, and modernization was prescribed for all forms of poverty.

The church followed the secular lead in modernization by initiating several development programs. Traditional charity gave way to contemporary models of development.

> The leitmotif of all these projects was that of the Western technological development model, which found its expression primarily in categories of material possession, consumerism, and economic advance. The model was based, in addition, on the ideal of modernization (Bosch 1991, 265).

Of all the approaches reviewed here, modernization response is probably the most analyzed by development gurus.

For churches involved in modernization, poverty has been essentially an economic phenomenon. Pursuing an Enlightenment-oriented emphasis on progress, the modernization paradigm measures and reads all of life within the context of an economic worldview. In this worldview human worth is largely derivative; one has worth only to the extent that one contributes to collective economic growth. Edgar Elliston, in assessing application of the Western model of development in Christian mission, points out that modernization has failed to fully serve developmental needs (1989, 169).

Second, churches involved in modernization have tended to neglect structural causes of poverty. Consequently, the benefits of modernization have not reached the poorest. Instead, modernization-based development initiatives of the church created more dependency. Modernization was basically a

> rhetoric [that] referred to progress and affluence for all, increased security, and benefits; in the final analysis, however, the issue was neither advantages nor affluence for all, but power, since selfishness called the tune (Bosch 1991, 266).

Third, the church's use of modernization strongly affirmed that poverty results from lack of potential among the poor to develop themselves. Development needed to be "taken" to the poor from outside. Modernization replaced the "official leader" of rural reconstruction with the technocrat. Church-based development projects became a conduit to instill a modernization mindset among the poor, who depended heavily on innovations from the outside. Early adopters of innovations then formed a new cadre of rich elite in the community.

Ministering to Victims

Another common approach by the church to issues of poverty involves relief to victims of society. Some serve the poor within the context of their community. Others have started homes and orphanages. The Indian church became known for its many hostels and orphanages started to take care of destitute children. The work of Pandita Ramabai is a case in point.

Pandita Ramabai was from the Chitpawn Brahmin caste of west India. She was born in 1858, and in the 1877 famine her parents died. In 1880 her brother died. Six months later she married a Bengali; he also died after 19 months. Picking herself up from these difficult circumstances, this young Hindu widow—who was not permitted to remarry—went to England. Contacts with the sisters of St. Mary the Virgin at Vantage gradually led her to be baptized into the Christian faith. She then went to live in the United States for three years. Ramabai returned to India with a passion for India's revival. In 1889, Pandita Ramabai started the Sarada Sadan, a home for learning for Hindu widows. The title *Pandita* was given to her in recognition of her proficiency in Sanskrit.

Ramabai focused on widows who were victims of society, "outcastes" within their own community. Hindu tradition based on Manu's edicts asserted that "though destitute of virtue . . . yet a husband must be constantly worshipped as a god by a faithful wife. . . . He is her guru" (MacNicol 1930, 88). In Ramabai's own words, "Childhood is the heyday of a Hindu woman's life. . . . Then, lo all at once the banns of marriage is pronounced and the yoke put on her neck forever!" (in ibid.).

Widows were taken into safe havens that Ramabai provided through her ministry. In 1896 a famine in central India left hundreds of children orphans, and a "brisk traffic was growing in the bodies and souls of young girls. Ramabai went forth into the stricken areas and was horrified at what she saw" (Neill 1934, 131). In 1900, after another famine in western India, more came to the Sarada Sadan for refuge. By the early 1900s Sarada Sadan housed 1,800 widows (Richter 1908,

239). The Sarada Sadan became a place of safety as well as a place of learning.

Ramabai's work emphasized prayer. In 1905 she formed prayer bands among the residents of her home. These were known as *Mukti Bands* (deliverance army). The Mukti Bands visited towns and villages, reporting extraordinary conviction of sin and confession, restitution, reconciliation and restoration with conversions and evangelism (Orr 1970, 114). The poor, in Ramabai's model, had the potential to become agents of mission.

In the final analysis, the Mukti model was an

Indian enterprise conceived in an Indian brain and carried out by Indian faith. But the Pandita was a special instrument raised up from most unlikely soil (Neill 1934, 133).

The rescue-mission approach suggests that society is a key force in perpetuating poverty and oppression. The Ramabai mission was a protest against male-dominated society, which perpetuated victimization of Hindu widows. Ramabai's efforts were supported by other social thinkers of her day. Eight years after Ramabai's death in 1922, India's government passed the "Sarada Act" restraining child marriage, based on the work at Sarada Sadan.

The rescue-mission model traced the roots of poverty to the religious system of a people. Ramabai recognized that "in India, religion sanctions social status and economic power" (Samuel and Sugden 1981, 30). Ramabai challenged the oppressive religious system. Recognition of the role played by religion and worldview in shaping poverty relationships is not new—Ramabai and her team encountered religion as a force in poverty situations in the early 1900s.

The rescue approach affirmed that the potential of the poor to be agents of transformation is not destroyed by their experience of poverty. Although Ramabai perceived the poor as "victims" of society, she was able to employ their potential to be a blessing and transform society through the ministry of the Mukti Bands.

The role prayer played in this ministry suggests that Ramabai recognized that poverty situations require prayer. Is there a suggestion here that prayer can serve as a tool in confronting causes of poverty?

Finally, the rescue dimension of this approach suggests that poverty is the result of the insecurity the poor experience. In response, the

Ramabai approach provided a safe haven for victims of society. However, this "home" approach had its negative implications. The poor who found security in the safe haven of Sarada Sadan later found it difficult to integrate back into society.

Social Service and Public Policy Initiatives

By the mid 1900s, some churches were involved in the public domain, both at micro and macro levels. Eli Stanley Jones's ministry through his public lectures, Round Table conferences and the popular Ashram movement is a classic example of this approach to the poor.

E. Stanley Jones came to India as a missionary at age 23 and served until 1973. His close association with Gandhi was also well-known.

Stanley Jones was driven by his passion for the "unshakable Kingdom and the unshakable Person." Paul Rees said of Jones, "he was intoxicated with Christ" (1983, 22). Stanley Jones served the nation primarily as an evangelist. His public lectures and Round Table conferences allowed him to interact with the heart of Indian public life. His ashram was an expression of a covenant with God and a fellowship to follow a disciplined life and habits (Jones 1983, 10). It provided mobile medical service to the community, and members were involved in developing the surrounding area. In this approach public policy and involvement at the community level were held together as a seamless whole. Jones saw both the poor and the complex issues of poverty demanding a response of compassion and change in public policy.

Stanley Jones's response to people was rooted in relationships. He was sensitive to issues India was struggling with at that time. He always sought to model a relationship marked by cooperation, complementing and contextualization. Stanley Jones expressed his desire to be part and parcel of the Indian soil:

India has become my home; India's people have become my people; her problems, my problems; her future, my future; and I would like to wear upon my heart her sins if I could lift her to my Savior. I told them I wanted to be thought of as at least an adopted son of India (Jones 1925, 104–5).

Stanley Jones's response to the poor was embedded in his relationship with the people. This was more than a program.

He did not imply passively glossing over inequalities in the nation he loved. As an adopted son of India, Stanley Jones told the nation,

> Brother, what can we do with the sixty million outcastes? They are a millstone around our national neck. Our country will never be strong until we lift them. How can we do it (Jones 1925, 104)?

Stanley Jones's model of involvement in both the public and personal issues of poverty expressed a clear bias toward the outcastes of society. This approach recognized that poverty was the marginalization of a people from the mainstream of a nation and society. Therefore, Stanley Jones "found[ed] the Christian movement largely among the outcastes and left it at the centre of India's life, a challenge and an issue for intellectuals and leaders" (Mathews 1944, 10).

Second, this approach affirms the link between poverty situations and national policies. Stanley Jones measured the health of the nation by the way it treated its outcastes and the poor. He called poverty a national shame, as well as a reflection of how the nation was managed. This assumption provided the basis for his involvement in the public domain.

Third, this approach assumed that "the degradation of the outcaste is not inherent. It is socially imposed" (Taylor 1973, 115). For Jones, "many of our captivities are rooted in their economic[s]. . . . We believe therefore, that one of the first things in order to do away with captivity is to do away with poverty" (ibid., 110). Stanley Jones reckoned,

> You cannot free the social and political captives unless and until you free the poor from their poverty, for the whole super structure of social slavery rests upon an economic slavery (in ibid., 25).

Fourth, this approach insisted that assumptions about poverty and response to poverty had to be holistic. In Paul Rees's analysis of Jones's contribution to mission, he quotes Jones as saying,

> The clash between the individual gospel and the social gospel leaves me cold. An individual gospel is a soul without a body, and a social gospel without an individual gospel is a body without a soul. One is ghost and the other is a corpse. Put the two together and you have a living person (Rees 1983, 24).

Fifth, this approach required addressing poverty as an issue of justice: the only adequate response to poverty is the removal of poverty (Jones 1935, 40). For Jones,

> If the giving of charity is the only goodness we have for the poor, then it is not goodness; for charity hurts the man who gives it and the man who receives it. . . . It is no remedy for poverty (in Taylor 1973, 109).

"Charity without justice is an insult" (Jones 1940, 98). Jones desired nothing less than the actual eradication of poverty. Poverty was not only an economic issue with roots in national policy but also an issue of justice at the micro level.

According to Jones, poverty is the result of a flawed order, and the kingdom of God is that new order that is breaking into, molding, changing and regenerating the lower order. The lower order is greed, unbrotherliness and selfishness (Taylor 1973, 107). Jones looked toward

> a world order in which these basic injustices, coming out of competition, will be replaced by an Order based on justice, love, sharing and equality. . . . We would not hesitate to embody the ideas of the Kingdom of God in legislative action (Taylor 1973, 119).

Terms such as *new order* and *lower order* suggest that this approach recognized that poverty is about oppressive systems, for which the kingdom-based order is the most adequate response.

To sum up, this social service–public domain involvement brings a new understanding of the poor and their reality. Poverty, in this reflection, is defined as the marginalization of outcastes from the public arena of the nation. Accordingly, poverty situations involve economics, justice, flawed national policies and structures and systems.

5

Four Contemporary Responses

A long with increasing numbers below the poverty line, the presence of the church among the poor has also increased remarkably in many parts of the world. This presence is marked by

> both continuity and change, both faithfulness to the past and boldness to engage the future, both constancy and contingency, both tradition and transformation (Bosch 1991, 366).

Inquiry into those "continuities and changes" within the church's search for a more effective way of responding to the poor reveals several types of ministries springing from mainline churches, Pentecostal churches, church-growth-oriented congregations and social action groups. The missional paradigms and assumptions about poverty of each are different. Four major assumptions at the grassroots level are represented in the following groups:[1]

1. The Evangelical Churches of India ministers to the landless poor in Mogalliwakkam.
2. The Church of South India ministers to the poor in Monnaivedu.
3. The Pentecostal Church in Chikkarayapuram ministers to quarry workers.
4. A Protestant action group called the Awaz ministers to the landless.

The Church-Growth Model

In this survey of contemporary responses, the Evangelical Churches of India (ECI) represents the church-growth approach to mission among the poor, characterized by a strong emphasis on people-group orientation as well as a passion for "winning the winnable."

The history of the Evangelical Churches of India is closely related to the life and ministry of the local ECI church in Porur, where the ministry began in 1957.[2] The national president of the Evangelical Churches of India, Ezra Sargunam, has said,

> It was here in Porur, that God gave the vision of the possibility of a church in every village and town. The affirmation that, if the Lord could call thirty out of one village, there must be hundreds of thousands of people out there if we could go and systematically evangelize every village and town. The vision caught on. . . . It all began in Porur, Madras (in Dhanraj 1992, 573).

The ECI began its ministry with the poor and the landless lower castes, since they were most responsive to the gospel. James, pastor of the Porur ECI church, says that the poor came to Christ "thinking that God will help them improve their life . . . and that they can find acceptance among the Christians."

The ECI has always been passionate about preaching the gospel. Traditionally, the ECI measured its effectiveness in the number of churches planted, attendance, baptisms and offerings. The ECI is the fastest-growing church in the Porur and Mannapakkam area. Today there are 680 ECI churches all over India.

The ECI is strong in its community orientation and in its affirmation of the "web of relationships." ECI pastors are highly relational, and church growth is their major measure of effectiveness. They also consider encounters with the principalities and powers an integral part of their mission.

Analysis of Assumptions

First, the ECI paradigm recognizes that poverty is the result of bad habits, large family size and wasteful expenditures. According to James,

"The poor do not have control over their lives, their habits, family size and spending. . . . In Mogalliwakkam, there are many poor people. They have a lot of problems like drinking and large families. They drink because they feel frustrated—because of their inability to provide for the needs of the family." He believes that the poor are heavily in debt because of expensive celebrations like *Adi kuzh ootharathu*, a festival for Mariamman (a Hindu goddess). However, to the poor in Mogalliwakkam, these celebrations are essential to please their gods.

This assumption has crucial consequences. The church affirms changes and improvements in the lives of individuals who have accepted Jesus Christ. Further, its definition of *improvements* includes primarily behavioral and moral change. According to James, "When [the poor] come to Jesus Christ they reduce wasteful expenditure and stop drinking." I observed at the time of data collection that some who had joined the ECI were constructing and renovating their houses. Joseph, a Christian community leader, commented, "Christians do well in life. They work hard and seek to live a better life." However, as James pointed out, "there has been no real income increase among the poor converts." In general, there is consensus that among the Christians in Mogalliwakkam, there has been a reduction in wasteful expenditure and increased regularity in working.

This assumption about poverty also affected their understanding of the recipients of transformation. Referring to the social changes, James stated, "These changes were only in those who had accepted Jesus Christ." The ECI paradigm affirmed that change in the larger society, such as reduction in the number of conflicts, was wrought through key people who had come to Christ.

Second, specifically referring to the role of the caste system in power structures, the ECI's dominant assumption is that

> though casteism is not encouraged or promoted in the church, it is often seen that caste does not become a barrier to people becoming Christians. . . . It is the prime duty of the Christian evangelist to see that he does not upset the long cherished customs and traditions but makes conversions with minimum social dislocations. This is religiously adhered to by the ECI in their ministry (Dhanraj 1992, 568).

In the ECI mission strategy, caste is a key variable used to define a people group. For the ECI, caste serves as a vehicle for people-group conversion. ECI strategy affirms the "web of relationships" prevalent in the community. Ezra Sargunam points out that "caste helps a society to make collective decisions. So let us learn to accept this 'order' rather than declare a war against it" (1974, 174). The ECI affirmed caste and other factors that "bind" the community so as to facilitate group decisions for growth of the church. Consequently, for ECI, poverty was not the result of inadequacies in relationships and did not involve structural issues.

This neglect of structural roles in poverty is most evident at the grassroots level. There is no overt critique of the local caste structure and little reflection on the role of structures in causing poverty in Mogalliwakkam. The pastor of the Porur church commented that he believed that "the Christians in Mogalliwakkam can be involved in politics and be honest there." For the ECI, politics was only an arena for practicing Christian ethics; political involvement was not considered a necessary part of mission strategy.

However, there have been some shifts within the ECI at the national level.[3] In a 1992 interview Sargunam said that the church is planning "to join the caste struggle. The church must stand with the oppressed." This indicates the ECI may be undergoing a major paradigm shift.

Third, at the grassroots level ECI leaders affirm that poverty is the result of the rejection that the poor face in society. The Porur pastor pointed out that the lower castes "turn to Christ because they think this God will help them improve their life . . . [and] they find acceptance with Christians." The ECI is very conscious of this need for acceptance among the poor and constantly seeks to meet this need. In fact, the ECI's emphasis on relationships and being accessible to the community during times of need has been a significant factor in the growth of the church. Members back up concern for the poor by emphasizing teaching and fellowship in the village and providing leadership opportunities in the church for lower-caste Hindu converts. Further, the fact that lower-caste converts can sit alongside higher-caste Christians has become a source of positive witness for the gospel in Mogalliwakkam.

Another assumption evident in the ECI paradigm is that poverty is the result of exploitation by principalities and powers. According to James, "These demons cause the poor to remain poor." He points out that the principalities and powers cause the poor to be ignorant through their belief in the Hindu gods. According to Joshua, pastor of the Mannapakkam ECI church, the principalities and powers bind the poor through different compulsions and habits. Ezra Sargunam also points out that the poor are kept vulnerable by principalities and powers. Therefore, within the ECI paradigm, poverty has clear cosmic dimensions. Mere mechanistic explanations of earthly forces do not seem adequate in the ECI's explanation of poverty.

Based on such assumptions about social reality, the ECI believes power encounters with principalities and powers is a key aspect of mission strategy. Signs and wonders play a crucial role in mission methods in communities like Mogalliwakkam. However, there is little evidence that ECI's grassroots practitioners recognize the role of principalities and powers in structures and systems.

Ultimately, for the ECI, poverty is the result of the poor not depending on God. The ECI believes that although the poor may come to Christ for various "social" reasons, they need to be taught to depend on God for their material needs, not on the church.

This assumption shapes the teaching ministry within the ECI. As James says, "Through teaching and testimonies, these poor Christians are constantly encouraged to look to God rather than depend on man." According to Joseph, a community leader, the Christians believe that God will help those in need. Gnanakkan, another local Christian, explained, with several examples, his belief that God had helped him and the other Christians in the village. He then commented, "It is beyond our understanding how God provides for our needs." Selvam, another community leader, said, "As a Christian, the little money I get, I take it to God to bless it and the money becomes enough to meet my basic needs." These comments suggest that the ECI's assumption that poverty is related to dependence on God has effectively shaped local church membership.

Impact

The Porur local church has 250 families as members; 80 of them are from a Hindu background, the majority from the lower castes, although today it has become more diverse.

However, response is not very positive among the Mudaliars or other higher-caste Hindus from this area. In fact, the higher castes feel that the church is for the lower castes. The pastor of the Porur church feels that higher-caste Hindus will need someone from the higher castes to witness to them.

While there is evidence of the growth of the church among the poor, James also expressed concern that "the poor [converts] are not active in reaching out to others." This lack of interest is significant, considering the fact that the poor were originally the focus of ECI ministry. Today they are not in the forefront of the mission outreach of the local church, which has shifted to the non-poor. James believes that the poor are "more concerned with their socioeconomic needs and do not have time for mission involvement . . . and they are disappointed that the church did not help meet their needs." Ezra Sargunam feels it is "probably because their foundations of faith were not firm and they suffer from inferiority complex." Two crucial questions must be considered. First, did this shift result from ECI's failure to meet the needs of the poor? Second, is this a natural outcome of strategies to "win the winnable" and "equip the equip-able" (the non-poor who can give time for mission)?

Although the local ECI has had positive impact on the lives of those poor who have come to Christ, primarily in the area of behavior, morals and reduction of wasteful expenditure, these changes were confined to the Christian poor.

Nevertheless, the converts in Mogalliwakkam now perceive a positive relationship between the God of the Christians and the poor. As Gnanakkan, a local Hindu convert, pointed out, "If we think about life's experience this way then our knowledge of God and our faith in God will increase." This attitude and awareness among Christians is different from the way their Hindu neighbors perceive the relationship between God and their poverty. The Hindu poor believe that God wills poverty and is the one who brings trouble. Converts' positive reading of the relationship between God and the poor is probably the result of the teaching of the local church.

Yet the local church is not included in the survival network of the community. The field study identified community leaders, political leaders and landlords, in that order, as key players in the community's network of survival. According to Selvam, a local Christian leader and ECI member involved in politics, "the ECI, the CSI and all the churches in this area have not done anything for our village." This comment from a church member who is also a community leader reflects the gap the

poor have discerned between the church's teaching and its active response.

Finally, this community is still in the grip of chronic poverty, gov-
ernmental neglect and inter-caste conflict. The ECI mission paradigm
at the local level does not provide a conducive environment to confront
these issues. The church is unaware of the powerlessness of the poor in
Mogalliwakkam, while the local factories, the landlords, the government and the political parties continue to perpetuate poverty in
Mogalliwakkam.

The Mainline Model

Among contemporary approaches to the poor in India, the Church
of South India (CSI) represents the mainline model, characterized by
the presence of a local church along with specific projects such as a
school and/or development project. Often the mainline church in a local area is part of a larger hierarchy.[4]

The Church of South India has been in Monnaivedu[5] since 1917.
Today 30 families make up its membership. The CSI also runs a primary school and implements a development project in Monnaivedu.
The school was started to serve the poorest in the village, who were
unwelcome in the schools in higher-caste villages. The development
project is comparatively new, implemented in this village in 1987, in
partnership with a Christian relief-and-development organization.

Monnaivedu is predominantly a lower-caste Hindu community of
465 families. Occupationally, it is a community of agricultural laborers
and a few small farmers. Several major political parties are represented
in this village, which is also characterized by low income and high incidence of debt.

Analysis of Assumptions

CSI leadership, community leaders and the development project staff
all agree that the poor in this village are unable to come together on
community issues. They are divided on the basis of political affiliations
as well as personal and family conflicts.

Responding to the disunity, the CSI church invests its time organizing the community through development programs. The formation of

a Village Development Association (VDA) was a step forward, especially in the absence of a local government body. Further, the VDA has become a forum to develop leadership within the community. However, according to a member of the VDA, the community still lacks unity and leadership.

According to the CSI's approach, poverty is also the result of ignorance, lack of education and superstition. Consequently, education became a primary concern for the CSI in Monnaivedu. Before the church started the school in this village, lower-caste Hindus were denied access to schooling. The CSI also responds to ignorance and superstitions among the poor through the development project's education and awareness-building programs. These suggest that poverty is the result of a lack of education, ignorance and superstition, and that the church must include response to these needs as an integral part of its mission.

The ministry of the CSI also believes that poverty is the lack of access to resources and the opportunity to develop. This assumption recognizes that the poor need resources from outside. The CSI plays the role of facilitator among the poor. The development project in particular is designed to help people tap resources available through the government and financial institutions. During my data collection, the community was organizing to access bank loans to purchase livestock. Because of the project's success in tapping external resources, the poor in the community do not come to the church for any economic assistance; they go to the church to worship.

Jayseelan, a local Christian politician, told me, "The church will take care of my relationship with God; in relation to the world and for doing good to my people I need to work through the political parties." This distancing of God and church from the good of the people is a cleavage with important ramifications at the grassroots level, suggesting that God is distanced from the day-to-day issues of poverty and the poor. Second, according to the area chairman of the pastorate, the local CSI church has nothing to do with the CSI school and development project. Again, this distancing of the local church has crucial implications. The poor see the church only as a place of worship and not as part of the survival network of the community. At the same time, the development project and school have been reduced to mere programs of the church. A third cleavage is between changes the gospel brings to the life of the poor and economic development. According to Rev. Prabhakar, "only behavioral changes result from conversion. Economic development is a different issue." This is the third fragmentation in the CSI approach to the poor: economic development was not included in the scope of transformational results of conversion.

These three assumptions suggest that God, church and conversion have practically nothing to do with the day-to-day economic good of the people. Poverty is an earthly issue for which God, the church and conversion are not the solutions.

Impact

Hindus in Monnaivedu are open and responsive to the church and the message of the church. Up to 60 or 70 Hindu families listen to the messages of the church regularly. Several even join the all-night prayer that the local church conducts every month.

The Christian poor in the village attend church regularly and contribute generously. Further, the poor from Monnaivedu no longer come to church looking for assistance, although they did so earlier.

Community initiative is high and the Village Development Association is confident of tapping government resources. The community is organized, including a women's association, village development association and youth club. In fact, the CSI approach emphasizes people's initiative as a key indicator to measure effectiveness of the church's mission.

The primary school has altered the community beyond imparting formal education. It has inculcated in parents a positive attitude toward education. The school has also helped improve the children's behavior and general cleanliness.

And the community includes the Village Development Association as an integral part of the community network, along with the village elders and political party representatives.

However, the local CSI church is not part of this community network, although it has been in the community for the last 75 years. As mentioned earlier, this could be the result of the cleavage between the local church and the mission of the church. In any case, this division seems to have had a negative impact on the image of the church.

According to the poor in Monaivedu the local government system is corrupt and will work only for the powerful. In the face of this, the CSI's local paradigm does not allow the local church to relate the work of God, the local church and the conversion of the person to confronting inadequacies in the local structure and systems.

The Pentecostal Model

This work among the poor is probably one of the more difficult models to stereotype because of its basic autonomous nature. However, some common features such as a deep desire to reach the unreached and to focus generally on the poor and not on any particular caste group allow us to say accurately that Pentecostal churches are among the more active among the poor today. The Pentecostal church based at Chikkarayapuram, India, is one such example.[6]

The church's life and history revolves very much around one person, the pastor of the church. After serving as a teacher for 15 years, Devakadatchium felt called to start a church in the area.[7] He observed that, during Jesus' ministry, "he spent his time among the common people and the poor who are most willing to trust in God." Therefore, he opted to start his mission with the poor. This option for the poor in the Pentecostal approach is similar to some radical social-action models. The Pentecostal intentionality in opting for the poor is more than a pragmatic choice for the poor based on positive response. Pentecostal ministry to the poor is preceded by conscious interpretation and obedience to the understanding that Jesus came to *be* poor. In this, the poor are more than a "responsive audience." This commitment of the Pentecostal church has enabled the church to remain a church of the poor in many places in the world.

Today about 40 families are members of the Chikkarayapuram Pentecostal church, and approximately 100 attend worship. The church draws members from all castes but predominantly from the lower socioeconomic class. According to the pastor, "Since we teach about Christ's love, both the lower and the higher castes learn to worship alongside each other here." Like other Pentecostal churches, this one seeks after those who are "prepared by God" and does not specifically adopt a community approach in its outreach.

The church places high emphasis on relationship, and the pastor invests much time in nurturing members and teaching the Word. Prayer and fasting form an important part of church mission strategy. Power encounters along with signs and wonders form a key component in the life of the church. Leadership of the church revolves around the pastor and his family.

The church ministers to several communities in the area, including a community of stonecutters (quarry workers). In Devakadatchium's assessment, these people are poor and are responsive to the message: "They listen to the message and come to the church for prayer." There is a primary school in the village and high school in the town nearby. There is no primary health center in the village. Scarcity of water is another issue with which the community struggles.

The Quarry Workers' Cooperative Society is a key people's organization in this community.[8] This government society has 314 members and is an active part of the community's life. The Quarry Workers' Cooperative Society leases the quarry hill from the government. Because of the physical labor involved, the quarry workers rarely work all the days in a week. Frequent injuries, unavailability of explosives, unavailability of the pump to drain water from the pit, and rain all prevent regular work. Balakrishnan, a quarry worker, explained that workers "need another job apart from the quarry work as an income source."

Analysis of Assumptions

According to the Pentecostal approach reflected in this context, poverty is the result of lack of belief. Belief requires more than an acknowledgment of God, and the poor are poor because they do not believe in the Bible. Devakadatchium commented, "They [the poor] have not believed in God's Word. God will lift those who trust him." He continued, "Since they do not believe in the Word, they do not have hope in life and their fatalistic mindset is not transformed." With these comments, the church places the blame for being poor on the poor themselves. Speaking of the behavior and wasteful expenditures of the poor, the pastor points out that "if they are released from their sin, they can work hard, save money and do well in life."

This understanding of poverty has several ramifications for the mission of the church. The teaching of the church encourages the poor to look to God as the giver of all blessing. The links among the Word, trust, sin, poverty and response to poverty are strongly maintained in the Pentecostal paradigm.

Consequently, a key element in the Pentecostal message seen here is that when the poor come to Jesus Christ, their lives will improve, that house construction, regular work and things like that will then be possible. In this paradigm the definition of "transformational results" of conversion affirms the materiality of salvation. Life is not divided into spiritual and material. Life is all spiritual, and the material is derivative and secondary to the spiritual. The Pentecostal paradigm, as expressed by Devakadatchium, defines transformation as behavioral, moral and value change—and includes finding employment, release from debts and getting assistance from the government. It is interesting to note that although the Pentecostals view transformation through the "conversion lens," the paradigm has a holistic scope beyond behavioral and moral changes. The Pentecostal paradigm affirms the materiality of salvation.

However, while the Pentecostal approach recognizes socioeconomic depravity of the poor and defines transformation in material terms, when it comes to the church's active intervention in these needs, the pastor responds, "We pray for the needy. . . . We do what we can. We can only pray for them." Accordingly, there is a clear division between becoming involved in socioeconomic issues and the spiritual ministry of the church. According to the pastor, "When we serve God, we cannot serve another master."

Second, in the Pentecostal approach prayer and fasting are linked to response to the poor. This suggests that poverty requires a response of prayer. "We keep the people in prayer, and God blesses them with a job. . . . One became a conductor, another got a job in an export company," the pastor said. "The Bible promises that 'I will bless the land.' So we pray for the community needs also." When the poor in the church apply for government loans, the church prays. They do so believing, as the pastor says, that "God who made the rulers and the kings is the One who is listening to our prayers."

In the Pentecostal paradigm, poverty and the lordship of God over the rulers are closely related, as are repentance and blessing. The church believes that the God who came for the poor will hear their prayers. According to the pastor, "When the poor cry and pray to God for healing and help, God hears their prayer and responds. Then they come to Christ and begin knowing that Christ is the only true God." Therefore, according to the Pentecostal reading of poverty, fasting and prayer are essential in mission among the poor.

The Pentecostal paradigm also suggests that poverty is the expression of the devil's control over a whole village. This assumption suggests that the first thing to be done in a village is "to tie the devil before going into any village." Apart from the personal captivity of the poor, this suggests the collective captivity of the whole community of the poor.

However, interpretation of the devil's work is more in terms of preventing the work of the church. Principalities and powers are seen as a possible threat to the work, and through prayer and fasting the Evil One needs to be tied. As a strategy, this church does not enter any village until church members have prayed over the village for at least a month. In this Pentecostal paradigm of poverty, principalities and powers are an important force to consider. However, the church does not explain the role of principalities and powers specifically in terms of perpetuating poverty.

Impact

The poor respond positively to the ministry of signs and wonders, of binding the Evil One both in the community and in the individual. This evokes a positive response from the Hindu poor. They request that the church pray for their needs also. One woman says the healing and conversion of her husband has resulted in the whole family being healed and becoming a witness for Jesus Christ in the community.

But the church is not part of the community's survival network. Political party leaders, village priests and the Quarry Workers' Cooperative Society are key players in this community network. The Quarry Workers' Cooperative Society is an economic institution that caters to social needs by providing loan facilities and meeting medical needs. Could neglect of the social needs of the poor be a reason the poor neglect the church?

The community continues to be powerless in relation to bureaucratic structures and political parties. The community was struggling to get ration cards and a health facility for the village. The people are oppressed by local political parties. However, Pentecostal assumptions about poverty do not consider these issues as valid mission involvement.

The poor here have been tied to the profession of stonecutting for generations. Women in the community asked, "What can we do? It is our fate. We have to go on working like this." Widows and the aged in the community who do not have strong sons are also marginalized by the quarry work.

Even the church points out that little change has occurred in the community. Devakadatchium says, "People are still very worldly and the devil is active among them." Such statements reflect the general mood of the community, as well as the overall impact of the Pentecostal church in the last eight years.

The Action Group Model

Many parachurch and action groups are involved among the poor. In India, Awaz is an evangelical fellowship of believers,[9] related to an organization called ADORE (Agency for Development of the Oppressed through Relief and Education). Awaz includes members of churches but is not organically related to a church.[10]

Cyrus, leader of the Awaz fellowship, explains the group: "Awaz is a fellowship where all brothers and sisters are equal." A lawyer who was instrumental in the founding of the Awaz mission,[11] Cyrus promises, "In the first half of the next century in India there will be a great Christian movement. We mobilize the youth . . . intensively."

Awaz's strategy for mission deliberately attempts to model the biblical description of the kingdom of God. Members engage in both micro and macro issues in the community. Simple lifestyle marks the fellowship. Legal aid and community organization are among methods used in Awaz's approach to the poor.

Josiprasda is one of 20 villages served by this fellowship. The area was Awaz's first mission field, where it initiated a peasant movement, organizing the poor against oppression by rich landlords and illegal government actions. Awaz was able to help the poor with legal advice and initiated a stay order on illegal proceedings against the poor. Some of Awaz's most effective work has been in Josiprasda and Gomma villages.

Awaz had been active among the poor in this area for almost 10 years. Their experience has been so effective that they have sought to replicate this approach in other places.

Analysis of Assumptions

A key theme in the Awaz paradigm is that poverty is the result of structural inadequacies. Cyrus asserts, "All sinful structures are a result of sin. [They are] exploitative economic structures, reinforced by graded social structures [that] are . . . sinful structures in the human community" (Awaz 1985, 8). These sinful structures then perpetuate, according to Awaz, 10 different kinds of bondage among the poor: "*adharma* (sin), ignorance, injustice, poverty, exploitation, oppression, bureaucratic tyranny, war, abuse of nature and male chauvinism" (ibid.). In Awaz, the poor are categorized into classes rather than caste groups.

Among structural factors, Awaz staff identify the *malgujari* system as the key force they encounter in their work. In the *malgujari* system, Ravi Das explains, "rich landlords exploit the poor. The rich buy the land and use it to set up factories." This is the "ghost of feudal structure," sustained by other power structures including "corrupt panchayat authorities . . . local government officials and cankered political leaders" (Awaz 1987, 9). Political parties play a key role also within poverty situations. "Politicians ensure that the people are divided. These parties exploit the village conflicts" (ibid.). Therefore, for Awaz, poverty is an issue of structure and exploitative systems.

Consequently, the mission of Awaz is shaped by this understanding of the context of mission. If poverty is about inadequate structures, the kingdom of God offers an alternative "system of righteousness, peace and joy in the Holy Spirit" (Cyrus 1992, 1). Awaz describes the kingdom of God as "socialistic structures or Christ structures . . . [where there is] collectivization of means of production and distribution." Second, Awaz equips Christians to participate actively in politics. Cyrus states, "I am convinced that unless Christians dominate the political field, there will be no salvation. So, in politics, Christians should be very active and wield great influence to cause structural changes."

Apart from describing poverty as a structural issue, Awaz's approach suggests that poverty is also the result of character inadequacies. Consequently, Cyrus commented, Awaz seeks to "transform the character of the people, struggle against the present exploitative structures and mold new socialistic structures."

For Awaz, poverty is the result of sin. People are self-centered and seek to monopolize God's earth and its resources to become rich. Hunger is a result of this self-centeredness. Inadequate structures are also a result of humans' sinful actions. So people need to be redeemed from sin. Therefore, in Awaz's paradigm, poverty is rooted in the fallenness of humankind with ramifications in their character and structures. "Any salutary changes wrought in the economic, social, political and religious structures without corresponding changes in the individuals who handle them are bound to fumble in the long run" (Awaz 1987, 7).

This understanding has crucial implications for Awaz's strategy among the poor, chiefly the role of staff and the training provided for youth in the villages. According to Cyrus, "*Dharma Palaks* are the heart and soul of the mission." These *Dharma Palaks* are "spiritually inclined youth" from among the poor who will listen to the poor, model lives like the early Christians, and organize the struggle to create Christian structures. "Our role is to train leaders. The intellect of the poor needs to be developed and their spirituality should be enhanced." This also implies that members of the Awaz fellowship "provide the moral and spiritual leadership for mobilizing the young people."

Awaz's approach to the poor also suggests that poverty is the result of exploitation of structures by principalities and powers. "Satan, an evil power opposed to God, is working in this universe, and he is striving to topple the cosmic plan of God by separating everything in the universe from Christ" (Cyrus 1992, 4). The mission paradigm of Awaz recognizes the role of principalities and powers in the exploitation of the poor. Structures are seen as being demonized, and in that sense become agents of the evil one. This understanding of the principalities and powers in relation to evil structures and the commitment of Awaz to the kingdom of God provide the basic framework for mission.

Awaz's paradigm suggests that religion (Hindu, Christian and others) is used by the devil to perpetuate poverty. According to Cyrus, "The Hindu faith causes us to believe that the earth is the domain of Satan, so we should not work against these structures." Therefore, Awaz responds by challenging the religious beliefs of the poor and non-poor.

However, in spite of this understanding of the role of principalities and powers, Awaz's paradigm does not adequately deal with the role of principalities and powers in the personal lives of the poor.

Awaz's approach does understand that poverty is an expression of distortions in spirituality. As Cyrus pointed out, one reason for poverty is the poor look to the rich for salvation and not to God. Poverty is also the symptom of the inadequate spirituality of the non-poor.

Therefore, in its response Awaz, says Cyrus, seeks to inculcate "real spirituality where both the material and spiritual aspects of our life are focused on Jesus and are directed God-ward." Cyrus calls this "socialistic spirituality," in which the traditional dichotomy between the spiritual and the material is not recognized and both are submitted to God.

Awaz also responds by instilling a form of spirituality Cyrus describes as "seek[ing] to harmonize everything so as to bring full justice, everlasting peace and eternal joy to all, everywhere, under the inspiration, guidance and power of God who is its proprietor, pivot and architect" (1992, 6).

Impact

First, the Awaz fellowship is an integral part of the survival network of the community. The poor perceive that Awaz is consciously on their side.

Second, the community is confident of dealing with issues of powerlessness in their context. The landless in Josiprasda are aware of the role of the government, local political leaders and community leaders of the higher castes in perpetuating their poverty. Because of the work of Awaz, the poor are not only aware of their powerlessness but also conscious of their legal rights.

Third, economically the community is still poor. Villagers have a high level of debt. Earlier, landlords were the primary source of loans. Now that the people have revolted against the rich landlords, the poor are compelled to go outside the village to borrow. There is a high incidence of migration. A villager observed that "employment in the village is becoming difficult. They migrate to towns nearby as well as to Nagpur and Bombay. The children's studies are affected." Could neglect of wealth creation be a natural result of emphasis on structural causes of poverty?

Fourth, in general the community does not recognize that the work of Awaz is motivated by God and that Jesus Christ is the God of the members of Awaz. "Cyrus came to work with us. I do not know who his God is. . . . Sometimes I think that they are like gods to us, for not many in the village work for us." About Jesus, one community member believed that "among the 33 *crores* [330 million] gods, Jesus is also one of the gods. We can worship him also. We do not *abhiman* [give special preference to] any one god." The work of Awaz does not seem to have altered the perception of God or enhanced awareness of Jesus Christ as God. During the field study, I had an opportunity to discuss this conclusion with Cyrus. He was particularly unhappy with the fact that Awaz's work did not enable the poor to know that Awaz worked out of a motivation directly resulting from belief in Jesus as God.

Finally, the poor in these communities still seemed to believe God was on the side of the rich. "We do not even have money to garland *Murugan* [one of the Hindu gods]. . . . The moneyed people dominate all areas of life." A woman said, "We do not worship any god," while her husband countered, "Our work is our God."

Notes

[1] The data on contemporary approaches to the poor was gathered through field study conducted in the summer of 1992. The primary purpose of the field study was to understand the church and its theology of poverty rather than to understand the poor. Further, the study specifically inquired into the theology of poverty of four contemporary ministries. It did not study the whole theology of ministry of these four ministries. There are three major biases to avoid while gathering qualitative data (Miles and Huberman 1984, 230): (1) The holistic fallacy (assuming events and processes as a patterned whole). During the study, and more specifically during the data collection, care was taken to minimize this bias. Care was also taken to report the seeming contradictions and loose ends without trying to mold them into one whole. (2) The elite bias (depending heavily on well-informed source). During data collection attempts were made to increase the number of sources and also to verify often by cross-checking. (3) "Going native" (being co-opted into the local perspective). Through constant cross-checking of tentative conclusions, this risk was minimized. However, the study tended to rely on the views of the community in two specific areas: the causes of poverty, and the impact of the ministries.

[2] Data regarding the ministry of the ECI was gathered from pastors of the ECI churches in Porur and Mannapakkam (James and Joshua), the district superintendent of the ECI Porur Area (Sadhu Singh), Ezra Sargunam (president of the ECI), community leaders (Joseph, Gnanakkan), representatives of different political parties (Selvam, Rajshekar) and families in Mogalliwakkam.

[3] This is an example of a "loose end" observed during the data collection and analysis. Any analysis of paradigms at the grassroots level will encounter such "loose ends" and even seeming contradictions.

[4] During the field study the focus was on the local church in Monnaivedu, part of the Ikkadu Pastorate of Madras diocese. The Ikkadu Pastorate is part of the central area of the Madras diocese. The Central area has 18 pastorates. Madras diocese has four such areas. All the pastorates report to the area council chairman and through him to the Bishop of Madras, the Rt. Rev. Azariah. In all, the Madras diocese has 104 churches, including Monnaivedu. Data about CSI ministry in Monnaivedu was gathered through interviews with the area chairman of the CSI, Ikkadu Diocese (Charles Prabhakar), local church catechist (Sirgurudass), school teachers, development project staff, community

leaders (Michael Raj), church leaders (Padmini), political leaders (Jayseelan) and other community members.

⁵ The Monnaivedu CSI is one of 24 churches in the Ikkadu Pastorate. According to the area chairman of the Ikkadu Pastorate, the Monnaivedu church is the most effective rural congregation, showing much initiative and also spiritually strong. The CSI church is the only church in this village and has been serving this community for 75 years. It has a catechist who provides leadership; he is assisted by a committee of four members. The Rev. Charles Prabhakar provides overall leadership for the pastorate.

⁶ The data about the ministry of the Pentecostal church was gathered from Devakadatchium, the pastor of the church in Chikkaryapuram; local community leaders in Kollaicheri (Aaron and others); and a local community member, the secretary and the president of the Quarry Workers' Cooperative Society.

⁷ The Pentecostal church started here at Chikkarayapuram. Later, in response to several requests, Devakadatchium moved the church to Poonamallee. Poonamallee is about 2.5 miles from Chikkarayapuram, where the pastor stays. This Pentecostal church (hereafter referred to as the Chikkarayapuram Pentecostal church) is an independent church without any organizational affiliation with similar organizations.

⁸ During the field study members of the Quarry Workers' Cooperative Society were interviewed. They were V. Aaron (ex-panchayat member of the Congress party), Balakrishnan (ex-panchayat member of the DMK party), and E. Shanmugam (ex-president of the Cooperative society).

⁹ The data about the work of Awaz in Josiprasda area was gathered through interviews with Cyrus (leader of the Awaz fellowship), Ravi Das and Mr. Santosh (members of the fellowship), Vicar Verghese (Marthoma church-treasurer of the Raipur unit of Awaz), Toli Ram (president of the Josiprasda Kisan Sangh), Asha Ram (a farmer from Josiprasda) and several families in Belvetta, Gatapar and Josiprasda.

¹⁰ Awaz is not a registered organization; it has remained as a fellowship. It does not raise any funds on its own. ADORE is based in Kerala and comprises leaders from different Christian groups who raise funds for organizations like Awaz. Awaz fellowship members are not allowed to have any financial transactions, and none of the Awaz members holds office in ADORE.

¹¹ Although Cyrus was instrumental in developing the vision behind the whole movement, including the forming of Awaz and ADORE, he does not hold any office. He is a lawyer by profession and sees a close link between work among the poor and the law. He provides "visionary leadership" for Awaz members. Awaz began its work in Ernakulam (Kerala) with ministry among those affected by Hansens disease. After some exploratory work, the fellowship decided to begin its north India work in Raipur, which it did in March 1983. The fellowship focused on Satnamis in Raipur district. As part of its initial strategy, Awaz started 25 fellowships, seeking to use these as forums to train villagers. However, Awaz abandoned the effort, since it did not address the real issues of the

poor. At the same time, one of the communities was struggling with an issue of injustice. A rich rice mill owner had tortured a Harijan boy, named Hemalal, aged 12. Police did not help the community, so the Harijans organized themselves to protest. The police were compelled to arrest the mill owner. Awaz was involved in the protest at this time. This event brought much good will for Awaz (Awaz 1985, 17) and changed the direction of its ministry.

PART TWO

LEARNING FROM THE POOR

In Part One we examined assumptions and theories that have guided reflections and ministries among the poor in the past and into the present. In Part Two we inquire into the meaning of powerlessness of the poor using these clues about dimensions of poverty as a frame of reference.

We start with the assumption that poverty is about power relationships. Reflections on insights from history suggest that poverty is no simple social phenomenon that can be explained using a few isolated variables. As we saw in Part One, development theorists; liberation, Dalit and evangelical theologians; and grassroots ministries among the poor all affirm the fact that authentic development is not possible without addressing power issues (Bosch 1991, 357).

6

Power, Worldview
and Poverty

Studies about power in relation to poverty have become a major theme
in poverty debates and in development circles. Strategies for participation are giving way to empowerment strategies. Poverty measurements are grappling with indices to measure power inequalities.
Sustainability standards are being redefined with power as a key variable (Chambers 1983, 112,116).

However, Sik Hung Ng points out that the focus has been on "what
kind of power" rather than on "power inequality" (1980, 189). John
Friedmann's "(dis)empowerment" model is a case in point; he develops
his thesis on power relations around eight bases of social power.[1] Others who have studied power inequality have focused on the creation of
power. Their views cluster around two major theories, namely, the dependency theory, and the trust theory of power creation. The former,
based on the early 1960s work of Richard Emerson, assumes that power
is created in the context of social interdependence, where "A uses B's
dependency to make demands on B that results in changes in B's actions
and ideas" (Olsen and Marger 1993, 5). The trust theory, on the other
hand, based on the work of Talcott Parsons in the same period, suggests
"power rests on people's involvement in social relationships in which
they trust others" (ibid.). Power structures have also been studied with
an emphasis on network and content analysis (Domhoff 1993, 170).
Others have studied decision-making patterns focusing on the issue of
who governs or who is in control or exerts influences." Powerlessness
was perceived merely as the negative image of powerfulness.

However, powerlessness is a reality in itself, that affects the lives of
many millions—one-fifth of the world's population.[2]

Poverty Relationships

Powerlessness is relational and is an integral part of poverty relationships. Poverty relationships are the context within which the poor experience powerlessness. Therefore, it is important to understand poverty relationships in order to understand powerlessness.

Basic Unit in Poverty Relationships

Most development studies affirm that the household is the basic economic and political unit within poverty situations. It is also the basic unit of community, social and religious life. Households, therefore, have become the frame through which poverty relationships are analyzed.

However, households do not exist in isolation, especially in poverty situations. Households are connected, and in their connectedness they form the substance of a community. Therefore, like households, the community is also an integral unit.

Finally, both the household and the community are formed of persons. People within the household and the community are the defining force within these units. Both household and community represent persons in relationship.

Therefore, the basic unit in a poverty relationship is a three-dimensional unit consisting of the household, the community and the individuals. Powerlessness is the experience of "a people," as liberation theologians suggest.

Domains of Poverty Relationships

John Friedmann defines four clusters of relationships—the state, civil society, corporate economy and the political community—as the "domain of social practice" (1992, 26–31).

Following Friedmann's analysis, I use the phrase "domains of poverty relationships" to refer to the many relationships that characterize poverty situations.

In the Indian situation, yet another significant set of relationships is with the religious world, establishing the norms, symbols and the leaders who govern the religion of the people. The life of the Hindu poor is dominated by their religion. This is surely true in many other cultures of poverty, as well.

Two characteristics of these domains of relationships must be mentioned at the outset:

1. Each of the domains of relationships (five, including social, political, economic, religious and bureaucratic) contains within it several centers of power (Friedmann 1992, 26). Hence, the term *domain* refers to a collection of powers.
2. Further, these five domains of relationships are in constant interaction with each other. They do not exist isolated from each other. They mutually reinforce each other. Various power expressions take place within these domains of poverty relationships.

Life Space in Poverty Relationships

Poverty is about real people, living in real life space. It is

> people [who] inhabit these spaces, and it is these flesh-and-blood people who suffer the booms and busts of the economy. . . . They are socially *connected* beings who live in families, households, and communities and who interact with neighbors, kinfolk, friends and familiars (Friedmann 1992, 90).

Based on insights from John Friedmann's works and my own learning from grassroots colleagues over the years, three aspects of "life space" need to considered.

First, the experience of powerlessness takes place in this real life space. Friedmann describes this space as the economic space over which both the political community and the state claim sovereignty (1992, 29). Only by examining the real life space of the poor can we recognize the "human depth and [the] toughness that are a promise of life" (Gutiérrez 1988, xxii).

Second, a cursory examination of the life space of the poor suggests that it includes micro, macro and global dimensions. The micro level refers to relationships the poor have with communities outside the basic unit. Macro refers to the national community and global refers to international communities. National and global political economies, legislation and structural adjustments initiated by global financial institutions and such other forces all affect the basic unit within poverty relationships.

Third, apart from these three levels, poverty situations are also influenced by the cosmic level.

> Day to day life is . . . lived in fear [of these forces]. People attempt to manipulate these forces to their benefit or to propitiate them when they have been offended (Samuel and Sugden 1987, 143).[3]

Rulers and authorities in the heavenly realms constantly impinge on the lives of the poor in their experience of their own poverty.

Components of Social Reality in Poverty Relationships

Thus far, we have identified the basic unit, the domains of relationships, and the real living space within poverty situations. Since chronic poverty is intergenerational, time-related forces also need to be considered.

I found a helpful frame of reference to exegete social reality in the works of the ancient sages of Hinduism, the *sastra-karas*, writers and teachers of the Hindu *sastras* or scientific treatises. According to them, social reality can be divided into four interrelated categories: *Srama* (effort), *desa* (place and region), *kala* (time), and *guna* (natural traits) (Prabhu 1940, 73).

Since my work has sought to understand and respond to the powerlessness of the Hindu poor, it would be appropriate to begin with categories that they use to classify their reality. Also, this frame of reference that Hindu teachers have used provides a more holistic frame of reference.

Therefore, applying the four components of social reality to my study, I have classified my conclusions into the following four categories:

1. *Srama:* effort of humans. I include various relationships and actions characteristic of poverty relationships. This inquiry into poverty relationships examines four specific aspects, namely, the god-complexes of the powerful, the exclusion of the poor, the fragmentation of community and depriving the poor of love and compassion.
2. *Desa:* place and region. This category examines spatial dimensions of poverty situations—the physical isolation of the poor, their vulnerability to natural disasters and their dependence on and depleting of natural resources.

3. *Kala:* the time dimension of the relationship between power and poverty. Here we inquire into present physical weakness, historical distortions and the hopelessness for the future.
4. *Guna:* character or natural traits. I include reflections on the deeper level issues of "being" of the persons involved in poverty. Because poverty is about persons in relationships, it is important to examine the basic nature, understanding, beliefs, and other traits that form the essence of these persons. Our inquiry will include the identity of the poor, the role of faith in private and public life and understanding of power.

Power, Poverty and Relationships *(Srama)*

Poverty is relational. Similarly, power is relational. Social power is an interactive process that resides within social interactions and relationships. *Srama* (the efforts of humans, including actions and relationships) within poverty relationships can give us important clues for understanding powerlessness.

Captivity of the Poor Within God-Complexes

Poverty is not about numbers. It is about inequality, and specifically about inequality in power relationships. It is about a minority, "less numerous, [who] performs all political functions, monopolizes power and enjoys the advantages that power brings" (Curtis 1981, 332). In rural India, this minority includes a triangular power bloc consisting of rich farmers, powerful industrial houses and professionals supported by the political system (Murickan 1991, 4). They systematically exclude the poor from access to education, wealth and benefits from the system. They seek to play god in the lives of the poor. They combine to form "god-complexes."[4]

The "God-Complex"

First, these powers seek to influence the future of the poor. The powerful within poverty relationships base their power on what Max Weber calls the "eternal yesterday" (Curtis 1981, 427), and they influence the "eternal tomorrows" of the poor. This ability to influence the eternal tomorrows, or future generations, of a people is normally attributed to gods.

Second, the powerful seek to influence multiple areas of life. For example, the influence of a landlord gradually begins to affect village politics on one hand and family celebrations of the landless, on the other. The influence of the powerful is pervasive.

Third, the powerful within poverty situations operate under the assumption that their power is immutable and can never be challenged.

Finally, in poverty situations, the powerful work in conjunction with others to keep the poor powerless. *God-complex* is a collective term, since it involves an interplay of several power holders and secondary players. As Wright Mills suggests:

> The power elite are not solitary rulers. . . .Advisors and consult-
> ants, spokesmen and opinion-makers are often the captains of their
> higher thought and decision. Immediately below the elite are the
> professional politicians of the middle levels of power (Mills 1959,
> 4).

T. K. Oommen comments that there are two kinds of groups that wield power in a village community: the "power reservoirs," who may not have formal decision-making roles, and the "power exercisers," who shape formal decision-making structures. Together they form the "power pool" in the community, and within the god-complexes mutually reinforce each other (Oommen 1990, 131). As Gunnar Myrdal observed, for example, "India is ruled by compromises and accommodations within and between the upper class and the various groups that constitute the bulk of the upper class" (1968, 766).

Through these different means the relative powers within poverty situations play gods over the poor, creating god-complexes within poverty relationships.

Walter Wink's work on the nature and unmasking of the "domination system" sheds more light on the nature of the god-complexes. Wink's primary thesis in his book *Engaging the Powers* is that we need to avoid

> cosmic personifications that disguise the power arrangement of
> the state . . . [and the] mystification of actual power relations that

provided divine legitimacy for oppressive earthly institutions (1992, 25).

Wink goes on to describe a strategy for "unmasking the powers" represented by the world's domination system. I personally do not see the need to depersonalize cosmic forces or principalities and powers to understand the relationship between cosmic forces and the structures and systems. I see in Wink's proposal to depersonalize the cosmic forces an attempt to demonize the "enemy" so that our response to the structures can be sustained and radical. However, Wink's description of the domination system appears to be about the power of structures rather than the cosmic powers in structures.

Nevertheless, Wink's description of the domination system is helpful for understanding the nature of the god-complex in poverty relationships. Wink suggests that the domination system of the world teaches us to value power (1992, 54). Second, the domination system is a contaminant; it requires a society to become more like itself (1992, 40). Third, this domination system acquires a sense of independence "beyond human control" (1992, 41); it assumes an identity of its own. Fourth, the domination system wounds the soul of its subjects; it makes them feel valueless (1992, 101). Such is the nature of the god-complex that keeps the poor powerless.

These god-complexes operate through all the domains of poverty relationships, including the religious system, to perpetuate powerlessness. A case in point is the way landlords avoid land redistribution in India by writing off surplus land to the *mutts* (temple trusts) (Farzand Ahmed 1992, 59). Laws, government policies, systems and structures all serve as tools to siphon benefits toward the powerful. Joe Remenyi points out that powerlessness and poverty are

a symptom of the existence of systems of injustice in our societies. No matter how much one wishes to avoid the rhetoric of the do-gooder fraternity, the reality is that the poor are victims of entrenched socio-economic systems that allow poverty to persist (1991, 31).

Another tool commonly used within the god-complex is the mass media. Through mass communication the powerful within the different domains of poverty relationships ensure that the "vast majority of the population . . . becomes relatively powerless and . . . increasingly manipulated by the power elite" (Mills, quoted in Olsen and Marger 1993, 155). The wants and aspirations of the poor are shaped in the name of "creating a market" through effective use of mass media in the god-complex (Ng 1980, 110). The different god-complexes use structures, systems and people in the different domains of poverty relationships to create and sustain themselves.

Within the different structures and systems is an ideological center or inner reality that shapes the various structures and systems. The structures, systems and people involved in the various social, political, religious, economic and bureaucratic relationships are influenced by this inner reality. This inner reality provides the inner logic for the structures and systems. It provides interpretations for issues in life that deal with ultimate values of life and events. For example, economic systems are not merely a combination of several mechanistic forces locked up in a cause-and-effect relationship. Different economic systems communicate different interpretations of life's ultimate value. This is the ideological center that shapes structures, systems and people. These ideological centers deal with ultimate values in life and are inextricably related to structures and systems. They form the "spirituality" of the various economic, social, political, bureaucratic and religious units.

Therefore, apart from structure, systems and people, there exists the "interiority of earthly institutions or structures or systems" (Wink 1992, 77). These "inner spiritualities" become the system above the systems. They provide that underlying "spiritual dimension in the victimization of the poor and the power accruing activity of the systems" (Linthicum 1991, 19).

To sum up, god-complexes are

1. Clusters of power (social, economic, bureaucratic, political and religious) within the domain of poverty relationships that absolutize themselves to keep the poor powerless;
2. A function of structures, systems, people and the spiritual interiority within each cluster of power.

God-Complexes and the Powerless

What implications for the poor are inherent in this understanding of their captivity within god-complexes?

First, issues of power and powerlessness cause discomfort among the structures, systems and the non-poor involved in the god-complexes. The powerful within these god-complexes (such as the elite, policy-makers and other power holders) are uncomfortable with issues of powerlessness. According to Robert Chambers, the elite would prefer to respond to the physical weakness of the poor, rather than deal with issues of powerlessness (1983, 164).

Second, the power of these god-complexes is comprehensive, intense and extensive (Wrong 1979, 14). Following Marvin Olsen's levels of social power,[5] the relationship between the poor and the powers within the god-complexes is such that the power holder lays the parameters for all relationships. These aspects of power in poverty situations qualify it to be considered a kind of "god-complex."

Third, the common tendency of these god-complexes is to blur the distinction between compliance based on fear of further deprivation and compliance based on rewards. For the poor, any reward helps them to survive their general deprivation. Therefore, when the powerful threaten to withdraw rewards, for the poor this becomes a choice between survival and death.

Summary

To sum up, these reflections suggest that powerlessness of the poor is relational. Powerlessness is the captivity of the poor within god-complexes created by the non-poor, built into structures and systems, shaped by the spiritual interiority within the power cluster. If poverty and powerlessness are about captivity of the poor to god-complexes, should not the response to powerlessness be defined as establishing the kingdom of God?

Exclusion from Mainstream of Life

An important hallmark of poverty relationships is that the poor are constantly excluded from what the powerful define as the "mainstream" in public life. The various clusters of power within poverty relationships are designed to exclude the many and protect the interests of the few. Technological revolutions tend to protect the interests of the few. Benefits of economic growth, poverty alleviation programs, the green revolution, and so forth all tend to gravitate toward the few rich. In the final analysis, it appears the playing ground is tilted against the poor,

excluding them from mainstream politics, religion, economics and social and bureaucratic relationships. As Shankar and Rajshekar, local
political leaders in Mogalliwakkam, said during an interview in July
1992:

> When we go to visit the government officers we realize that we do
> not have the financial capability to command their respect. If we
> went to these leaders in a car or on a motorbike, they will respect
> us. We can only go by bus and then we have to walk to the offices
> . . . and then they will know that we do not have the money to give
> them . . . and will ignore us.

Mogalliwakkam is a microcosm of communities experiencing this form
of exclusion from various arenas of public life. Such exclusion is brutal,
in that no niceties are involved.

Exclusion of the poor is part of a "systematic process of disempowerment" (Friedmann 1992, 30) from the economic, political, social, bureaucratic and religious life of the community. When it is time for
elections and for organizing political rallies, the poor are the most
important targeted participants. But when the dust settles after these
elections and rallies, passion for the poor also settles down. When the
poor flee from rural poverty to towns and cities, "it turns out to be a
transfer . . . to a slum in the town. In both places they are considered
encroachers" (Fernandes 1988, ii). The poor have no hope of getting
credit, nor can they receive "protection from the police or the judicial
system" (Llosa 1989, xiii). Exclusion follows the poor wherever they
flee.

The Process of Exclusion

How does this process of exclusion work? First, in the eyes of the
world, the wisdom of the poor is not considered worthy of attention.

> If the voice of the people is regarded by government as damaged
> goods to begin with—blemished either by ignorance or self-in-
> terest—then it is hardly surprising that abuses of power and in-
> trusions into individual liberty follow (Doyal and Gough 1991,
> 11).

Among the Hindu poor, this perception of the poor is further reinforced by caste-related issues. In all societies class segregation intensifies the process of exclusion.

Next, the poor exclude themselves by not participating in social and political processes. They do not give much importance to participating in local associations or political parties, to voting in elections (unless there are other incentives), or to engaging in micro and macro affairs.

> The poor do not speak up. With those of higher status, they may even decline to sit down. Weak, powerless and isolated, they are often reluctant to push themselves forward (Chambers 1988, 18).

Even when nominated to local government bodies, the poor often remain on the "fringe," thus intensifying their powerlessness in society (S. P. Gupta 1987, 323; also see Olsen and Marger 1993, 322). The poor have little surplus time after earning a livelihood to participate in social life (Friedmann 1992, 68) or in politics (S. P. Gupta 1987, 323; also see Olsen and Marger 1993, 63). Pluralists point out that multiple group memberships help breed a spirit of moderation and reduce intense commitments in political activities (Wrong 1979, 17). However, in the case of the poor, they are socially "unattached" because they do not have the surplus time for such attachments and do not see the process serving their interest.

Third, various systems are used to exclude the poor.

> When legality is a privilege available only to those with political and economic power, those excluded—the poor—have no alternative but illegality (Llosa 1989, xii).

Although the founding fathers of our nations have thoughtfully built into their constitutions provisions to protect the interest of the poor, grassroots interpreters of the law use the law to exclude the poor. In communities like Josiprasda, the landless poor are prevented from cultivating the same waste land that rich landlords are allowed to cultivate. Hernando De Soto, in his analysis of the working of the Peruvian economy (1989), suggests that the legal formality of economic systems tends to exclude the poor.

Finally, educational systems also ensure intergenerational exclusion of the poor from the mainstream. Thus, children are sorted into the future poor and non-poor. Arguing that curriculum development is always a political-pedagogical process, Paulo Freire concludes,

> It is the very structures of society that create a serious set of barriers and difficulties, some in solidarity with others, that result in enormous obstacles for the children of subordinate classes to come to school (1993, 30).

Summary

Systematic, selective exclusion from the mainstream of public life becomes a source of intergenerational powerlessness for the poor.

Community Becoming Non-community

Community within poverty situations is often threatened when power encounters poverty. When the sense of community among the poor is broken, the poor are kept powerless.

A basic assumption of the evangelical theologians considered earlier, in their reflections on missions and poverty, is that poverty involves the marring of the image of God in humans. This is distinctly a Christian affirmation. However, this belief that we are made in the image of God does not imply that we are finished products; we are *being made* in the image of God. This shaping of humans into the image of God is accomplished in the context of the church (that is, community). Therefore, community is an essential corollary to belief that we are made in the image of God. As discussed earlier, community is also integral to the basic unit in poverty relationships.

However, in poverty relationships, when power encounters poverty, community comes under attack. Power expressions almost always require that the community be divided: poor and non-poor, power holders and power subjects, powerful and powerless. Even language comes to reflect these divisions. Sik Hung Ng, reviewing several sociolinguistic studies, points out,

> Within the same culture, the poor and the powerless speak a different language from the rich and powerful. . . . The language of

the hard-core poor is restricted speech code. . . . At the same time, it inhibits the development of his political consciousness (1980, 113).

Let us briefly examine four ways power keeps the community divided in poverty relationships.
First, power itself is divisive.

Power breeds privilege, and enables its wielder to dominate over others. As a result it leads to political conflict on two planes. On the horizontal plane, man opposes man and group opposes group, in the struggle to attain, share, or influence power. On the vertical plane, there is opposition between those who hold power and others who are subjected to it. Power is therefore divisive and leads to antagonism and conflict (Ng 1980, 85).

Even the social balance that power holders seek to establish invariably implies status quo. While the utopianist school[6] emphasizes that power serves to integrate (Ng 1980, 66, 70), among the poor this merely means integrate according to rules laid out by the powerful.

Second, common responses to power also result in disintegration of community. Often the poor either "exit," express "loyalty" or "voice" their response (Chambers 1983, 142–43). The poor *exit* through migration, express their *voice* through protests and collective action, and express *loyalty* by accommodating themselves to fit within existing demands of society. However, when they voice protest, power holders counteract. Through exiting or voicing protest or submitting in loyalty, community within poverty relationships is further divided.

Third, power in poverty situations assumes a divided community. The elite are an inevitable part of any society.[7] The rationalist school within the elitist tradition.[8] affirms that power is an integral part of any relationship, and that conflict is a reality within all power relations.

The role of the elite in fragmenting the community can be seen in suggestions that the elite are "called to govern" because they (1) are educated to assume that role; (2) possess a superior quality of personality; (3) come from a privileged family background that gives them an advantage; (4) strive harder; (5) are more capable of organization and collective action; (6) represent the dominant interest in society; (7) are a necessity for any hierarchical structure within any society; (8) occupy functionally key positions in society; (9) are required by society to be leaders and make decisions; (10) acquire control over important resources; (11) are perceived by the non-elite as indispensable; and (12) are welcomed by the non-elite as willing leaders (Olsen and Marger 1993, 80–81). The masses are seen as "incompetent and thus incapable of 'acting in default of an initiative from without and from above'" (Prewitt 1993, 131). In short, these theories suggest that for the elite to govern, the masses need to be perceived as incompetent. Thus, the community is fragmented into the competent powerful and the incompetent powerless.

Fourth, not all disunity among the poor is created by the elite and the powerful non-poor. The poor themselves fragment the community. Studies about peasant movements suggest that the poor often segregate their relationships on the basis of caste, political affiliation, family feuds, competition for scarce resources and other reasons (Oommen 1990, 91). In this way, the poor themselves contribute to the weakening of community fabric.

Non-community and the Poor

When power encounters poverty, the very nature of power, the role of the elite and the response of the poor all contribute toward eroding community.

Traditional securities break down. The community's ability for collective action is weakened. The poor grow dependent on outsiders to mobilize them and voice their concern. This sense of powerlessness is expressed by the poor in Mogalliwakkam when they say that they are powerless to do anything on their own. This is the powerlessness of a fragmented community.

Summary

The onslaught against community within poverty relationships renders the poor vulnerable to further exploitation.

Lack of Love, Compassion and Consequent Insecurity

Most analyses of the causes of poverty tend to be insensitive and academic. One can never overemphasize that poverty, in the ultimate analysis, is about people. Therefore, any analysis of poverty is inadequate that ignores the emotional dimensions of poverty.

Lack of Compassion and Insecurity of the Powerless

The poor rely upon traditional sources of security, such as the extended family, traditional patron-client relationships and so on. However, when power expressions bring various pressures on the poor, these traditional sources of security break down and force the poor to seek security elsewhere. Consequently, the poor become compelled to depend on outsiders in times of family crisis. Sickness and accidents remind them that they have no traditional networks to fall back on. The socioeconomic cost of the community breaking down is high. Without community, "coping with contingencies . . . costs more" for the poor (Chambers 1988, 15).

The emotional costs of this captivity by god-complexes, exclusion, and the breakdown of community are high. The fragmenting of the community affect hurt and pain. Although such experiences of lack of love and compassion impact all, the poor do not have the same options as the non-poor to fill the vacuum created by this lack of love. The poor slip into greater frustration and perhaps death-dealing habits. This is one reason, I believe, that there is greater appreciation among the poor for expressions of love. Years of mission work among the poor in India and elsewhere indicate that there is more to poverty than numbers or cold analysis of political relationships. Flawed relationships involve hurt. This hurt further weakens the poor and destroys any potential for a security net.

Summary

Examining the *Srama* dimension of the social reality of poverty, we identified four specific expressions of powerlessness:

1. Powerlessness is the captivity of the poor within god-complexes of the non-poor, structures and systems;
2. Powerlessness is the exclusion of the poor from the mainstream of life;
3. Powerlessness implies a community of persons becoming non-community; and
4. Powerlessness involves lack of love and compassion, and consequent insecurity.

Power, Poverty and Environment *(Desa)*

Powerlessness, apart from being relational, is also a spatial. With recent concerns about environmental degradation there is a new interest in the ecological and spatial dimensions related to poverty (see Korten 1990; Boulding 1984). At the grassroots, the physical location of the poor is always a crucial issue in analyzing poverty. Human costs incurred due to recurring natural disasters have caused the development community to examine issues of environment seriously.

Physical Isolation of the Poor

A common phenomenon in poverty is the physical isolation of the poor. Most poor communities, especially those of lower castes, are located away from the main road. Often they are far from the marketplace, drinking water sources and transport facilities.

Physical Isolation and the Powerless

Basic services and community life both become inaccessible to the poor, who are generally tucked away from the rest of the village. Isolation of the poor makes concrete their marginalized status in the society. Moreover, at times of crisis, like illness and natural disasters, remoteness causes the poor to be more vulnerable.

Physical isolation also affects participation in socioeconomic and political life. Considering that the poor lack the surplus time to participate, distance and isolation serve as further barriers.

Physical isolation is a sociopolitical issue. Who decides where the poor should live? Is this decision to isolate the poor physically another expression of captivity within the god-complexes?

Acute Vulnerability to Natural Disasters

Natural disasters are a common phenomenon, affecting both the poor and the non-poor. However, a quick survey of natural disasters will show that the poor take the brunt of these natural disasters.

Natural Disasters and the Powerless

First, natural disasters intensify the vulnerability of the poor. Their safety net weakens after a relatively minor disaster. Further, it takes longer for the poor to recover from natural disasters than it does for others. The economic costs of disasters are normally beyond the capacity of the poor. Apart from the epidemics that commonly follow, the poor are also forced into greater debt, with higher interest rates, in attempts to recover after natural disasters.

Second, the poor often live in areas more vulnerable to natural or manmade disasters. Fisher folk living close to their workplace (the sea) are easy targets for a tidal wave and consequent floods (for example, the 1977 tidal wave on the coast of Machilipatnam, Andhra Pradesh, in India). Slum dwellers take the brunt of manmade disasters like industrial accidents (for example, the Union Carbide gas leak in Bhopal, Madhya Pradesh, in India).

Third, relief assistance reaches the poor last. Official relief programs tend to ignore those who are not a priority for their political bosses. This neglect further delays recovery of the poor from natural disasters.

Summary

The last line of defense of the poor is weakened through repeated natural disasters. Added to this, the poor are also powerless in terms of accessing assistance after disasters. In this sense, the powerlessness of the poor is their acute vulnerability to the combined impact of repeated natural disasters and official neglect.

Extreme Dependence on Depleting Environmental Resources

The issue of poverty and environment is an integral part of the larger discussion on global environmental degradation. However, with the 1987 report of the World Commission on Environment and Development titled "Our Common Future," focus shifted to tracing the relationship between development and environment. Difficult questions emerged regarding the negative impact of years of development and economic growth (Korten 1990, 26). It was recognized that any effort to deal with poverty while neglecting the environment question was self-defeating (Doyal and Gough 1991, 143).

Environment and the Powerless

The poor are generally more dependent on the environment than the non-poor, who have other fuel alternatives and employment options. The poor are dependent on the weather for uninterrupted employment. The virtual landless (small and marginal farmers) have disproportionately little access to natural resources (Lewis 1988, 180). By and large, "the poor to a much greater extent than the rich, are dependent on their immediate environmental setting for their livelihoods" (Korten 1983, 203).

Poverty worsens the environmental situation. "As more and more people in poverty situations press upon limited natural resources in rural areas, they begin to deplete the stock of renewable resources" (World Bank 1989, 15). The large family size that is characteristic of poor communities adds to the pressure of depleting ecological resources.

Often the absence of a safety net in times of crisis causes the poor to exploit natural resources. During dry seasons, the poor

> have to scrounge the farthest and hardest for fuel. In turn, in their marginal circumstances, they become degraders of resources and despoilers of forests (Lewis 1988, 18).

As noted earlier, the poor often live in environmentally vulnerable locations, making their homes outside factories, along sea coasts, on street sidewalks and other such vulnerable locations. This is not just peculiar to the Two-Thirds World. As Al Gore in his analysis of environmental challenges facing the world suggests, in the United States

> a hugely disproportionate number of the worst hazardous waste sites are in poor and minority communities that have relatively little political power because of race or poverty or both (1992, 179).

In India, the gates of Bhopal Union Carbide stand as a reminder that the poor have no power to decide where they should build their homes, rendering them vulnerable to the threat of environmental waste and disasters.

In many ways the unemployment and low income of the poor have roots in the quality of the environment.[9] In India

> over half of the land suffers from degradation in one form or the another; farmers there face steadily declining productivity without major new investments (Lewis 1988, xi).

Economic loss tends to trickle down faster than economic development. It is not just the landowner who is affected; the landless farmer who looks to the land for his daily wages also suffers. Further, as Len Doyal and Ian Gough point out, when the "environment is seriously polluted, increases in real income will not necessarily lead to an improvement in individual health and autonomy" (1991, 143). Environmental degradation sets off a chain reaction leading to poor health, low work output, low income, low food intake and even worsening health. In this circular causation, environmental degradation plays a determining role.

Summary

This late entry—environment—into the poverty debates sheds new light on the meaning of powerlessness. The poor are dependent on the environment in normal circumstances and become more dependent on it during times of crisis. The powerlessness of the poor is intensified by worsening ecological imbalance and environmental degradation.

Power, Poverty and Time *(Kala)*

A key contribution of Marxist models of development and liberation theologies has been the consideration of time. Most other models explained poverty as though it were merely a static concept, but the Marxists and liberation theologians were interested in historical process.

In their analyses of social reality ancient Hindu sages always included the dimension of time *(kala)*. For them, experience of the present is integrally related to historical processes and is influenced by perception of the future.

Further, any study that seeks to understand the powerlessness of those who are locked in intergenerational poverty must raise the question of time. Poverty is a time-related concept.

Three aspects related to *kala* offer clues to understanding powerlessness:

1. The present weakness of the poor.
2. The distorted interpretation of history.
3. The hopelessness of the future.

Present Weakness of the Poor

Analyses of poverty generally tend to read poverty as a present reality. This is only appropriate, in that the experience of poverty and powerlessness is indeed a present reality for one-fifth of the world's population. The poor are disempowered through a web of flawed relationships; they are weak socially, physically, politically and economically in dealing with today's challenges.

Present Physical Weakness and the Powerless

Physical incapacity is a typical characteristic of the poor and their deprivation. Len Doyal and Ian Gough, arguing that physical health is the most basic of all needs, suggest that physical health needs must be satisfied before any other needs are addressed (1991, 56). Among the stonecutters of Kollaicheri in Chingleput District, Tamilnadu, India, accidents and prolonged periods of physical illness are common. These accidents, along with physical illnesses and poor postnatal care for women contribute to lower income, lower food intake and greater physical weakness.

The poor lack the "social muscles" to respond to physical violence. In spite of their numbers, the poor often lack not only physical strength and health but the ability to muster strength for collective action.

Even within the context of the present, poverty is seasonal; consequently, powerlessness is seasonal. Robert Chambers suggests there is a "time of year when many dependent and exploitative relationships begin or are reinforced and deepened" (1984, 129). Apart from considering seasonality in calculating income and setting the poverty line, it is important to recognize that there are certain seasons when the poor are more vulnerable than at other times to all sorts of power encounters. For example, the stonecutters of Kollaicheri are most vulnerable during monsoons, when their part of the quarry is flooded and they are unemployed.

Distorted Interpretation of History

Marxists, the dependency school and liberation theologians have contributed much to our understanding of the role of historical processes in causing poverty.[10]

History and the Powerless

Although all humans are free to make history, some humans are much freer than others to do so. Further, those who "do not make history . . . tend increasingly to become the utensils of history-makers as well as the mere objects of history" (Mills 1993, 162). The very process of history-making becomes a source of powerlessness for the poor, because the way history is written assigns an identity to the poor.

The substance of remembered and interpreted history also tends to perpetuate powerlessness by setting the agenda for poverty relationships. Marvin Olsen calls this power to set the agenda as the "meta power." Olsen defines meta power as the ability to "shape the aggregate action and interaction possibilities of those involved in the situation" (Olsen and Marger 1993, 36). Those who hold meta power not only shape the rules for relationships and define the wants of the poor, but they also ascribe meaning to life situations—and interpret life situations in a way that ensures continued powerlessness of the poor. A classic example of this is the way in which the non-poor influence the identity of the poor. It is common in a variety of cultures to see the poor going to their landlord to ask him to name their newborns. However, the powerful in some instances give names that are derogatory and communicate a low image of the poor. These children of the poor may be named for their darker skin color or their supposed mental ability or their caste or some other "identity." The children then carry these scars through life. Through such subtle but powerful means, the non-poor continue to shape the history of households and persons in poor communities.

Opportunity to independently read the world is also curtailed for the poor. Paulo Freire in *Pedagogy of the City* (1993) defines literacy as the "reading of the world." Considering the way education systems are designed, often the poor are taught to read someone else's reality rather than their own. Categories the poor learn from their schools do not help them understand their own reality any better, instead causing them to understand their reality using a lens that the powerful have lent to them. This lens distorts the reading of history. It focuses on a history that only the powerful write.

However, not all remembered history is distorted. Some near-accurate readings of history are remembered by the poor. Furthermore, the powerful do not create all distortions of history; the poor also play an active role in distorting history. However, it must be mentioned that the socioeconomic costs of distortions the powerful create are extremely high for the poor.

Summary

To sum up, powerlessness causes the poor to become mere tools in the hands of history-makers. History-makers frame the rules for all relationships. They provide interpretations for life's events in a way that the poor are kept powerless. This "history" affects future generations through the educational system.

Hopelessness of the Future

Hope and hopelessness are often thought of as belonging to the realm of the future. However, human experience suggests that these two are more than a state of mind. Hope and hopelessness shape present reality; they shape the powerlessness of the poor today.

Hopelessness and the Powerless

Hopelessness prevents meaningful action in the present, expressing itself in disinterest, lack of desire for change, and low aspirations. Second, hopelessness about the future is rooted in the distorted readings of history, which shape perception of the future. In this sense, hopelessness and powerlessness transcend time. The relationship between marred history and hopelessness causes further powerlessness, powerlessness further destroys hope, binding the poor within a vicious circle of deprivation. And without a "minimum of hope, we cannot so much as start the struggle" (Freire 1994, 9). Gradually the powerless poor lose even the inner energy to hope.

Summary

Lack of hope for the future is the flesh-and-blood experience of the poor today. This hopelessness perpetuates powerlessness, and powerlessness in turn perpetuates hopelessness. *Kala* (the time dimension) sheds new light on poverty relationships as a present experience that is continuously shaped both by history and perception of the future.

Power, Poverty and "Being" (Guna)

Reflection on the nature of persons (guna) was an integral part of ancient social studies, forming the cornerstone of Hindu theory of social organization (Prabhu). The term guna refers to a person's natural traits, disposition and attitudes. I use the term guna or being to mean the essential core of a person. This includes his or her beliefs, understanding, worldview, religious beliefs and other such aspects.

The nature of persons[11] in poverty relationships and the reality of poverty mutually reinforce and shape each other, affecting, at the very least,

1. The identity of the poor.
2. Faith in public and private life.
3. Understanding of power.

Marring of the Identity of the Poor

Response to poverty calls for more than politics or even affirmation of simple dignity. The poor explain their condition often by tracing the direct relationship between their identity (caste, location, family background, and such other descriptions of themselves) and their poverty. They suggest that the "problem" is with their identity. They say, "We are not treated as equals in the corridors of bureaucratic power because we are Harijans."

Lack of independence, self-respect and humiliating subservience causes greater pain than high interest rates and debts (Chambers 1988, 16). Identity becomes the cause and the target of all poverty-creating efforts and relationships. Poverty mars the identity of the poor and hurts the soul of all involved.

Identity and the Powerless

In the Indian context, the caste system is the mold used for shaping social norms. Religion and traditions often reinforce these norms. For example, caste tradition, reinforced by fear and shame, shapes the identity of temple prostitutes in Kolar, Karnataka, India.[12] When traditions, fear, shame and marred identity combine, intergenerational powerlessness results.

Years of poverty leave a negative imprint on the minds of the poor. This is more than the stunting of aspirations and awareness. The ability of the poor to reflect critically and to analyze their situation has also been retarded. Paulo Freire, in his conscientization *(conscientizacao)* strategy for liberation from oppression, advocates, "Each man [must] win back his right to *say his own word, to name the world*" (1990, 13). But years of intergenerational poverty seriously cramp the ability of the poor to even name their reality. The Mushars of Bihar, India, are a case in point. The Mushars are rat-eaters who live far below subsistence levels. Years of exploitation have "reduced the Mushars into dull, submissive living objects. Their perpetual exploitation froze their minds" (Farzand Ahmed 1992, 13). John Sewell, then president of the Overseas Development Council, in his survey of global poverty challenges also points out,

> physical and mental capacity of much of the future labor force has suffered in at least 8 countries in Latin America, 16 in Sub-Saharan Africa, 3 in North Africa and the Middle East, and 4 in South and East Asia (1988, ix-x).

Hurt and pain, shaped by the distorted shared memory of the community, dulls the mind and serves to perpetuate powerlessness among the poor.

When the poor are simply used or ignored within a network of relationships, the poor become less than human in the process. Their identity is defined by the mere object status assigned to them.

> In their unrestrained eagerness to possess, the oppressors develop the conviction that it is possible for them to transform everything into objects of their purchasing power. . . . For the oppressors, what is worthwhile is to have more—always more—even at the cost of the oppressed having less or having nothing. For them, *to be is to have* and to be the class of the "haves" (Freire 1990, 44).

Marring of the identity of the poor becomes a prelude to further exploitation. Exploitation and oppression must deal with the question of the identity of the oppressed. Once an exploiter or oppressor ascribes a "low identity" for the poor, then all the exploiter's consequent acts become "legitimate" behavior. Low identity sanctions all forms of oppression. The landless have to become "tools for production" before they can be exploited by landlords. Wives of the poor must become "property" before the landlord can abuse them sexually. The landless become "debtors" before they are abused and humiliated by the money-lender. The question of identity is also closely tied to the worldview of a people.

Summary

Oppressive social norms of the community stunt the mind, retard reflective ability of the poor and reduce the poor to being mere objects. thus marring the identity of the poor.

Erosion of Faith in Public and Private Life

Discussions and studies on power often focus on power bases, the will and ego of the power holder, and the reaction or response of the poor. These reflections on power relations assume the existence of trust and involvement on the part of the power subject (Olsen and Marger 1993, 5).

Within poverty relationships powerlessness is characterized by lack of trust. A common phenomenon in poverty relationships is lack of unity among the poor. Political affiliations divide the poor. Employers divide laborers using trade unions. Ethnicity, religion and other such factors also keep the poor divided. Power tends to be naturally divisive. The power of the non-poor in poverty situations thrives in the midst of mistrust and deceit. Trust between people becomes alien to power relations in poverty situations.

Additionally, the world's power does not nourish faith in God. Jacques Ellul contends, "Political power cannot recognize the true God for what He is. It can only use Him, incidentally, for its own reinforcement" (1988, 164). Power itself seeks to claim absolute status and play god among the poor. In poverty situations, moneylenders and landlords nurture dependence among the poor. They make gods of themselves. Power does not in its normal course require faith in God. God or faith in God is not an essential prerequisite in most power relations. In fact, faith in God is constantly at risk in power relations.

The world's powers seem to prefer force to ideology, especially when challenged. Force constitutes the final court of appeals in power relations within poverty situations (Olsen and Marger 1993, 61). Power, force and might gradually become closely equated, and reason and ideology shrink to the sidelines as effective modes of domination (Mitra 1992, 279).

Having devalued truth, reason and ideology, power proclaims itself to be the truth. Truth as a point of reference outside the axis of power-powerlessness has no value in power encounters.

Next, the world's powers convert willing obedience to absolute duty. Mutuality of purpose or free acceptance of authority does not serve as an adequate basis for compliance. As Rousseau says, "The strongest man is never strong enough to be master all the time, unless he transforms force into right and obedience into duty" (quoted in Wrong 1979, 85). There is no mutuality of goals or reciprocity of influence in poverty relationships. Instead, the ego and desires of the power holder take precedence over persons. Persons do not matter in the world's understanding of power.

It follows that choice belongs to the powerful, the non-poor. The poor are called to accept the changes and desires of the powerful. Power survives by limiting choices available to the poor.

The relationship between wealth and power within poverty relationships is explicit. Possession of resources, economic goods and services are often used to measure power (Liddle 1992, 795). Amitai Etzioni traces the relationship among assets, wealth and power, and suggests that conversion of assets to power is not an abrupt jump but rather a process of transformation. Etzioni points out that this conversion or transformation of wealth and assets to power is most evident during times of conflict (1993, 25). Assets and wealth are activated on behalf of a power-yielding state when the powerful foresee a conflict or see their position being threatened by the poor. Power attempts to buy the compliance of the poor with wealth and assets that the powerful possess and the poor need.

The world assumes that power is a scarce commodity. The nature of power has been the center of popular debates among academicians. Wright Mills takes the position that power is scarce and can only result in a win-lose relationship. Talcott Parsons, on the other hand, proposes that power is not a zero-sum product but more like wealth in an economic system, where wealth is produced according to the structure and type of economic organization that exists. Parsons prefers to believe that sharing of power never reduces power. According to Parsons, then, it is possible to have a win-win relationship (Cassell 1993, 212–13). However, within poverty relationships the governing assumption appears to be the zero-sum understanding of power.

The powerless often believe the only way to respond to expressions of power is to internalize those distorted power expressions. The ideal of the poor, then, is to be powerful. To be powerful would mean becoming like the oppressors who have dominated them for generations (Freire 1990, 29). Among the poor, men often express this understanding of power within their homes. The landless in a village exploit migrants who come to their village in search of employment. Thus the poor, too, play hosts to the world's distorted understanding of power (ibid., 33). Consequently, equality becomes "the point of transition through which *superordination* can be gained" (Ng 1980, 97). This causes ripples of powerlessness in and around poverty relationships.

Summary

Misuse of power within poverty relationships is usually preceded by misconceptions about power. Roots of misuse of power are found in the world's distorted understanding of power. Powerlessness springs from these distortions.

Worldview and Poverty

With growing commitment to understand poverty from the perspective of the poor, the development community and missiologists faced new questions and concerns. Practitioners, recognizing the human cost incurred in development, began considering questions of ethics (Crocker 1991, 458). Poverty is not just a matter of economics, technology or even politics.[13] Community psychologists searching for effective empowerment strategies recognized that empowerment is essentially worldview-related (Rappaport 1987, 139–42). Evangelical missiologists also looked to worldview-related clues in their continued debate on bridging evangelism and social action (see Bradshaw 1994).

Worldview

Worldview refers to the assumptions, values and commitments or allegiances that shape perceptions and responses of the persons in poverty relationships (Kraft 1989, 20, 1992a, 56).[14] Michael Kearney defines worldview as people's

> way of looking at reality. It consists of basic assumptions and images that provide a more or less coherent, though not necessarily accurate way of thinking about the world (Kearney 1984, 41).

Worldview is rarely reasoned out; it serves as the lens through which people perceive; it organizes people's responses to life's experiences and events and becomes the most critical element in shaping relationships. It is like the personality of culture. Worldview serves as a framework to explain, evaluate, validate, prioritize commitments, interpret, integrate and adapt to various realities and pressures of life (Kraft 1989, 183).[15] Worldview influences at least six other areas of life: categorization, person-group, causality, time-event, space-material and relationships (Kraft 1989, 195ff.; Kraft 1992a, 68–69).

Worldview does not do anything on its own. People are the doers.[16] If we do not allow this "space" between worldview and people's relationships and behavior, we will soon be blaming victims (the poor) for inadequacies in their worldview. Consequently, it is possible to conclude that the poor are poor because of their inadequate worldview. Hence, this study affirms that worldview does not use people; instead it is people who use the worldview.

Sociocultural and geographic environments also play an important role in shaping the worldview of a people. Among the Hindu landless, for example, the dominant sociocultural factor is religious life, as shown in Figure 6–1 on page 145. The size of each "slice" varies, of course, depending on the amount of influence each system exerts on the culture represented.[17]

Notes

[1] John Friedmann identified the following bases of social power in his (dis)empowerment model: (1) financial resources, (2) social networks, (3) appropriate information, (4) defensible life space, (5) knowledge and skills, (6) social organization, (7) instruments of work and livelihood, and (8) surplus time over subsistence requirements (1992, 66ff.).

[2] Since poverty and power are relational concepts, this inquiry examines various dimensions of poverty relationships within a poor Hindu community. Information sources included the author's 13 years of experience with grassroots

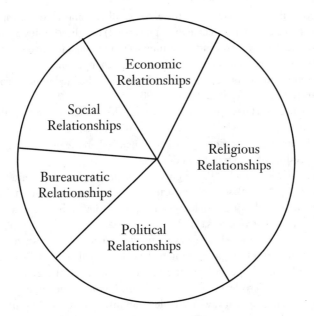

Figure 6–1: Sociocultural Factors Among the Hindu Landless.

staff who work among the poor. This analysis of power expressions in poverty relationships among the Hindu landless is presented here as conclusions of an inquiry.

[3] The next chapter deals with the issue of principalities and powers and the powerlessness of the poor.

[4] I have borrowed this term from Jürgen Moltmann, who defines "god-complex" as humans and powers seeking to become gods. See Jürgen Moltmann, "Thine is the Kingdom, the Power and the Glory" in *The Reformed Word* 37, nos. 3, 4 (1982), 3–10.

[5] Marvin Olsen suggests that the first level of social power is when power holders make decisions and take actions that affect others; the middle level is when power holders prevent decisions from being made; the third level is when power holders shape the overall setting and set parameters for the exercise of power (Olsen and Marger 1993, 34–36).

[6] According to utopians within the elitist tradition, power is a means for accomplishing the common good rather than dominating others (Talcott Parsons). The rationalist school suggested that power is primary and always serves the elite (Wright Mills). The latter recognized that power relations always involve conflict.

[7] Basic principles of the elite perspective are: (1) the masses cannot and do not govern themselves; (2) the elite may be a tiny minority, but they control a

large proportion of resources; (3) the elite use all available resources and means to protect, preserve and enhance their powers; (4) the elite employ a wide range of techniques from controlling governments to forming ideologies; (5) the elite may permit or even encourage limited social change; and (6) over time the power of the elite becomes less visible since it is embedded in numerous organizations (Olsen and Marger 1993, 79–80).

[8] R. Dahrendorf has done much work on elitism. According to Dahrendorf (quoted in Ng 1980, 47ff.), "The 'Utopians' view society as being based on consensus among its members. The 'Rationalists,' on the other hand, see society as a product of constraint and domination."

[9] Gopal K. Kadekodi, "Paradigms of Sustainable Development," *Development* (1992), 3. "It took several centuries of intellectual pursuit for human society to realize that the origin of hunger and poverty lay in the degradation of the eco-system and not vice versa" (72).

[10] In the past the focus has been very much on macro-level historical process with very little attention given to micro-level historical process. By focusing on the micro level, I hope to keep the focus of inquiry at the grassroots level. Second, at the micro level (and macro level) history is never available as an objective reading. It is always available as an interpretation of events. Therefore, this study understands history as interpreted, and in that sense it shapes the present and the future. While history itself is objective reality, what we get to know is essentially interpreted aspects of history. It is perceived history that shapes the day-to-day life of the poor, stored in the memory of the community. Therefore, in this brief inquiry the focus is on micro-level, interpreted-perceived and shared aspects of history that have shaped poverty relationships.

[11] This discussion on "being" should not be construed as meaning that poverty and powerlessness in the final analysis are about individual choices and beliefs. Like all other forces and factors discussed in this study, any factor on its own will distort the meaning of powerlessness and our understanding of causes of poverty.

[12] Journalist Saritha Rai, narrating the story of a community of prostitutes in the Kolar area, points out that the caste tradition has been used to maintain this institution of prostitution in this village for generations. Caste traditions require that poor families dedicate at least one girl to the trade of prostitution. (see Saritha Rai, "Turning a New Leaf: A Village Steeped in Prostitution Finds a New Life," *India Today* [1992], 10).

[13] Dennis Goulet suggests moral options ought to be exercised around three vital issues: criteria of the good life, basis for just relations in society, and principles for adopting a proper stance toward forces of nature, including technology (1989, 45).

[14] In their endeavor to explain differences between people, especially in the way they perceive reality, anthropologists stumbled over the concept of worldview. Ruth Benedict in the 1920s looked for underlying configurations and emphasized patterns in culture. Morris Opler, reacting to the improbabil-

ity of an entire culture being dominated by a single pattern, suggested that cultures are shaped by multiple themes. In the 1960s and 1970s ethno-semanticists focused on identifying people's perception about the world as reflected in names and labels they used. For them the labels and names were important indicators for cognition (Kearney 1984, 32–37). Redfield's concept of worldview was descriptive. He defined worldview as "the picture the members of a society have of the properties and characters upon their stage of action . . . the way the world looks to that people . . . a man's idea of the universe" (in Dennis Brown 1991, 3). In the early 1980s Francis L. K. Hsu suggested that underlying all cultures is a "core value," which then becomes the foundation for the basic values of a culture. Robert Redfield from the University of Chicago did not follow the single or multiple theme tradition or the ethno-semantic approach to cognitive anthropology. He inquired into the way people divided and categorized the reality they perceived.

[15] Paul Hiebert in his model of worldview identifies the different levels as foundations, processes, states, values/allegiances and explicit beliefs and value systems (Hiebert 1982). Charles Kraft suggests worldview consists of assumptions that underlie values and allegiances/commitments (1992a, 57). These assumptions are then clustered around themes.

[16] A common question debated among anthropologists is whether people are determined by cultures and their worldview, or the other way around. Worldview conditions and does not determine the person. People use worldview to explain, evaluate, validate, prioritize, interpret, integrate and adapt. Kraft points out that any supposed power of worldview is really the power of habit formed by the conditioning of the worldview (Kraft 1992a, 56).

[17] Cultural anthropologists have debated much on the relationship between the various sociocultural systems and worldview. Several anthropologists have suggested that religious systems and beliefs in some cultures form the core values. Others suggest that all systems including religious systems are external to worldview. This would mean that worldview themes, allegiances and values influence the different systems. Systems in turn also influence worldview. Further, in some cultures one or more systems may be emphasized over others. That dominant system will exercise greater influence on worldview than all other systems (Kraft 1992a, 55–56).

7

Principalities and Powers
and Poverty

Any effort to understand the meaning of the powerlessness of the poor must grapple with poverty the way the poor experience it in all aspects of their reality, which includes the whole realm of authorities in spiritual places.

Mission anthropologist Paul Hiebert's survey of the different perceptions of reality and the "excluded middle" triggered several reevaluations of traditional perceptions of causes of poverty. According to Hiebert, the influence of Enlightenment thinking, dualism and mechanistic perceptions of reality influenced Christian mission thinking, consequently excluding important dimensions of reality. Hiebert describes this exclusion as including

> beings and forces that cannot be directly perceived but thought to exist *on this earth*. These include spirits, ghosts, ancestors, demons, and earthly gods and goddesses who live in trees, rivers, hills and villages. These live not in some other world or time, but are inhabitants with humans and animals of this world and time. . . . This level also includes supernatural forces such as mana, planetary influences, evil eyes and the powers of magic, sorcery and witchcraft (1982, 41).

Through the ages, most Christian mission was built on a flawed reading of history and reality. Even today, for those of us who were products of Enlightenment-oriented education, this middle tier that Hiebert calls the "excluded middle" never exists.

This fragmented perception of reality and the resulting fragmented missional involvement exerted a far-from-Christian influence. Missionaries became agents of secularization in spite of all their good intentions. To the Hindu poor, Christians appeared godless, or at least as a people who "did not need [a] hypothesis of God" to explain their reality (Newbigin 1966, 17).

Hiebert's insights triggered a paradigm shift in Christian mission, at least among theologians. Poverty and powerlessness cannot be fully understood without considering the role of forces in the "excluded middle," particularly principalities and powers. For the Hindu poor, and most poor peoples of the world

> sickness, a failed business, and social ostracism are the results of spiritual power working against them. This spiritual power is mediated by demons, shamans, witch doctors and gods (Myers 1991, 3).

In the final analysis, then, poverty is not only rooted in the Fall of humans but is also a result of the present working of the Evil One. Missiologists and grassroots practitioners came to affirm that "behind all poverty is the devil. . . . The ultimate cause of poverty is the devil himself" (Duncan 1990, 9). Evidences of the destructive role of the Evil One in the horrors of war, poverty, financial exploitation and racial discrimination were also recognized (Arnold 1992, 122). Authentic mission among the poor was seen as involving confrontation with the powers of the Evil One. For "the Son of God was revealed for this purpose, to destroy the works of the devil" (1 John 3:8b). Any attempt to respond to the powerless poor will be inadequate without consciously addressing the relationship between principalities and powers and poverty.

Identity of "The Powers"

Early studies on the powers can be traced to the work of Otto Everling (*Die paulinische Angelologie und Damonololgie*, 1888), who suggested that the language of power is rooted in pre-Christian Jewish and heathen religious and cultic activity (Arnold 1989, 42).

Through the years debates have raged on the identity of the cosmic powers. A common view is that the powers were created by God and meant to serve God's purposes (Yoder 1972, 143; Hawthorne 1993, 750). However, after the Fall they were set against God's purposes and were particularly directed against God's creation (Wagner and Pennoyer 1990, 117). "Now they are 'behaving' as though they were the ultimate ground of being" (Mouw 1976, 89). They are enemies of Christ (Ps. 110:1, Eph. 6:11–12, 16; 2:2; 4:8, 27) (Arnold 1989, 56). The powers belong to the kingdom of Satan and wield control over people, structures and systems.

On the nature of the powers, there are different views.[1] For the purposes of this study, principalities and powers are considered personal beings that have a dominating influence on persons, social organizations and groups, and structures.

The following section examines the work of these created fallen members of the kingdom of Satan in relation to the powerlessness of the poor.

Principalities and Powers and Persons in Poverty Relationships

The devil and his forces influence persons in any situation by seeking to

separate us from the love of God (Rom. 8:38); we find them ruling over the lives of those who live far from the love of God (Eph. 2:2); we find them holding men in servitude to their rules (Col. 2:20); we find them holding men subject under their tutelage (Gal. 4:3) (Yoder 1972, 143).

They hurt people's health and bodies; at other times and instances they possess people's minds and bodies. Within the context of poverty relationships, cosmic powers influence people's mind, health, habits, relationships, exploitation of curses, will and identity.

The Mind

Inquiries into poverty have often concluded that a common effect of the role of principalities and powers is reflected in ignorance and superstition among the poor. Beyond this general conclusion, let me examine four ways by which cosmic principalities and powers affect the mind[2] with particular reference to the context of poverty.

First, the powers reinforce various deceptions that have roots in a people's belief system. They "blind the mind of unbelievers" (2 Cor. 4:4). For example, the poor are made to believe that their identity is defined by their caste, or race, or place in life. The devil and his forces are great deceivers (2 Tim. 2:26; Gal. 4:3; Eph. 2:12). They keep the poor enslaved and deceived about their rightful role in society, their place in the hierarchy of this world and their place in God's presence (Arnold 1992, 93).

Second, the poor are kept powerless through the deception even outside their belief system. "Ever since the garden of Eden, Satan has continued to use his diabolical method of deception, causing people to believe a lie" (ibid., 128).

A third impact is the blinding of the mind from the Truth. As 2 Corinthians 4:4 teaches, Satan has blinded the minds of people from seeing "the light of the gospel of the glory of Christ, who is the image of God." This is not confined to the poor.

Finally, the devil influences the mind of people in poverty relationships by offering an alternative interpretation for life's experience. Often this interpretation leads people away from God. As Heinrich Schlier suggests, the nature of these powers is to "present and interpret everything in the universe which they dominate in their own light and in their own way" (1961, 32). The devil and his forces shape the people's worldview so that they explain, evaluate, interpret and prioritize reality in a way that takes them away from God's intention for them.

Health

Demons are said to have the ability to attack the body through disease (Matt. 9:32-33; Luke 13:16; 2 Cor. 12:7). This is probably why a church that ministers to the health and physical well-being of its members attracts many poor. We have learned this important lesson through the years from Pentecostals' work among the poor (Davids 1990, 204). The poor and non-poor alike are vulnerable to exploitation of the principalities and powers in this area of their life.

However, in the case of the poor such sickness carries greater socioeconomic costs. Ill-health pushes them to the edge of survival. Dependence on moneylenders, high debts, absence from work and other such negative economic implications result from attacks on health. The poor may also become dependent on village priests or witchcraft, which becomes another drain on already meager financial resources.

Habits and Actions

The role of powers in influencing people through compulsive dependence on certain habits also causes dependence and ruins lives. The cost of maintaining compulsive behaviors is high and erodes the financial base of the poor. However, in the context of this inquiry into the meaning of powerlessness of the poor, another important impact of the powers on habits and actions is exploiting common frustrations among the poor by offering them escape via death-dealing options.

A common source of frustration these days is the result of exposure to mass media. In remote villages of India today television is shaping values and life. Multinational media networks expose the poorest to lifestyles of the rich and urban worlds. This exposure is fast changing aspirations of the young in poor communities. Aspirations shaped after the rich do not match the low-income reality of the poor. Frustration sets in and grows.

The poor do not have the same options that the non-poor have. Therefore, the devil, the well-known tempter (1 Thess. 3:5) entices the poor to choose destructive options. When the poor respond to their frustrations under the influence of the devil, death and destruction follow. Compulsive habits or behavior then results in the further socioeconomic captivity of poor households.

Relationships

The devil attacks the very relationships that were meant to serve as positive agents in our journey toward becoming what God wants us to be.

The devil is busy in poverty situations reinforcing divisive forces and creating new ones. He sows seeds of enmity between people and keeps the poor, who are already on the fringes of society, divided. Unity and brotherhood are not the devil's cup of tea. For unity and brotherhood spell life, and marred relationships keep the poor divided, a mark of abiding in death (1 John 3:14).

Curses

The devil also exploits the curses that people cast on each other. "A curse is the invocation of the power of Satan or of God to affect negatively the person or thing at which the curse is directed" (Kraft 1992b, 75).

Will

Cosmic principalities and powers seek to control the will of the poor and non-poor. "The ultimate aim of the enemy is not simply to control people's minds but to get at their wills" (Kraft 1990, 272). By capturing the will of a person, the devil then seeks to influence the various choices that he or she makes through life.

The devil's access to the will of the poor has ramifications for how they perceive their future. Principalities and powers attack the hope of the poor; the poor often see no reason to hope for a better future.

The devil and his forces specifically seek to destroy the will to face the future.

Identity

The devil and his forces also seek to cripple the identity of those in poverty relationships. The powers seek to deceive the poor into believing they are not made in the image of God.

The "poor . . . feel nonexistent, valueless, humiliated. . . . [They believe they] are stupid, ignorant people who know nothing . . . like oxen who know nothing" (Wink 1992, 101). In this context powerlessness is an issue of identity and reinforced by cosmic powers.

Often the powers "piggyback on problems already in the person, rather than originating problems" (Kraft 1992b, 104). In this sense the devil and his forces are opportunistic (ibid., 41). They give the impression that poverty is by and large the result of a simple combination of natural forces.

The devil feeds on "spiritual garbage" (Kraft 1990, 276) believed by the person and the community. This further abuses the marred identity, hurt from broken relationships, and captivity to harsh religious belief systems.

Powerlessness is a spiritual disease. The scars of powerlessness can be seen on the will and identity of the poor. Principalities and powers play a crucial role in intensifying the powerlessness imposed by society on the poor by reinforcing the oppression and internalizing it within poor communities and cultures.

Principalities and Powers in the Context of Poverty Relationships

Apart from influencing those involved in poverty relationships, principalities and powers also influence the structures and systems within which these relationships take place. Recent interpretations suggest that the powers work through economic, social and political structures as well as by influencing social patterns, cultural norms and group habits. "These 'structures of existence' are then viewed as the objects of our spiritual struggle and may be regarded as demonic" (Arnold 1992, 167).

On the other hand, others suggest that powers must only be dealt with in the context of setting individual souls free from the grip of darkness (McAlpine 1991, 55).[3] C. Peter Wagner points out that the devil and his forces influence nations and keep the minds of the unreached blind. Wagner argues, based on passages such as Daniel 10:10–21, that "territorial spirits and their dominance of geographical areas are taken for granted as the history of Israel unfolds" (Wagner and Pennoyer 1990, 79).

However, Walter Wink (as discussed earlier) is of the opinion that the powers are the inner spirituality inhabiting structures and systems. He suggests that unless we depersonalize cosmic powers, it will be difficult to justify any involvement in setting right the inadequacies in structures and systems (1992).

Clinton E. Arnold, commenting on the influence of the powers over nations and territories, suggests that the powers influence the structures and systems by influencing people. Thus the influence of the powers "extends to human institutions and organizations, the social and political order" (Arnold 1992, 81).

As we can see, there is much ambiguity about the role of the powers in relation to structures and systems. Richard Mouw points out that this ambiguity is not due to defects in current theological understanding but rather due to "the perils inherent in attempts to duplicate Paul's exact views, given his lack of systematic presentation on the subject" (1976, 88).

Douglas Pennoyer suggests that the powers actively manipulate the social, political, economic, religious and even artistic subsystems of a culture by "acting through individuals" (Wagner and Pennoyer 1990, 256). Following reflections in the last section, we may conclude that the powers influence the context of poverty relationships through people.

Thus, principalities and powers exploit belief systems and worldviews to manipulate the context of poverty relationships. Several who have inquired into the relationship between powers and non-Christian religions have concluded that there seems to be a connection between them. They point to Paul's argument that there is a demonic character to non-Christian religions (1 Cor. 8:4–5; 10:19–20) (Arnold 1992, 94). However, the powers seemingly exploit any form of idolatry, irrespective of which religious system nurtures it. In fact, when we "deal with domains of the Powers . . .we are taking an inventory of various possible objects of human idolatry" (Mouw 1976, 89). The powers exploit and reinforce any challenge to the sovereignty of God. In poverty relationships, when the non-poor along with their structures and system claim status over the lives of the poor, the powers are there to reinforce those god-complexes.

Finally, the devil and his forces have access to poor families through many symbols and articles of significance. The powers empower various symbols and forms within religious systems. These symbols and forms are not neutral. Within the Hindu religious system, for example, the symbols, articles and other items are dedicated to the gods. These include symbols that children wear that are dedicated to the gods. Kraft rightly cautions that these symbols, articles, buildings and places can be under the authority of the powers (Kraft 1992b, 19). The powers seek to manipulate places and articles of significance in order to manipulate people.

For the religious poor who have very few options when crisis strikes, such symbols are of great value.

Notes

[1] Hienrich Schlier develops the thesis that the "air" in Ephesians 2:2 is the principal medium by which the powers exercise their control on the affairs of humans (1961, 12). H. Berkhof proposed that these powers are structures of earthly existence, and that Paul's emphasis is not so much on personal-spiritual aspects of nature as on the role of the powers in conditioning earthly life (1962, 18). Oscar Cullmann (in *Christ and Time*, 1950) proposed that the powers were

both human authorities and angelic powers. Wesley Carr claims that powers should not be understood as referring to any evil or demonic force but as pure angelic beings who surround the throne of God (1981). John Howard Yoder focuses his attention on "revolutionary subordination" of the church to the powers. With reference to the identity of the powers, Yoder says that they are fallen. However, "the Powers [are] not simply something limitlessly evil. The Powers, despite their fallenness, continue to exercise an ordering function" (1972, 143–44). Richard J. Mouw suggests that Paul depersonalizes the power while he identifies these powers as forces that "'stand behind' and 'influence' the political life . . . [and] other areas of human social life" (1976, 87). Clinton E. Arnold, in his survey of the concept of power in Ephesians, concludes that Paul does not "demythologize the 'powers' and make them equivalent to the abstract notions of 'flesh' and 'sin' or see them as some kind of spiritual 'atmosphere.' The flesh and the devil (with his 'power') work in confluence leading humanity into disobedience from God (Arnold 1989, 69). Finally, Walter Wink's three-part work suggests that spiritual powers are not some separate heavenly or ethereal entity but the "inner aspect of material or tangible manifestations of power" (1984, 104). Wink identifies such an understanding about powers as a mark of an integral worldview based on the views of Carl Jung and others. They are the "withinness or interiority in all things, . . . [the] inner spiritual reality [that is] inextricably related to an outer concentration or physical manifestation" (1992, 5). Wink suggests three types of manifestations of powers: outer personal possession, collective possession and the inner personal demonic (1986, 43). For Wink, powers are that spiritual interiority of the domination system that shapes the day-to-day life of all humans.

[2] There is need for some caution here. The reflections may suggest that this influence is on the cognitive aspects of humans. However, *mind* must not be confined to meaning the rational and logical aspects of knowledge. The knowledge of the poor is experiential; it is not a mere theoretical truth that is at stake. Their truth-acquiring mechanism is deeply rooted in their day-to-day experience. Therefore, it is their whole life that is at stake.

[3] In his review of various traditions in relation to beliefs about the powers, Thomas H. McAlpine suggests that the "Third Wave" tradition teaches that "powers" become an issue only as they hinder the church from evangelizing (1991, 55).

8

The Meaning
of Powerlessness

Thus far our inquiries suggest that powerlessness is a present state of being as well as the result of an ongoing process of disempowerment. Situations of powerlessness for the poor involve

1. captivity within the god-complexes of the non-poor, structures and systems,
2. exclusion from the mainstream of life,
3. community of persons becoming non-community,
4. lack of love and compassion with resultant insecurity,
5. physical isolation,
6. acute vulnerability to natural disasters,
7. extreme dependence on limited environmental resources and vulnerability due to depleting environmental resources,
8. present physical weakness,
9. distorted interpretations of remembered and shared history,
10. hopelessness,
11. marring of their identity,
12. erosion of faith in the private and public arenas of life, and
13. distorted understanding of power.

In this chapter, we bring together the following key themes discussed up to this point:

1. Powerlessness is the result of a multifaceted process resulting in fragmentation of relationships.
2. Powerlessness is captivity in god-complexes.
3. Powerlessness is the experience of real persons.
4. Powerlessness is the result of inadequacies in a people's worldview.
5. Powerlessness is the result of exploitation by principalities and powers.
6. Powerlessness is captivity in a web of lies.

Powerlessness Is the Result of a Multifaceted Process

Our study demonstrated that the poor are disempowered through their various social, economic, political, bureaucratic and religious relationships. We also pointed out that in poverty situations, these different domains of relationships tend to become clusters of power. These clusters of power are products of interaction among structures, systems, people and the spiritual interiority within the social, economic, political, bureaucratic and religious units of poverty situations. We also recognized that powerlessness is a relational concept *(srama)*, with spatial *(desa)*, time *(kala)* and being *(guna)* dimensions. These different forces interact to create poverty through disempowerment.

In Josiprasda, the legal system of the bureaucracy works with the economic system to prevent the landless from using waste land productively. Macro-level policies of the government (for example, pricing policies of agricultural goods) affect the wages of the poor in the village. Cosmic activities, including demon possession and illness, cripple the economy of households. In this sense, powerlessness is a dynamic process with many dimensions.

Second, in the process of disempowerment, time-related factors interact in and through various relationships at different levels in the life space. For example, caste relationships in a community like Josiprasda have a history of distortions behind them. The future interests of the non-poor and the hopelessness of the poor play a key part in the political process in Josiprasda.

Third, the process of disempowerment involves persons in relationships. Interaction among people within each of the five clusters of power (social, economic, political, bureaucratic and religious) create powerlessness for the poor in the basic unit of households, within communities.

Fourth, in the process of disempowerment, cosmic forces influence and interact with other forces to perpetuate powerlessness. While concrete human events and experiences can explain micro, macro and global levels adequately, the understanding of powerlessness will not be complete. Cosmic principalities and powers express themselves in and through the social, economic, political, bureaucratic and religious units, but they are not confined to these. Activities of cosmic powers go beyond the finite understanding of time.

Powerlessness Is Captivity in God-Complexes

As the world's powers play god in the lives of the poor, god-complexes are a product of the interaction among structures, systems, people and the spiritual interiorities within the domains of poverty relationships. The worldview of a people sanctions the hierarchical relationships of that people and forbids the poor from seeking any change. Finally, principalities and powers in poverty situations, being fallen beings themselves, tend to reinforce any effort by relative powers to play god, thus ensuring that the god-complexes are sustained.

The term *god-complexes* serves to bring together many themes, suggesting that the poor are powerless captives within these god-complexes.

Powerlessness Is the Experience of Real Persons

Because powerlessness is the experience of a people who live in real life space, issues of compassion, insecurity, hurt and exclusion are as real as any other factors involved in poverty relationships. Powerlessness is the experience of real flesh-and-blood people who need healing.

Powerlessness Is the Result of Inadequacies in a People's Worldview

Powerlessness is more than a socioeconomic and political phenomenon. The implications of worldview on poverty relationships can be seen at two levels.

First, inadequacies in worldview enable the non-poor and the poor to validate and explain poverty and powerlessness, suggesting that

1. Poverty, caste/class groupings, occupation are all a result of their own past bad deeds and their *varna*.
2. The riches of the non-poor are divinely ascribed to them, and therefore there is no causal relationship between poverty and wealth.
3. Basic identity is defined by status within one's people groups.
4. Poverty and social status as well as occupation (consequently, income level) are divinely sanctioned.
5. Stratifications of people groups are divinely sanctioned.
6. Physical isolation and exclusion of the poor are part of the divine order.

Second, the worldview of a people tends to reinforce the powerlessness of the poor, suggesting that

1. Poverty is the result of *karma* and part of the natural cycle of life; therefore, little can be done to change the present.
2. One has to go through the life one's been given; therefore, there is no gain in trying to struggle against the present.
3. Those who desire "too much" or "don't know their place" will get burned, as in variations on Icarus-type myths; therefore, it is important that the poor not desire change. Consequently, there is no motivation for action toward change.
4. Action for change is not desirable, since the future will essentially be an extension of the present.
5. Liberation lies in fulfilling one's duty in life; therefore, challenging occupational hierarchy and status quo is not desirable.
6. The wealth of the rich and the poverty of the poor are not causally related; hence, there is no place for accountability within poverty relationships.

Through the interplay of all these worldview themes in poverty relationships the poor are kept powerless. These themes reinforce and are reinforced by forces in the social, economic, political, religious and bureaucratic realms. In conjunction, they ensure intergenerational powerlessness of the poor.

Powerlessness Is the Result
of Exploitation by Principalities and Powers

If principalities and powers influence the mind, health, relationships, habits, will and the identity of the poor as well as the spiritual interiorities within structures and systems by manipulating symbols, articles and places, then we should not be surprised at the staggering socioeconomic costs of the activity of these powers and principalities.

Powerlessness Is Captivity in a Web of Lies

The various power expressions, worldview themes and role of the principalities and powers in poverty relationships indicate that the poor are captive within an oppressive set of relationships. These oppressive relationships are sustained by flawed assumptions and interpretations rooted in religious systems, worldview and the work of principalities and powers.

A helpful image to represent the captivity of the poor in a world of flawed assumptions and interpretations is the web. In the context of poverty relationships, this web is a "web of lies." Both the poor and the non-poor believe these lies and thus ensure perpetuation of the powerlessness of the poor.

Therefore, powerlessness is captivity of the poor within such a web of lies. This web is nurtured by different structures, systems, people and principalities and powers in poverty relationships. The web affirms the status quo and is seen as an expression of the justice of God. For the poor, their captivity within this web of lies is nurtured by the many forces involved in poverty relationships.

PART THREE

LEARNING ABOUT THE KINGDOM OF GOD

M issiologist David Bosch points out that for authentic develop ment to take place, transfer of power is essential (1991, 357). Empowerment is not a new theme in the field of development and mission among the poor. There is an increased focus on responding to the poor with empowerment strategies and power shift.

Robert Chambers calls for empowering the poor to enhance resources and resist the rich and powerful (1991, 5). John Friedmann suggests that development initiatives must "above all, give them [the poor] a voice, [which] articulates their immediate interests, and creates the conditions for a more adequate and meaningful livelihood" (1991, 7). David Korten identifies empowerment as a critical piece in any people-centered development (1984, 241) and describes empowerment as a "power building effort . . . best served through action to hasten creation of the new, rather than through political confrontation to hasten the passing of the old" (ibid., 309).

Julian Rappaport, a community psychologist, points out that empowerment suggests both individual determination as well as participation in one's community. It is both psychological and social, and responds to people in context (1987, 121).[1]

In Search of an Alternative Response

Alvin Toffler's analysis of trends and tendencies in global events suggests that the next era be called the "powershift era." He suggests that "powershift . . . presents a new theory of social power, and explores the coming shifts in business, the economy, politics and global affairs" (1990, xx). What is interesting about Toffler's reading of world trends is his differentiation between "power shift" and "powershift." He proposes that the term *power shift* describes "transfer of power" while the *powershift* refers to "a deep-level change in the very nature of power" (ibid., 16). Following this cue from Toffler, we recognize that the challenge before the church is not just empowerment or transfer of power. The challenge before the church is the transformation of the very nature of power.

There is a wealth of Christian thinking on power from the point of view of leadership, management and organizational development.

However, to consider the question of power from within the context of the poor, there is a need for an "*alternate* consciousness, which in the spirit of the Magnificat and Beatitudes puts the poor and the powerless at its centre, that is the true task of the Church in development" (Elliott 1987, 118). This requires more than just adding the spiritual as an additional dimension.[2] As David Korten proposes, an alternative human consciousness enables one to

> view power not as a club to be used in the service of personal aggrandizement, but rather as a gift to be held in stewardship to the service of the community and human and spiritual fulfillment of all people—especially the powerless (1990, 168).

Beyond mere strategies for empowerment, the very nature of power needs redefinition.

9

The Kingdom of God:
A Brief Survey

Kingdom of God motifs have become common in recent theological inquiries. Evangelicals have studied the kingdom motif with great passion, especially after their recovery from the Great Reversal. As a key theological frame of reference for the mission of God, it defined the identity and mission of the church as the "instrument, witness and the custodian" of the kingdom (Ladd 1974, 262; see also chap. 11). It is important because "our vision of the future molds and determines the content of our mission" (Samuel and Sugden 1987, 148).

Over time, the focus of kingdom studies broadened. John Bright argued that the "reign of God" motif was not confined to the New Testament, suggesting that it served as a unifier of the Old and the New Testaments. According to Bright, Old Testament understanding of the reign of God provides a necessary background for a clearer understanding of *he basileia tou theou* (the kingdom of God), *he basileia ton ouranom* (the kingdom of heaven) and *he basileia* (the kingdom) (Bright 1953).

The kingdom of God was central in Jesus' ministry. It comprised the very purpose for his coming (Luke 4:43) and "His preaching and His miraculous healing are signs of the Kingdom" (Sider 1993, 51). Liberation theologian Leonardo Boff suggests that the kingdom of God is

all-embracing, proclaiming the deliverance of every human and cosmic reality from all sin—from the sin of poverty, from the sin of starvation, from the sin of dehumanization, from the sin of the spirit of vengeance and from the sin of the rejection of God (1988, 2).

Scholarship in the past, by and large, interpreted the kingdom motif from each age's particular understanding of the millennium.[3] Some scholars describe the kingdom in relation to the present as the shadow cast by the kingdom that is at hand. Others see the present as a foretaste of what is to come or as a sign of the kingdom. George Kummel proposes that the "Kingdom is itself present. It is not merely the signs of the Kingdom or the powers of the Kingdom, but the Kingdom itself which is said to be present" (1957, 107). In Old Testament teaching, says George Ladd,

> the cleavage between history and eschatology is never radical. The God who will manifest Himself in a mighty theophany at the end of history has already manifested Himself during the course of history (1974, 59).

Moving beyond the issue of timing, this section specifically examines the understanding of power in kingdom theology. A review of contemporary evangelical scholarship suggests the following descriptives of the kingdom of God.

The Kingdom of God Is Theocentric

Abraham Kuyper captured the focus of the kingdom well when he said, "There is not a thumb-breadth of the universe about which Christ does not say, 'It is mine'" (in Clouse 1977, 179). The psalmist captures this spirit, saying, "The earth is the Lord's and everything in it, the world and all who live in it" (Ps. 24:1, NIV).

The life and ministry of Jesus Christ also strongly affirmed that the kingdom of God is the dynamic rule of God, not the product of historical process.

> History will not produce the Kingdom, not even history as an instrument of the divine activity. Only the direct visitation of God

can bring the divine purpose to its consummation and transform the present order into the Kingdom of God (Ladd 1974, 59).

Neither is the kingdom of God the result of the religious consciousness of humans.

It is not a program for human rescue. . . . It is, rather, one inaugurated and consummated by a King who has nail prints in his hands and who rules his subjects from a higher world (Henry 1992, 49).

Hans Küng describes the kingdom as the *"sovereign act of God himself.* There is no one who can invite himself to the eschatological banquet" (1967, 76).

The Kingdom . . . will not come through an immanent earthly evolution; not through human moral action. . . . Its coming is only to be understood on the basis of [God's] miraculous and all powerful action (Ridderbos 1962, 23–24).

Jürgen Moltmann suggests that the kingdom of God is essentially an expression of the promise of God, rooted in the "credibility and the faithfulness of him who gives it" (1967, 119). Therefore, any inquiry into the kingdom's understanding of power must affirm the theocentricity of the kingdom.

The Kingdom of God Opposes All Other Kingdoms

The kingdom of God "is a rule for which all other rules will come to a standstill; it is not simply a rule alongside the other rules" (Henry 1992, 41). In this sense the kingdom of God will always be confrontational. The kingdom is the

question mark in the midst of established ideas and answers developed by people and societies. The Kingdom is the appointed challenger of all sacralizing myths and systems and the relentless unmasker of all human disguises, self-righteous ideologies or self-supporting powers (Arias 1984, 46).

The kingdom of God is the challenger of all the god-complexes that exist within poverty situations that keep the poor powerless. The kingdom constantly challenges

the sin of the world in its enslaving effects: injustice and powerlessness, sickness and ignorance, hunger and thirst, hatred and violence, endemic fear of those in power who torture and kill are all signs of the anti-kingdom (Marcella 1982, 62).

In such a kingdom "tension is unavoidable because the mission of Jesus was not one of withdrawal from the world but being sent to confront it" (Glasser 1991, 76). In the words of Mary in Luke 1:46–55, there will be a scattering of the proud, bringing down of rulers, sending away of the rich. In fact,

the thought of the coming of the Kingdom of God over the whole world, for the good of his people and the overthrow of any power that opposes his rule has from olden times been one of the central motives of Israel's expectation of salvation" (Ridderbos 1962, 8).

Reign or Realm?

The issue of realm or reign has been debated among scholars who have researched the kingdom of God motif. There are at least four different usages of the idea of the kingdom of God in the Bible: (1) In a few places the phrase is used to refer to the abstract meaning of reign or realm (Luke 19:12, 15; 23:42; John 18:36); (2) kingdom is also used to refer to a future apocalyptic order that the righteous will enter at the end of the age (Mark 9:47; 10:23–25; 14:25; Matt. 8:11; Luke 13:28); (3) the kingdom is introduced in the gospels as being present among us (Mark 10:15; Matt. 6:33; Luke 12:31; Matt. 11:12; 12:28; Luke 17:21); and (4) the kingdom is represented as a present realm into which people are now entering (Matt. 11:11; Luke 16:16; Matt. 12:31; 23:13) (Ladd 1974, 123).

Scholars suggest that in the kingdom, "it is the glory of God, not the pre-eminence of the people, which is placed in the centre" (Ridderbos 1962, 20).

In the last analysis all details of the Kingdom of God are unimportant (cf. Mark 12:24–27) by comparison with the single fact that it represents the time when God will reign (Küng 1967, 78).

As missiologist Newbigin points out, the kingdom is

not a new "movement" in which those interested may enlist. It is not a cause calling for support, a cause which might succeed or fail according to the amount of support it attracts. It is, precisely, the reign of God, the fact that God whom Jesus knows as father is the sovereign ruler of all people and all things (Newbigin 1978, 37).

This is a crucial affirmation for the powerless poor.

While inquiring into the nature of kingdom power, care must be taken that the reign of God is not reduced to a program. God is always the prime mover in a kingdom-based response to the powerless poor.

The Kingdom of God Is Relational

Recent works on the kingdom of God emphasize the relational dimensions of the kingdom. Evangelical theology has made a definitive shift from an individualized reading of the kingdom to a community or body of Christ-based understanding of the kingdom of God.

The Kingdom of God is that new order of affairs begun in Christ when finally completed by him, will involve a proper restoration not only of man's relationship to God but also of those between sexes, generations, races and even between man and nature (Verkuyl 1979, 168).

Jürgen Moltmann argues that the kingdom of God is the kingdom of the Tri-unity. This Trinitarian kingdom invites and influences people to enter into a relationship with the Trinity and among themselves. "The

Trinitarian hermeneutics leads us to think in terms of relationships and communities" (Moltmann 1981, 9). The Trinitarian kingdom calls people to focus on human relationships and not on human individuality (ibid., 199).

Moltmann goes on to suggest that the mark of this Trinitarian kingdom that Jesus preached is "God's Fatherhood" (ibid., 70). In the kingdom, then, God is not just the Lord; God is also the merciful Father.

For Ron Sider, the kingdom of God is not a concept or a doctrine or a program. It is

> before all else a person with the face and name of Jesus of Nazareth the image of the invisible God. If the Kingdom is separated from Jesus then it is no longer the Kingdom of God which he revealed (Sider 1993, 59; also see Arias 1984, 69).

The kingdom is deeply relational; it belongs to the merciful Father; it is the kingdom of Jesus of Nazareth.

The God of this kingdom is a king who invites and who seeks a response from his people. William Dyrness in his search for a theology of holistic mission suggests that the kingdom of God assumes an intimacy between God and God's people (1983, 132).

This relational kingdom opens up the possibility of transformed relationships among the community of the free. Metropolitan Geevarghese Mar Osthathios emphasizes the relational nature of the kingdom when he mentions that "the Kingdom is the community," with a caution that the community is not the kingdom of God (1980, 1). Moltmann argues that Trinitarian hermeneutics enables us to think more naturally of the kingdom in terms of relationships and community (1981, 19). Johannes Verkuyl affirms that this "restoration of man's and woman's relationship to each other and even with nature" is the righteousness we await (1979, 168).

> Kingdom demands a transfer from "self" to "other," from an individualistic and egocentric consciousness to one communally and fraternally oriented (Costas 1982, 92).

Kingdom relationships are covenantal.[4] Reflections and conclusions about the nature of power in the kingdom of God must be consistent with this overall nature. Power in the kingdom must always build relationships.

The Kingdom of God
Is Political

It was liberation theologians who brought the political dimension of the kingdom of God to the fore of contemporary scholarship, evangelical and otherwise.

Jesus' action and prophecies, especially those directed against the ruling institutions of his society, suggest that he was mounting a more serious opposition than a mere protest. It is certain that Jesus was executed as a rebel against the Roman order (Horsley 1993, 320).

Jesus was interested in politics. He challenged political structures by challenging the meaning of political relationships and the way power and leadership were exercised. Jesus' whole life and relationships were different from all other militant groups.

If politics is indeed a matter of who has power over whom and who can decide what for whom, it is obvious that the whole mission of Jesus was inextricably bound up with such concerns (Prior 1987, 139).

Jesus called society to live with a different frame of reference—the kingdom of God. Rather than heed his call, we preferred to kill him.

The crucified God is in fact a stateless and classless God. But that does not mean that He is an unpolitical God. He is the God of the poor, the oppressed and the humiliated (Moltmann 1974, 329).

However, kingdom political involvement transforms the very nature of the political arena. The kingdom, for example, redefines the concept of freedom. Freedom is more than liberation from the "realm of necessity"[5] (Moltmann 1981, 213). The kingdom defines freedom as restored relationships between God and all God's people.

The Christ of the kingdom is political. He deals with issues of power, poverty and powerlessness.

The Kingdom of God Focuses on the "Inner"

Contemporary evangelical scholarship strongly affirms that in Jesus' response to the law he emphasizes "what [lay] behind the specifically ethical aspect and really concentrate[d] on the religious root of obedience to the divine will" (Ridderbos 1962, 318). Jesus differed from rabbinical ethics precisely in this focus on the inward. Jesus demanded inner righteousness in the restructuring and shaping of external behavior and relationships.

Both oppressor and the oppressed need more than new and improved social structures. Sin is deeper than the very evil social systems. Therefore, they need both better social systems and also a new living relationship with Christ that . . . transforms at the core of their personalities (Sider 1993, 153).

Conclusions about kingdom understanding of power must address the "inner" as it challenges the world's power.

The Kingdom of God Is Redemptive

God's redemptive action is rooted in his desire for intimate relationship with us. The quality of that redemption is the "radical difference" that comes from submitting to the reign of God.

At the heart of Jesus' message is his assurance

that God has once again been redemptively active in history. . . . The eschatological Kingdom has itself invaded history in advance, bringing to men in the old age of sin and death, the blessings of God's rule (Ladd 1974, 326).

This redemptive presence of the kingdom[6] expresses itself

in liberated relationships which actually challenge the distorted personal, social, economic and religious relationships which express rebellion against God. God's Kingdom is His ongoing invasion of liberation (Sugden 1981, 23).

God's kingdom is a rule intended to redeem and transform persons and their situations—

> break[ing] down the hierarchical relationships which deprive them of self-determination, and . . . develop[ing] their humanity (Moltmann 1974, 318).

The Kingdom of God Demands a Response

The kingdom is the gift of God and it is to be received (Mark 10:15; Luke 18:17; Matt. 18:3; John 3:3; Mark 15:43; Luke 23:51), appointed to humans by covenant (Luke 12:29, 32), and entered into (Matt. 5:20; 7:21; 18:3; 19:23f.; 23:13; John 3:5)(Colin Brown 1976, 2:385). The kingdom of God is a divine initiative that seeks a response. The emphasis on human response does not preclude the earlier affirmation that the kingdom of God is essentially theocentric, always focused on the reign of God. This response has to be an irrevocable decision that expresses repentance. Hoest Marcella, education director of the Maryknoll Sisters, New York, states: "There is no credible way of proclaiming the Kingdom or of denouncing injustice without conversion. There is no conversion without the 'dangerous remembering' of the imperatives of the Kingdom" (Marcella 1982).

The Kingdom of God
Is Redemptively Biased Toward the Marginalized

Not much was said in early evangelical scholarship on the kingdom of God's preferential option for the poor. Herman Ridderbos in *The Coming of the Kingdom*, discusses the role of the poor as a preferred audience for Jesus' proclamation (1962, 185–92). In recent reflections on the kingdom, however, there are clear evidences of a shift in perceiving the poor as more than a preferred audience. "The poor were the only group [Jesus] singled out especially to receive the Good News. Why? Because of their poverty and vulnerability, they had no other security and hope than God" (Sugden 1981, 35). The coming of the kingdom is a tangible manifestation of God's attitude toward the poor and toward injustice. Ron Sider argues,

The biblical insistence on God's concern for the poor is first of all a theological statement about the Creator and the Sovereign of the universe (1993, 33).

This God in Jesus is "strangely moved at the cries of the oppressed, particularly when His people collectively make no sacrifice to relieve their anguish (Glasser 1991, 24). God's kingdom is particularly good news for the poor.

Nothing is more liberating to the poor, oppressed folk than the full biblical message that the One who dies for their sins is the God of the poor, who abhors unjust structures (Sider 1993, 178).

This bias for the poor within the kingdom is a redemptive bias. It does not suggest that God passively takes the side of the poor, as the world understands it. Instead, by taking a stand alongside the marginalized, the kingdom of God radically challenges the values that the powerful have used thus far to exclude the poor.

This aspect of the kingdom's values makes it difficult to explain the nature of kingdom power without recognizing Jesus' special concern for the poor and the oppressed.

The Kingdom of God Seeks to Reverse the Status Quo

Contemporary scholars reflecting on the relationship between the kingdom and worldly structures point out that reversal is the kingdom's way of confronting inadequacies in structures. Emilio Castro writes, "to pray today 'Your Kingdom Come' is to raise the banner of concrete hopes: it is to announce freedom to the captives" (1980, 32).

His Kingdom, His power and His glory are already in the midst of this world in the midst of us. This means liberating judgment on the rich, the violent and the oppressors. This means gracious liberation for the poor, the weak and the downtrodden (Moltmann 1982, 8).

Jesus challenged the status quo. His attitude toward the Temple is a case in point.

Temple was clearly the basis of an economic system in which the agricultural producers supported the priests, particularly the priestly aristocracy who administered the system, and were its chief beneficiaries. . . . The system had the political backing of the empire. . . . Temple was thus functioning as an instrument of imperial legitimation and control of a subjected people (Horsley 1993, 286).

Jesus, by attacking the use of the Temple as a den of thieves, was attacking

not things peripheral to the system but integral parts of it . . . a prophetic act symbolizing the imminent judgement . . . of the temple system (Horsley 1993, 300).

Jesus challenged the institution of Sabbath in his encounter with the woman who for 18 years had been possessed by a spirit that left her enfeebled (Luke 13:10–17). For religious leaders during Jesus' time, this was no ordinary good deed of healing. Jesus challenged religious leaders who oppressed the marginalized to maintain their power. When Jesus "saw her" and "called her over" and healed her, he disturbed the complacency of synagogue officials regarding the Sabbath.

Jesus was a revolutionary in violating Sabbath laws, criticizing the greedy, eating with sinners and provoking the Pharisees. His message of the Kingdom threatened the power of vested interest groups (Kraybill 1990, 58).

Jesus and the message of the kingdom of God also challenged the powers and ideologies of this world that keep the poor powerless. Brueggemann calls this the

assault on the consciousness of the empire, aimed at nothing less than the dismantling of the empire both in its social practices and in its mythic pretensions (1978, 19).[7]

Jesus challenged the status quo and its leadership by raising fundamental questions of meaning. These questions made the leaders and the powerful uncomfortable. The leaders complained (in Luke 5:21), questioned (6:2), grew furious (6:11), rejected God's purposes (7:30), ridiculed (7:39), were perplexed (9:7), then surprised and insulted (11:45), opposed fiercely (11:53), became indignant (13:14), remained silent (14:4), muttered (15:2), sneered (16:14), were saddened (18:23), sought to rebuke (19:30), tried to kill (19:47), became afraid (22:2), and mocked and beat Jesus (22:63). Some of these tensions resulted from questions initiated by the Pharisees and scribes; others resulted when Jesus corrected their statements and behavior (Tannehill 1969, 169–99). Jesus intentionally created dissonance by raising these uncomfortable questions, resulting, finally, in the cross. He was "perceived to be a threat to law and order, which could not be tolerated. So he was liquidated" (Stott 1986, 47). Mortimer Arias points out that Christ's kingdom permanently subverts human orders (1984, 43). It introduces a "new upside down Kingdom based on new power" (Kraybill 1990, 87).

Therefore, inquiry into the kingdom's understanding of power must involve calling upon all powers to submit to the claims of Christ's kingdom and "to treat all its citizens equally or rather to be biased towards the less privileged" (Bosch 1987, 14).

Summary

This brief survey of contemporary reflections on the kingdom of God establishes a frame of reference for the concluding chapters of our inquiry into the kingdom's understanding of power and its relevance for the powerlessness of the poor.

Notes

[1] Rappaport's work as a community psychologist in the context of urban America is a helpful resource on empowerment. He suggests guidelines for empowerment: (1) Empowerment is a multi-level construct. (2) The radiating impact of one level of analysis on the others is assumed to be important. (3) The historical context in which a person, a program, or a policy operates has an important influence on outcomes of the program. (4) Cultural context matters. (5) Longitudinal research, or the study of people, organizations and policies over time, is at least desirable, and perhaps necessary. (6) Empowerment theory is self-consciously a worldview theory. (7) It is assumed that conditions of participation in a setting will influence empowerment of members. (8) Other things being equal, an organization that holds empowerment ideology will be better

at finding and developing resources than one with a helper-helpee ideology. (9) Locally developed solutions are more empowering than single solutions applied in a general way. (10) The size of the setting matters. (11) Empowerment is not a scarce resource that gets used up but rather, once adopted as an ideology, empowerment tends to expand resources (Rappaport 1987, 139–42).

[2] David Korten proposes that voluntary action needs to move into the fourth generation. According to Korten, this fourth generation voluntary action will involve global change emerging from people movements (1990, 124). The goal of the fourth generation efforts will be "to energize a critical mass of independent, decentralized initiative in support of a social vision" (ibid., 127). Korten then goes on to outline an "agenda for a society in transition," in which he proposes that there is a need for spiritual development—an essential additional step (ibid., 168).

[3] "The Kingdom expected by the premillennialist is quite different from the Kingdom anticipated by the postmillennialist . . . in regard to its nature and the way Christ will exercise control over it" (Clouse 1977, 7). Personally, I view the question of time and the consequent interpretation of the substance of the kingdom of God as a question those who belong to the kingdom would tend to ask. However, of what relevance is the question of time to those poor who seem to live forever on the margins of society and the margins of time? Should we not, like the prophets of old, examine the state of people of our day and God's will for them?

[4] Mortimer Arias (1984) states that the term *kingdom* is an unfortunate one. He points out that the monarchical political connotation and patriarchal structures and language are being questioned by some. Charles Van Engen responds to this concern well when he suggests that we need a *"covenant/kingdom* theology [that] would take seriously the role of refugees, women, the poor, the marginalized, the weak, and the foolish in understanding the church's participation in God's mission" (1993, 258, emphasis added).

[5] Kingdom intervention is deeper than external freedom. Jürgen Moltmann's hermeneutics of the inadequacies in society includes five vicious circles: (1) poverty, (2) force—domination of the upper classes, (3) racial and cultural alienation, (4) industrial pollution of nature, and (5) senselessness and the god-forsaken (Moltmann 1974, 331). Moltmann goes on to trace the response of the crucified God to those vicious circles. Another contribution Jürgen Moltmann makes to our understanding of freedom is the moral choice involved in sustaining freedom. The new community comes into being which is without privileges and subjection, the community of the free (ibid., 211). But this realm of freedom would be "torment . . . if it were not for the realm of good, beyond necessity and freedom. The realm of good means the place from which moral purposes and values shine into the realm of freedom so that freedom may be used properly" (1981, 213).

[6] The Evangelicals in Social Action and the Charismatics conference affirmed that "God's intention is the transformation of the whole of society and

that is inseparable from the transformation of the inner, spiritual life of people, families and communities" (Hathaway 1990, 9).

[7] Brueggemann has a helpful analysis of what he calls the "royal consciousness." He refers to the kings who ruled the nation of Israel, especially during Solomon's period as the case in point. This royal consciousness exploited the poor of the time, first by an "economics of affluence" (1 Kings 4:20–23), then by the politics of oppression (1 Kings 5:13–18, 9:15–22) and finally by the religion of immanence (1 Kings 8:12–13) (Brueggemann 1978, 36).

10

Power in the Kingdom of God

The kingdom of God "has a face and Name: Jesus Christ" (Arias 1984, 69). Therefore, it is appropriate for us to search Jesus' life and ministry for clues to understanding the kingdom's view of power. Expressions of power in Jesus' ministry were totally different from the world's understanding of power (Prior 1987, 13).[1] Jesus' understanding of power also differed from Old Testament perceptions[2] and the Judaic perception of power.

> From the perspective of the OT and Judaism, the biggest surprise about the NT view of power is the type of power exhibited by the Messiah. Under the domination of Rome, the covenant people looked for an heir of David who would deliver them through a display of military and political might. . . . But Jesus marshaled no troops and attained no recognized political office. This does not mean that Jesus was apolitical, but that He transformed politics (Bromiley 1986, 928).

When Jesus came onto the scene, he redefined power. In Jesus, power was the

> totally unexpected laying down of His life in apparent weakness, giving Himself into the hands of His enemies, human and super-human. At no point is the difference between the concept of power

in the Old Testament and New so pronounced. Here, in what represents the greatest paradox and surprise of all time is discovered—the supreme demonstration of power (Powell 1963, 117).

Jesus' understanding of power included rather strange symbols and practices. These included the towel and wash basin, the servant, and the cross. The cross was Jesus' decisive criticism of the world's understanding of power. His crucifixion was more than the death of a noble man; it was the ultimate act of prophetic criticism.

Without the cross, prophetic imagination will likely be as strident and as destructive as that which it criticizes. The cross is the assurance that effective prophetic criticism is done not by an outsider but always by one who must embrace the grief, enter into the death, and know the pain of the criticized one (Brueggemann 1978, 95).

The cross redefined the very concept of power and made powerlessness an authentic expression of power, albeit a strange form of power.

Kingdom Power Rereads History

Chapter 6 pointed out that history plays a crucial role in perpetuating the powerlessness of the poor. Interpreted history, which is remembered and shared among the poor, is systematically distorted to perpetuate their powerlessness. How will a kingdom-based response to the poor deal with these distortions of history?

In Jewish and Christian tradition, God in history and God's lordship over history were symbolized as belief in the "hand of God" (Weber 1989, 29). Liberation theologians called on the church to be involved along with the poor in the task of rewriting history from the perspective of the poor.

However, kingdom theology affirms that history must be viewed from God's perspective, and neither the view of the victors nor that of the vanquished is a valid reference point. We need an alternate view on history. We need a fresh understanding of the future. This foundational affirmation that God is active in the history of the poor has several ramifications.

Imagining the Future Anew

The powerless are constantly denied history-making roles. The poor become tools in the hands of the history-makers of the world. However, God's action in history opens up the possibility of the powerless imagining the future anew, based on the coming of the kingdom. What Walter Brueggemann calls the "prophetic imagination" must precede any concrete response (1978, 45). This imagining is now a possibility for the poor, because it is God's reading of history, finally, that will shape the end of time.

In this task of imagination, the "prophet of God" provides leadership.

It is the vocation of the prophet to keep alive the ministry of imagination, to keep on conjuring and proposing alternative futures to the single one the king (referring to the kingdoms of Israel, particularly King Solomon's time) wants to urge as the only thinkable one (ibid., 45).

An Alternate Reading of History

Such imagination provides a remedy to the reading of history from the perspective of the powerful—a radical alternative. This imagination affirms that history can be read from a perspective other than that of the winners. However, neither is this kingdom alternative a history written from the perspective of the powerless. History written from the perspective of the powerless would mean only reversal, not transformation of history.

A kingdom reading of history must be from the perspective of the One who has a special concern for the poor and the marginalized. Kingdom power enables the powerless to reread history from God's viewpoint, including the "adventus and futurum" dimensions of God's acts—"surprises" of the Spirit's movement in history, as well as "normal" events. Not only is the possibility of an alternate reading of history prophetic, but the substance of that reading is also prophetic, challenging the power of the powerful.

An Alternate Way of Reading the Present

Kingdom affirmations about God's action in human affairs also insist that we read present reality differently. The kingdom suggests that we read the past and present with God's intended future as the primary point of reference. The world compels us "to absolutize truth from a snapshot of the events in history" (Kamaleson 1993). However, we have a God who is active in history. In kingdom readings of history the future is an important point of reference. It enables us to take a long view of the present that is crucial for the poor. As Robert Chambers suggests, the solution to powerlessness,

> is empowering the poor in a manner which encourages and enables them to take the long view, to enhance and not degrade resources (1991, 5).

Very often the poor are prevented from taking a long view of reality; their actions are often merely reactions.

Cross and Empty Tomb as Reference Point

Any reading of history, present and future from God's perspective, must also include the Cross and the empty tomb beyond the Cross. The empty tomb and the resurrection it signifies are decisive in kingdom power. The Cross is neither the last word nor a sign of ultimate defeat. As Ron Sider suggests, the resurrection of Jesus is powerful evidence that even the last enemy called death "will be but for a moment" (1982, 1108). Therefore, the kingdom and God's action in history reinterpret the pain of powerlessness with the Cross and the empty tomb as reference points.

History Cannot Redeem

Belief in the history-forming power of God recognizes that history itself has no power to redeem. The powerless need not be slaves of any particular understanding of history, for history is powerless to bring the kingdom's purpose to fulfillment (Ladd 1974, 56). Only God, acting in history, can cause the kingdom of God to be realized. Our history in the final analysis cannot determine our identity.

This source of power, that God is active in history, including the history of the poor, enables the poor to "imagine the future anew," bringing a new sense of dignity where the poor are no longer the passive objects of oppression and humiliation; they are now their own conscious subjects, . . . [with] the assurance of their indestructible dignity in God's sight (Moltmann 1993, 101).

A kingdom response to poverty should therefore always call the poor and the non-poor to read time and events in a way that affirms the existence of a living and loving God, who broods over the affairs of the poor and the powerless.

Kingdom Power Affirms Relationships

Most definitions of power presuppose relationships. The powerlessness of the poor is a relational concept. Kingdom power is also relational. The kingdom of God affirms relationships and builds community.

Kingdom Power and the Community

Community is integral to understanding the Trinitarian kingdom of God. When kingdom power is expressed, it always creates community. The world's power

cannot create community. It is always in tension with the power of the servant, the power of love and of the finer aspects of justice (West 1975, 8).

In the kingdom the "we" is prior to the "I" (Ray Anderson 1982, 169).[3] Further, in the kingdom freedom is not defined as lordship but as community (Moltmann 1981, 215). The Wheaton '83 declaration comments on Jesus' attitude to power structures,

His was a prophetic compassion and it resulted in the formation of a community which accepted the values of the Kingdom of God and stood in contrast to the Roman and Jewish establishment (Samuel and Sugden 1987, 260).

In fact, kingdom power can only be understood in the context of a community. However, the community that kingdom power builds is qualitatively different. It is a covenant-quality community.

In the kingdom of God, the concept of community (covenant community) does not recognize the need for winners and losers, nor power over the powerless, nor lord over subjects. Instead, kingdom power is fully realized only within a relationship in which covenant precedes power (Elliott 1987, 152).[4]

Covenant Does Not Exploit Inequality

Kingdom theology affirms that a covenant is between unequal partners. Taking our cue from the covenants Yahweh[5] entered into with Abraham, Moses and the people of Israel, this same "inequality" becomes the springboard for redemptive involvement. In the kingdom of God, inequality is never the basis for relationships or for breaking relationship or for any exploitation. The covenant-quality community transforms all relationships. There will be no need for winners and losers in the kingdom.

Covenant Does Not Destroy

A covenant-quality relationship seeks to build (2 Cor. 13:10) and not destroy anybody. Here kingdom power clearly differentiates itself from the world's understanding of power. Often the poor do not have access to worldly bases of power. Kingdom power does not seek to manipulate power but rather builds and affirms the personhood of the other without reducing the other to a mere power base. Further, kingdom power affirms commonality as well as diversity.

Covenant Redefines Solidarity

In the context of the covenant, *solidarity* is understood as being a community "with" the poor, not just operating a program "for" the poor. The covenant-quality community challenges the traditional understanding of solidarity with the poor. The mandate here is to be in solidarity with the poor.

> Born in a stable, introduced to the agony of refugees as a child, raised in the economic backwater of Galilee, Jesus, the wandering teacher, had no house of his own (Matt. 8:20) (Sider 1993, 63).

Jesus chose to become an outcaste. In a covenant there is a need for such intentional giving up for being in solidarity "with" the poor.

Covenant Challenges Issue-based Community Organization

The covenant-quality community emphasizes that solidarity with and among the powerless should never be reduced to an issue-based social program. Most development theoreticians and sociologists who have studied movements imply a need for an issue-based ideology. They suggest that community organization efforts must be built around issues. However, in responding to the powerless, whose relationships are already hurting, issue-based response can deepen the wound. Such programs tend to fade away after the issue is resolved. The covenant calls for authentic relationship-based involvement among the poor. Issues are secondary to relationships in the kingdom.

Covenant Will Not Exploit Numbers

Covenant-based solidarity does not exploit the numbers game that is so integral to this world's understanding of power. For the poor, their numbers are a source of power. However, when this power is exercised or exploited by politicians and others, their very personhood is reduced. In the kingdom's expression of power, based on covenant-quality relationships, the powerless are first and foremost seen as persons. Kingdom power never damages their basic personhood.

Kingdom Power and Its Inclusive Intent

The world's power is built on excluding the many poor so that the few powerful can rule. The kingdom of Satan is "based upon the exclusive and selfish solidarity of groups" (Nolan 1976, 60). A key characteristic of poverty relationships is that the poor are constantly excluded from the mainstream.

The kingdom of God, on the other hand, seeks to include. It is based on an "all inclusive solidarity" of the human race (ibid., 1976, 60). Inclusion, or embrace, as Miroslav Volf refers to it, is integral to the Bible's frequent reminder that in the kingdom of God there will be people from "every tribe and language and people and nation" (Rev. 5). Exclusion of the "other" is sin (Volf 1993).[6]

In its inclusive intent, kingdom power is radically different from the world's power, which seeks to keep the poor powerless by excluding them. Fundamental to the fact that kingdom power affirms inclusion is its attitude toward barriers that divide people.

> [Jesus] refuses to recognize any social, ethnic, political, or religious barriers. In his boundary breaking ministry Jesus embraces all. In doing so, he affirms [people]; more importantly: he empowers [people] (Bosch 1989, 8).

The kingdom of God refuses to recognize barriers that divide people. Jesus' refusal to endorse society's barriers resulted in a transforming experience for those on the other side of those barriers, enabling them to

> lift up their heads and hold them high, to recognize their own dignity, to begin to see themselves in a new light. After their encounter with Jesus, they are transformed into people who know themselves to be God's children (ibid., 8).

Further, in Jesus' ministry he intentionally challenged these barriers, accepting and freely mixing with those on the other side of the world's boundaries, the marginalized. As Lesslie Newbigin writes,

> The scandal, the stumbling block which Jesus presents to his contemporaries is that on one hand he simply ignores the lines which every society draws to separate the good from the bad and accepts freely into his company those on the wrong side of the line (1980, 31).

This intentional mixing radically criticized the lines themselves, and this inclusive nature of the kingdom challenges the reality of powerlessness in many ways.

Kingdom Power Challenges the Dividing Lines

Jesus went further than just ignoring the lines that have divided people since the beginning of human history. Jesus not only mixed with the poor intentionally, but he "angered the religious leaders (by) making his association with the sinners a religious issue" (Ladd 1974, 175). For Jesus, this erasing of the lines was integral to his understanding of mission.

God's kingdom challenges those lines, not just because of God's special concern for the poor but because those lines are contradictory to the reign of God. The kingdom of God challenges the power of oppressors to divide and rule. This is essentially an expression of God's redemptive plan for people of all nations, tribes and languages. As Jürgen Moltmann points out, through all these boundary-breaking ministries Jesus

> is not justifying the sin, the corruption of the prostitution. But he is breaking through the vicious circle of their discrimination in the system of values set up by the righteous. In this way he is also potentially rescuing "the righteous" from the compulsion of self-righteousness, and saving "the good" from the possession of the good (1993, 114).

Kingdom Power Includes All

The inclusive intent of the kingdom also affirms that the "Kingdom of God . . . will be a society in which there will be no prestige and no status, no division of people who are inferior and superior" (Nolan 1976, 58). The poor, who have been excluded thus far, will be included in the kingdom of God.

The key question, then, is, How did the kingdom, which "belonged" to the poor (Luke 6:20), become the kingdom in which all peoples of "all languages, nations and tribes" are included (Rev. 5:9)? The inclusive intent of the kingdom is best expressed in this shift. First, the kingdom of God belongs to the poor, who were once excluded by the rest of the world (Luke 6:20). Second, these excluded poor, to whom the kingdom now belongs, have the joy of including the very nations and languages and tribes and peoples who excluded them in the past. This shift from Luke 6:20 to Revelation 5:9 unequivocally describes the radical nature of the kingdom. All are included in the kingdom of God, which "belongs" to the poor.

The inclusive intent of kingdom power causes ripples of transformation. Sider describes Jesus'

> unbiased concern for the poor, [which] demands fundamental change in distorted values and systems that favor the rich and powerful. Jesus and the whole Bible's "preferential option for the poor" calls us to overturn poverty and correct justice. It summons us to a fundamental reversal of distorted views and practices (1989, 165).

God's concern for the poor is deeply rooted in the affirmation that "God so loved the world." This was and is a concern with a redemptive intent. This love challenges the distorted values that have ruled the world, including the distorted understanding of power.

Kingdom power is never self-serving. Jesus, after washing the feet of his disciples (John 13), did not exploit the moral advantage he had just established. Instead, he commanded them, "You also should wash one another's feet. . . . You should do as I have done for you" (vv. 14–15, NIV). There are other feet that need to be washed. In this understanding of transformation, the "powerless" servant is a key agent. The powerless are not on the margins of God's agenda for transformation.

Consequently, kingdom power does not need "enemy" labels to sustain emotion or motivation. Sociologists inquiring into the nature of social movements suggest that popular movements need to identify a common enemy. Effective movements need both sacred persons, events and objects, and demonized enemies to sustain themselves (Oommen 1990, 290). In the context of poverty situations, this "enemy" may be the government, the non-poor, the economic structures, the political groups or even distorted history. However, in the kingdom economy there is no need for demonization. Kingdom power will refuse to demonize any potential member of the kingdom. Kingdom power will declare the truth about exploitative relationships without sacralizing or demonizing any. The kingdom places no value on the "enemy" label.

Summary

To sum up, the kingdom affirms the potential in the "other" to be a member of the kingdom even as it challenges inadequacies and reverses status quo. The kingdom's affirmation of the covenant-quality community redefines the standards for all community organization interventions among the poor. Kingdom interventions will refuse to exploit the numbers of the poor, or to seek power through connections, or to manipulate the "other" in any power relationships.

In the process of dealing with power issues among the poor, kingdom power will always communicate and affirm the inclusive intent of the kingdom, refusing to consider anyone as the "enemy." Kingdom power will challenge the lines that divide and break the community in poverty relationships. Kingdom power will cause ripples of transformation as a community of "unequals" who do not exploit their inequality. Kingdom power will spread redemption.

Kingdom Power Is Based on Truth

In the world's understanding of power, truth is the first casualty. Truth is defined by the winner, and the losers views are ignored. The world's power always seeks to justify its own position. Power constantly seeks to absolutize itself and, as discussed earlier, helps create a "web of lies" within which the poor are held captive.

In the kingdom of God, truth is foundational.

> The only authority that Jesus might be said to have appealed to, was the authority of the truth itself. He did not make authority his truth, he made truth his authority (Nolan 1976, 123).

Kingdom power is based on Truth with a capital T. John 8:32 promises that we will know the Truth and the Truth will set us free. Kingdom power locates this Truth in the person of Jesus Christ (John 8:36) and in relationship with him. Therefore, the source of kingdom power lies outside the power-powerless axis of the world. It is in the Truth that is found in the Son. This understanding of power as rooted in the Truth challenges all other structures and powers—including rulers and authorities in the heavenly realm (Eph. 3:10)—who do not acknowledge the Truth.

Second, kingdom power is founded on a clarified understanding of self—the truth about self. While the world's understanding of power is built on the marred identity of the poor (which simultaneously mars the identity of the non-poor as well), kingdom power is built on a clarification of identity that enables the condemned to say with confidence "in all these things we are more than conquerors through him who loved us" (Rom. 8:37). This clarification enables one to say, "So, I will boast all the more gladly of my weaknesses, so that the power of Christ may dwell in me" (2 Cor. 12:9b).

> Such humble acceptance of our natural powerlessness, such genuine poverty of spirit, could alone provide the springboard for true faith in a God who can make mountains move (Prior 1987, 81).

We are "more than conquerors," as well as powerlessly dependent on God. Only through genuine recognition of powerlessness can we discover kingdom power.

Third, in the kingdom of God, truth is not only an absolute concept but is also a functional value in public life. In a world of winners and losers, ultimately truth is banned from public life. Moltmann refers to this phenomenon as the "loss of center" (1967, 307). Kingdom power will always seek to restore truth to its rightful place in the public arena.

> When dominating power is understood to be the truth it becomes the only way because it is the only *officially sanctioned* way of doing things (Fletcher 1992, 184).

The kingdom of God calls our bluff on assumptions about the officially sanctioned way of power. Francis Watson describes this as the comprehensive "divine unmasking of the conventional assumptions about wisdom and power" (1992, 140). Kingdom power challenges the distortion of truth in the world.

Truth and Fearlessness

Since Truth is the basis for the kingdom's understanding of power, the power wielder need not fear. Fearlessness (not arrogance) is the chief characteristic of one who has Truth as a power base. Jesus' opponents clearly perceived this relationship between his honesty and his fearlessness.

> Teacher, we know that you are sincere, and show deference to no one; for you do not regard people with partiality, but teach the way of God in accordance with truth. Is it lawful to pay taxes to the emperor, or not? (Mark 12:14).

In some versions the phrase "for you do not regard people with partiality" is translated as "you are not afraid of anyone." For Jesus, his relationship with the Father was the basis of all his teaching and ministry. This foundational relationship, this Truth, "made of him a uniquely liberated man, uniquely courageous, fearless, independent, hopeful and truthful" (Nolan 1976, 125). Therefore, kingdom power, based on Truth, can be exercised without fear.

Truth Leads to Prophetic Involvement

A key expression of kingdom power based on truth will be prophetic involvement among the poor. A prophet is one who declares the truth about a situation. Not only does the prophet express God's mind about issues but he or she also reads the issues as God would read them. A prophet raises the question of meaning. Walter Brueggemann described this role of the prophet as "articulating grief." The prophet grieves over people because of genuine care for the people (Brueggemann 1978, 52). Grief articulation is a natural result of recognition that truth is at stake in power encounters. This grief articulation is by no means a passive and helpless weeping over concerns of the day. Instead,

> weeping is a radical criticism, a fearful dismantling, because it means the end of all machismo; weeping is something that kings rarely do without losing their thrones. Yet the loss of thrones is precisely what is called for in radical criticism (ibid., 61).

Therefore, the focus and the act of grieving the loss or absence of Truth is in itself is a radical criticism of the world's exercise of power.

Truth and Cosmic Implications

The kingdom's affirmation that Truth is the foundation of power has cosmic implications. To begin with, the ruler in the heavenly places is the "father of lies" (John 8:44). Therefore, in the battle with principalities and powers (Eph. 6:12), Paul calls us to "stand firm then, with the belt of truth buckled around your waist" (Eph. 6:14, NIV). We must stand where kingdom power challenges the distortions that the cosmic powers perpetuate to keep the poor powerless.

Summary

Kingdom power seeks to break the "web of lies" and proclaim liberty to the prisoners, the poor. This would mean that kingdom involvement among the poor is essentially an effort to establish truth and righteousness. Earlier analysis of historical models and global reflections likewise affirmed that mission among the poor is essentially an effort to establish truth and righteousness.

Further, kingdom power allows fearless involvement in a prophetic ministry of articulating grief over the distortion of truth (and its implications among the powerless), by this means challenging the deceiver, the devil himself.

Kingdom Power and Identity Clarification

A key characteristic of kingdom power is that it "purchases" humans for God (Rev. 5: 9) and makes of them a kingdom and priests to serve God (Rev. 5:10).

Central to the Christian understanding of identity is the affirmation that humans are made in the image of God. "Being in the image of God is not a religious overlay on our natural humanity. On the contrary, being in the image of God is itself fundamental to our true humanity" (Ray Anderson 1982, 84). However, within poverty situations this understanding that the poor are made in the image of God is constantly attacked. Powerlessness is the marring of the image of God in the poor. In the kingdom, transformation involves being made into a new creation (2 Cor. 5:17) and into the image of the Son Jesus Christ. Transformation implies restoration of the image of God among the poor.

Anderson provides a helpful framework to understand this process of restoration. He suggests that the Bible understands the humanity of persons first as an "actuality" before becoming a possibility. The poor are made in the image of God—this is reality in the kingdom of God. The poor "can become human because [they] . . . are in fact divinely determined to be human and are human" (1982, 165). The poor are human in spite of all the violations of their identity by the powers. Kingdom power operates from this fundamental truth—that persons are first and foremost created in the image of God.

Image of God and "Response-ability"

The kingdom affirms the "response-ability" (Ray Anderson 1982, 83) of the poor, seeking a response from all, including the poor. The poor (perpetually on the margins of society), whose opinions are disregarded or disparaged are now called on to respond to the King of the kingdom. This ability to respond is endowed in humans and affirmed by the kingdom. The Good News is to the poor. It affirms their ability to respond and thus their humanity. The world, on the other hand, constantly seeks to mar this ability of the poor to respond. The poor are considered mere numbers when it comes to elections. The educational system stunts the reflective ability of the poor. Kingdom power seeks to reverse this marring by affirming that the Good News of the kingdom is directed to the poor and that they too have the ability to respond.

Identity and Community

Moltmann points out that in the kingdom human freedom is defined in the context of community (1981, 19). Affirmation of humanity in the kingdom will never imply the freedom to be human in isolation or having power over others.

Kingdom power always seeks to affirm the essential humanity and ability to respond within the context of a community, among the poor. For the poor whose identity is marred within poverty relationships, this affirmation means clarification of their identity—that they too are made in the image of God.

The Process of Identity Clarification

Paul's reflections on new life in the Spirit in Romans 8 help us understand the processes involved in this identity clarification in the kingdom.[7] The shift from being condemned in verse 1 to becoming "more than conquerors" in verse 37 is an example of identity clarification. Becoming "more than conquerors" is the result of the work of the Trinity. Christ Jesus, the Spirit and the Father engage in this sacred exercise of clarifying the identity of those whose identities are marred. The whole of the kingdom appears to be eagerly involved in restoring the image of God to humans.

Romans 8 provides further clues about this identity clarification. The move from being a condemned sinner to "more than conquerors" is gradual. We are declared "not condemned" in Jesus (v. 1), the Spirit indwells us (v. 9), we belong to Christ (v. 9), we are called children of God (v. 14), are heirs and joint heirs (v. 17), have the first fruits of the Spirit (v. 23), are helped in weakness (v. 26), have the Spirit interceding for us (vv. 27, 34). Thus no one can be against us (v. 31) or can bring any charge against us (v. 33), and nothing in all creation can separate us from the love of God (v. 39). This, according to the Spirit, is the meaning of identity clarification in the kingdom. For us, who were once condemned sinners, to experience all this and go through life as "more than conquerors" is truly an empowering clarification of our identity.

In the process of these shifts the Spirit addresses several forces seeking to mar the identity of the one made in the image of God. These forces are sin (v. 3), mindset (v. 6), sinful nature (v. 9), slave nature (v. 15), present suffering (v. 18), weakness (v. 26), others who seek to be against us and charge, condemn and separate us (vv. 31–35), and all other time-related, spatial, earthly and cosmic powers (v. 38). Kingdom power in its identity-clarifying role does not run away from real-life issues. It deals with them and goes deeper to address the "inner," which forms the basis for the outer realities.

An important piece in the kingdom's effort to clarify identity is the role of hope. Paul in Romans 8 describes this hope as the desire of all creation (v. 20). Hope is the response of the kingdom to the groaning of all creation (vv. 22, 23). This hope is redemptive and affects the whole of life (v. 23), including the body (see Sider 1993, 89). The link between identity and hope is crucial while addressing realities of the powerless. The powers within poverty relationships often mar the identity of the poor in the workshop called hopelessness.

Paul positions identity clarification (Rom. 8) between two seemingly contradictory human experiences (Rom. 7 and 9). At the end of chapter 7 Paul describes the struggle between his mind and the members of his body. He begins chapter 9 by expressing his unceasing anguish for the sake of his people (vv. 2–4). Analysis of this shift suggests that the move from focusing on personal struggle to concern for others involves a clarification of one's identity (Rom. 8).

According to Paul this clarification of identity is an integral part of the kingdom's transformational work, the result of the work of the Trinitarian God. It involves the condemned sinner becoming able to declare, "We are more than conquerors." Focus on personal struggle is transformed in a glorious giving away of oneself in service to others.

Political sociologists also affirm the need for identity clarification. T. K. Oommen in his survey of social movements points out that identity clarification is a crucial dimension in any effective movement. Social movements reinforce the identity of members by using symbols of identification and adopting a new lifestyle. Oommen then explains that this process of creating a new identity "invariably leads to the sacralization of persons, events and objects crucial to the movement . . . and demonization of the enemy" (1990, 290). However, identity clarification that needs "demons" and sacred "symbols" will tend to further fracture society.

Kingdom power, by contrast, does not clarify identity through sacralization and demonization. Kingdom power instead clarifies the identity of the powerless by affirming their humanity and the image of God in them. This affirmation about the identity of the poor attacks the root of bondage to the identity assigned them by structures, systems and the non-poor.

Kingdom identity clarification of the powerless will not result in fracturing the community. This does not imply glossing over oppressive relationships within poverty situations. As discussed earlier, regarding the power-poverty encounter, the presence of oppression and poverty within poverty situations may mean "social balance" or even "peace" as desired by the powerful. Kingdom power, however, affirms human freedom in the context of community—a community of freed people.

Summary

In the kingdom of God, the marred identity of the poor is continuously healed and clarified without fragmenting the community. The poor are empowered to give of themselves to be "healed agents" of transformation (for example, see the discussion of Pandita Ramabai's Mukti Mission in chapter 4).

Kingdom Power Redefines Power

The extraordinary nature of kingdom power is most obvious when the frame of reference used to define power itself is challenged. Jesus reversed the world's understanding of power.

In the world power is characterized by domination and oppression. The lines between force and ideology and between obedience and duty often get blurred. "Human fear and arrogance . . . create structures of domination and exploitation" (Schmidt 1992, 71). Jesus held these and other distortions of power up to total ridicule (Ellul 1988, 167).

Walter Wink reflects:

Jesus, in short, abhors both passivity and violence. He articulates .
. . a way by which evil can be opposed without being mirrored, the
oppressor resisted without being emulated, and the enemy neu-
tralized without being destroyed (1992, 189).

Wink reflects on three of Jesus' injunctions—turn the other cheek, give
the undergarment and walk the second mile (ibid., 175–84) to develop
his thesis on nonviolent response to domination systems. Wink points
out that Jesus' affirmation of nonviolence was for ordinary people—a
third way between "fight" (armed revolt, violent rebellion, direct retali-
ation and revenge) and "flight" (submission, passivity, withdrawal and
surrender) (ibid., 187). Wink then concludes,

> Our goal must be training of millions of non-violent activists who
> are ready, at a moment's notice, to swing into action on behalf of
> the humanizing purposes of God (ibid., 192).

Jesus' way is more than nonviolence; it is an active, positive powerlessness that radically challenges the world's understanding of power.

Kingdom Power in Weakness

Jesus' perception of power seems more like powerlessness in the eyes
of the world. J. B. Webster states that Jesus challenged the world's notion of power by affirming "power in weakness." Jesus was the *servus
servorum* (1988, 18). This was a reversal of power and a reversal of Old
Testament portrayals of liberation and salvation. In Jesus, victory

> will be won not through a holy war and God's avenging hand or
> by the Qumranite war. . . . The struggle for liberation is won by
> the agony on the cross and the vindication of the crucified Christ
> through resurrection (Weber 1989, 46).

This strangeness of Jesus' power was lived out on the cross. Yoder says
this reversal was more than a strategy. "He [Jesus] does not just tell us 'I
am on the other side; I am in favor of the other people who had been
victims.' He *becomes* the victim" (1978, 34).

For Jesus, living out this reversal involved being a defenseless baby.
The helpless baby was precursor to the helplessness of the crucified

Christ (Prior 1987, 29). This reversal for Jesus meant the washbasin and the towel. It meant being misunderstood and ridiculed before men. It involved being treated as an "option" by Pilate, to be considered for release, or not. When this option was finally exercised showing preference for Barabbas, the key decision-maker (Pilate) knew there was no fault in the man called Jesus. When Jesus was rejected, it meant the experience of the Cross. For Jesus, all this was part of a journey in powerlessness, from defenseless baby in Bethlehem to victim on the cross at Golgotha. Moltmann describes the implications of this journey:

> This changes our whole concept of glory, greatness, achievement, and the development of power. Normally we look upward. . . . In the case of Jesus we have to look *downwards* (1983, 24).

Jesus' Cross suggests that "mission cannot be realized when we are powerful and confident but only when we are weak and at a loss" (Bosch 1991, 515). The Cross is the most appropriate stance to confound the wise and the strong (1 Cor. 1:18), to confound a people who build their confidence and their whole life on a distorted understanding of power and wisdom. The hardest lesson the church will

> have to learn in the coming years (is) how to become again what it originally was and was always supposed to be: the church without privileges, the church of the catacombs rather than the halls of fame and power and wealth (Bosch 1987, 15).

Apart from challenging the stance for mission, the Cross also challenges the means in mission. It preempts the need for guns and swords in the kingdom's mission. Jesus testified to power of a different sort, the power of powerlessness.

Power Redefined as Positive Lowliness

The Cross defines power in the kingdom as powerlessness. Powerlessness or submission in the kingdom is different from the powerlessness of the poor. The powerlessness of the poor is imposed by the non-poor and the powers of the world. Kingdom power, in contrast, intentionally submits. In John 13:3 we see Jesus affirming his power and his relationship with the Father. Then Jesus takes the washbasin and towel as a natural consequence of this deep assurance of his power and his relationship with the Father (v. 4). The washbasin and the towel were deeply related to his recognition of the power that the Father had put behind him. Jesus chose to be a servant. This intentionality differentiates the powerlessness of the poor from the powerlessness that is characteristic of kingdom power. David Bosch calls the former "negative lowliness" and the latter "positive lowliness." He then proposes that the poor need to shift from the "negative lowliness" of their poverty to the "positive lowliness" characteristic of the kingdom of God (Bosch 1989, 8).

In the kingdom of God powerlessness and submission are more than a strategy. Submission is a genuine expression of kingdom lifestyle (Kamaleson 1993). For Jesus, submission and servanthood were not manipulative, but an authentic expression of kingdom lifestyle.

Submission and powerlessness in the kingdom does not distort God's nature. Servanthood expresses God's nature. God's strength is expressed in powerlessness. In and through powerlessness we express our dependence on God. God's power is also expressed in our weakness and transformation (1 Cor. 1:19). David Prior, referring to the "power of the baby" in Bethlehem, comments:

> It has been traditional to see this self-humbling as God in some way hiding or suspending or adding to or relinquishing his divinity in order to become man. But what if he was in Jesus, actually *uncovering* his divinity? Does the baby of Bethlehem not reveal God rather than obscure him? Is God's nature not seen in the powerlessness (to human estimation) of the baby? (1987, 24).

Jesus held to light the real intentions of the world's power. The kingdom challenges the world's understanding of power by redefining power as "self-giving emptiness of Jesus, about dominion through the loss of dominion, and about fullness coming only by self-emptying" (Brueggemann 1978, 94).

The Cross and its powerlessness were authentic expressions of Jesus' power to lay down his life and take it up again (John 10:18). Against this power—the power to invest life and to lay it down for others—there is no greater power.

Finally, powerlessness is essentially an act of faith. In our powerlessness we express our dependence on God. By refusing to play the power game with the powerful, the Christian makes a political statement. Kingdom power proclaims the sovereignty of Jesus' way over against the powers of this age. Kingdom power proclaims that the way of the kingdom expressed in submission and powerlessness is a more excellent way, a glimmer of the glory of the coming kingdom.

Summary

Intentional powerlessness is in fact a radical criticism of the world's power. It expresses God's true nature, our dependence on God and the lifestyle of the kingdom. Intentional powerlessness requires a shift from negative powerlessness. In the final analysis this understanding of kingdom power (as powerlessness) suggests it is a faith act, an affirmation that the kingdom way is a higher road.

Kingdom Power Challenges Principalities and Powers

Cosmic powers play a key role in poverty relationships and the powerlessness of the poor. They piggyback on the hurt, curses and weakness of the poor in poverty situations. Principalities and powers exploit structures and systems to keep the poor powerless. They work through people and shape the institutions involved in poverty relationships. They manipulate the spiritual interiorities of structures and systems and are, therefore, a key force to be dealt with in poverty situations.

The kingdom of God challenges the power of evil in all its manifestations. Conflict with the cosmic powers is an expression of the reversal the kingdom of God seeks to bring. The announcement of the reign of God means reversals and conflict, both in sociopolitical realms and in the kingdom of Satan. Jesus moved "to defeat God's enemies, acting in and securing the divine sovereignty at all points" (Powell 1963, 81). The breaking down of the kingdom of Satan has come with the coming of God's kingdom.

This conflict with the kingdom of Satan is also an expression of the theocentricity of God. The kingdom of God does not coexist along with other kingdoms, but seeks instead to "destroy the present course of the world . . . and thereby terminat[e] all pain and sorrow" (Küng 1967, 76).

The theocentric kingdom confronts all "contradivine" satanic power under which the present world groans (Küng 1967, 76). At the crux of this announcement of the coming of God's kingdom is total warfare with the Evil One, who introduced devastation into the good creation.

These confrontations with principalities and powers are expressions of the birthing of a new order in which God reigns supreme. God's kingdom is the new order. Arias suggests that since the coming of Jesus, all other orders are under a spell of "planned obsolescence" (Arias 1984, 43). Jesus recognized that "behind all wicked persons and twisted social patterns . . . was the works of Satan and his demonic forces" (Sider 1993, 62). Tracing the corruption of power and structures and the role of the demon, Charles Elliott concludes,

> As long as our structures are in the grip of demonic powers, the stuff of our politics, the way power is acquired and used, will be crude (1987, 152).

Integral to the kingdom's restructuring presence is its confrontation with the devil and his forces. Missional response to the poor is a battle against principalities and powers. It is a battle that seeks to establish the kingdom of God and bring peace. Kingdom mission recognizes that

> At the heart of all these complex difficulties [global problems] is a fundamental spiritual reality. We are not just dealing with facts and figures, people and issues, but with spiritual principalities and powers (Foster 1981, 164).

Missional response to the poor is a confrontation with the powers that keep them in a state of disempowerment. The poor are a natural prey to the devil, and we are called to unmask these powers. My personal opinion is that shalom and kingdom power are not contradictory. The quality of shalom that the kingdom of God envisages will put the kingdom directly in conflict with the powers of the world.[8] The radical nature of our involvement does not lie in the fact that we are involved in justice issues and empowerment initiatives. It lies in the fact that we are confronting the whole gamut of the causes of poverty. In this, development theories based on an Enlightenment-oriented analysis of structures and causes of poverty fall short (Duncan 1990, 10). To confront the powerlessness of the poor without being aware of these spiritual factors [spiritual powers that work in and through those who exercise worldly power], is to run the risk of being blind both to the ingredients of human power and to the radical contrast afforded by Jesus' power (Prior 1987, 156).

Therefore, involvement in issues of powerlessness of the poor "is a cosmic battle between God and Satan" (Linthicum 1991, 96).

Kingdom power also seeks to reverse the "spiritual interiority of institutions" that shapes structures, systems and people. This makes the conflict with principalities and powers a battle between differing spiritualities—between the spirituality that liberates the poor and the spirituality that disempowers the poor.

Battle or confrontation with the devil and his forces requires prayer and fasting. Only

through prayer, we as his redeemed people, reassert our God-given dominion over the world, ruling and reigning with Christ "far above all authority and dominion" (Eph. 1:21 and 2:6). Through believing prayer, we open the door for God's intervention in our troubled world (Robb 1993, 180).

Kingdom Power Affirms That Power Belongs to God

Thus far I have suggested that kingdom power rereads history from God's perspective, creates covenant community, is inclusive, is based on Truth, clarifies identity, defines itself as powerlessness and confronts principalities and powers. Each of these marks of kingdom power redefines the very notion of power itself. More than a mere transfer of power to the powerless, the kingdom of God calls for, in the words of Alvin Toffler, a "powershift" in which the nature of power itself is transformed.

In the theocentric kingdom of God power will always belong to God. Transformation of the very nature of power cannot happen by mere human ingenuity but is the result of the Spirit's work among us (Elliott 1987, 15). A transformation that will equip the powerless to know the power of the kingdom cannot happen without the intervention of the Holy Spirit. For it is "not by might, nor by power, but by my spirit, says the Lord of hosts" (Zech. 4:6). The Spirit's work among us is the source of kingdom power.

In the final analysis it is the Holy Spirit who empowers the kingdom. Transformation is perceived as the result of the Spirit's anointing. Only with the anointing of the Holy Spirit can there be preaching of the Good News, proclaiming freedom for prisoners, recovery of sight for the blind, release for the oppressed, and proclaiming of the year of the Lord's favor (Luke 4:18, 19, NIV). In Luke 4 the "ministry of the earthly Jesus is portrayed in terms of the initiative and guidance of the Spirit" (Bosch 1991, 113). Without the anointing of the Holy Spirit the rest of the Nazareth manifesto is merely an agenda for social activists. In the kingdom's response,

> the Spirit becomes the catalyst, the guiding and driving force of mission. At every point, the church's mission is both inspired and confirmed by manifestations of the Spirit (ibid., 113).

Kingdom power follows God's initiative. God hears the cry of the oppressed (Exodus 3:7, 8) before calling for our involvement. God makes the first move. We are invited to work along with God in this awesome task of building the kingdom with a redemptive bias toward the poor. The Spirit's kingdom power affirms that involvement among the poor is an active response rather than simply a reaction. Neither compelling statistics about poverty nor our empowerment strategies will be the motivation in kingdom-based response to the poor.

Because all power belongs to God (Ps. 62:11) we take our cues from God incarnate—Jesus. David Prior suggests that the "secret of power in the Kingdom of God is to put Jesus first" (1987, 87). This act of putting Jesus first is more than ritualistically starting with the sacred. We must truly acknowledge our powerlessness and affirm that all expressions of power in the kingdom of God consistently reflect the theocentricity of the kingdom.

Kingdom power recognizes that it is God who takes the initiative in history and that all empowerment in the final analysis is the work of the Holy Spirit.

God a Key "Player" in Power Relations

Since power belongs to God, all kingdom power relationships will include God as a key player. Exercise of power can no more be a bilateral relationship between the powerful and the powerless poor. The role and presence of the divine that transforms power must be an integral part of all kingdom power relations. This expansion of the "power triangle" affirms two key aspects of Christian mission. First, it affirms the fact that in any context, including the power-powerless situation, Jesus is the Lord. Second, mission and response to the powerlessness of the poor are God's mission.

Power Belongs to God

It is no longer "power to the people" when kingdom power is exercised. Most participatory development strategies communicate the message that power belongs to the poor. Modernization strategies suggest that power belongs to the development and technical experts. Sometimes it seems that the church has bought into this philosophy of power rather naively.

It is imperative that the church among the poor always communicate that the kingdom and the power do not belong to us (Elliott 1985, 16). As Yoder points out, even as we verbalized the slogan "power to the people," we were absolutely conscious that mere transfer of power without the transformation of power does not result in transformational quality reversal (1978, 33). Power is a gift of God. Man "would trespass his role if he regarded himself as the source of power" (Study Encounter 1975, 3). This supernatural power is absolutely natural for God.

Dependence on God

Among the poor, exercise of kingdom power requires closeness to the Father and dependence on the Spirit. That closeness to God is an absolute prerequisite for expressing kingdom power, calling for a centering around God instead of centering around people and strategies. This calls for solidarity with God. Solidarity with the poor is an unworthy substitute for solidarity with the God of the poor. Only in the context of this solidarity with the God of the poor can we know the full potential of kingdom power to empower the powerless.

Prayer and Fasting as Tools for Social Action

Following from the affirmations that all power belongs to God and that we have a need for closeness with the Father, kingdom power involves a commitment to prayer and fasting. Mission history teaches that "history belongs to the intercessors" (Wink 1992, 298ff.). We join our prayer along with that of the Intercessor (ibid., 305). Prayer and fasting are essentially expressions of our dependence on God, to whom all power belongs. Prayer defies the cosmic powers that keep the poor powerless. Prayer is an act against the powers who, through their rebelliousness, resistance and self-interest, hinder the redemptive intentions of God (ibid., 311).

A Prophetic Act

The kingdom's assertion that all power belongs to God is also prophetic, turning the world's focus to spiritual issues. This heals the world's "loss of center" (Moltmann 1967, 307) and restores its eroded faith. Kingdom spirituality emerges from following the Spirit into mission. This is the spirituality of a God who is involved in history. And mission spirituality has to "be a spirituality of engagement and not of withdrawal" (Costas 1982, 172).

Power Is Only Penultimate

Because in the kingdom, power will always belong to God, all exercise of power will have a ring of "penultimacy" to it. Among the poor, this would call for evaluation of paradigms used for our participatory methods in development projects. Does missional involvement among the poor communicate a truncated holism? Does it communicate "power to the people" through the various participatory methods or the message that "power belongs to God"?

Summary

When the Lamb sits on the throne (Rev. 5:) and leads us to springs of living water (Rev. 7), power will look very different. The kingdom redefines the very nature of power. Power in the kingdom rereads history from God's perspective, affirms covenant-quality relationships, includes all, is based on truth, clarifies identity, defines itself as powerlessness, confronts principalities and powers and, in the final analysis, affirms that all power belongs to God. This is a strange form of power that will appear like powerlessness to the world, yet it will challenge and reverse all inadequacies. In its strangeness, this kingdom power serves as a prophetic critique of the world's understanding of power that effectively perpetrated and perpetuates the powerlessness of the poor.

The final chapter focuses on constructing an alternative paradigm for responding to the powerless poor, built on the lessons of history, responding to new questions raised from the poor, and rooted in our reflections about the kingdom of God and its understanding of power.

Notes

¹ Definitions of power in leadership literature vary, although there are some common themes. Max Weber (1864–1920) defined *power* as the "possibility of imposing one's will upon the behavior of other persons" (in Galbraith 1983, 2). Yukl suggests that power is "an agent's potential influence over the attitudes and behaviors of one or more designated target persons" (1989 14). James McGregor Burns defines power as the "possibility that one actor within a social relationship will be able to carry out his own will despite resistance, regardless of the basis on which this probability rests" (1978, 11). Donald E. Messer points out that power is a neutral term. He suggests that negative connotations are seen when power is used for control and that examples of positive use of power emerge when it is used to serve others (1989, 104). Dennis Wrong suggests, "Power is the capacity of some persons to produce intended and foreseen effects on others" (1979, 4). Wrong goes on to suggest that any definition or description of power must deal with five issues: intentionality (intended or foreseen as against unintended influence), effectiveness (success or failure in use of power), latency (dispositional, or the tendency to use power, as against episodic or specific behavioral acts), asymmetry and balance in power relations between power holder and power subject and, finally, the nature of effects produced (ibid., 4–17). Hersey and Blanchard defined power as "influence potential"— the resource that enables a leader to gain compliance or commitment from others (1988, 202). Galbraith distinguishes among three instruments of power: "condign power," which wins submission by ability to impose an alternative to the preference of the individual or group (an overtone of punishment pervades this definition); "compensatory power," which wins submission by affirmative reward; and "conditioned power," which is exercised by changing belief through persuasion, education or social commitment (1983, 4–6).

² In the Bible the Hebrew words for power are *hayil*, *hazaq* and *yad*, and the Greek words for power are *dunamis* and *exousia*. The basic meaning of the Hebrew *hayil* is "strength," from which comes the derived meaning of "army" and "wealth." Wealth is often related to power, and *hayil* occurs with that meaning 30 times. The adjective *hazaq* is used·57 times in the Old Testament and 23 times in the New Testament. It refers to "strong hand" and most often to God's power, as in the Exodus. The Hebrew *yad* refers to the human hand performing normal work functions. In the New Testament the Greek *exousia* or *dunamis* are

used. *Exousia* means either conferred or derived authority, indicating the right to do something (Matt. 21:23–27). *Dunamis* implies ability (2 Cor. 8:3) or strength (Eph. 3:16) or powerful acts (Acts 2:22) (Myers 1987, 844). *Dunamis* most often denotes ability to carry out an action but can also refer to an act expressing power or to a supernatural being with great power (Bromiley 1986, 927). In the New Testament *dunamis* is found 118 times, relatively frequently in the Pauline writings; there is no use of the noun in Johannine writing. In the synoptic Gospels it denotes the power of God, heavenly power and the power that brings salvation to completion (Brown 1976, 2:603). Words for "dominion" in Hebrew, meaning God has supreme dominion, are *masal* (Job 25:2) or *meluka* (Ps. 22:28) or *memsala* (Ps. 145:13); or *rada* (Gen. 1:26–27), meaning human stewardship of natural order and political power of monarchy; or *salat* (Ps. 119:133), meaning control of sin over human lives. Words for "dominion" in Greek are *kratos* (1 Tim. 6:16), meaning God's dominion, or *kyrieuo* (Rom. 6:9, 14), meaning control of sin over human lives, or, as in Ephesians 6:12, meaning an hierarchy of angels (Myers 1987, 290). *Authority* is another word in the Bible that communicates use of power. The Hebrew words used are *raba*, meaning "be great" (Prov. 29:2) or *toqep*, meaning "validity," as used in Esther's ratification of the letter from the king. In the New Testament the Greek word *exousia* is used to mean "valid inner authority" (to teach Mark 1:22; to forgive Matt. 9:6; Mark 2:10; Luke 5:24; and to judge John 5:27 (Myers 1987, 108).

[3] Ray Anderson develops the idea of co-humanity and the covenant as a theological paradigm to understand authentic personhood. He suggests that all our brokenness and alienation has much to do with our belonging. Our believing comes out of our belonging, and individuality was not the original intention of creation (1982, 161–70).

[4] Van Engen develops the relationship between the kingdom of God and the covenant as he rethinks the purpose of the local church in *God's Missionary People* (1991). In *The Good News of the Kingdom* he suggests, "Kingdom thinking tends to support concepts of hierarchy and order. Covenant, on the other hand, tends to empower the weak and strengthen them through new relationships. The biblical idea of covenant is impossible without the broader concept of the reign of God in Jesus Christ" (Van Engen et al. 1993, 258). We need a fresh understanding of the covenant within the broader framework of the reign of God. This understanding has to be sought, in this case from within the context of the powerless—those who have traditionally been on the margins of all human covenants and reigns in the world.

[5] "Covenants imply several things. They imply God is a person. He is Spirit to be sure (John 4:24), but He can think, and He made plans, modified procedures as necessary to complete those plans, and felt joy, frustration, satisfaction and anger through it all. Covenant presupposed free moral agency in man. He was accountable. Covenant became the objective standard by which man became morally responsible. Thus far in the biblical history any relationship to God was first and foremost a covenanted relationship" (Smith 1981, 127).

⁶ Miroslav Volf suggests that exclusion of the "other" is integral to Scripture's understanding of sin and consequently "inclusion" of the other would be part of salvation. He develops this thesis well as he reflects on ethnic cleansing in the former Yugoslavia (Volf 1993).

⁷ Identity clarification involves more than what is discussed here. For example, identity clarification involves dealing with distortions in history, distorted understanding of power, worldview inadequacies and roles of principalities and powers. Here we seek simply to set a basic framework for effort to clarify identity.

⁸ Hiebert reviews the perception of encounter and conflict in the Indo-European world and the biblical world. He asserts, "The central issue in the Scripture is not power but shalom" (1992, 43). However, the shalom the kingdom ushers is in conflict with the ways of the world, directly challenging the popular, religious revolutionaries of Jesus' day (Sider 1993, 69). The shalom of the world is built to keep the poor poor. Therefore, to usher in the shalom of the kingdom of God implies conflict—a conflict with the powers (Eph. 6:10–12) that keep the poor powerless.

11

A Kingdom-Based Response
to the Powerlessness of the Poor

My search for a more effective and authentic way of responding to the powerlessness of the poor began at the very doorstep of the powerless. Part One examined assumptions about poverty that shaped historical and contemporary models of ministries among the poor. Part Two inquired into various expressions of powerlessness. Part Three examined key aspects of the kingdom of God reflected in contemporary scholarship before exploring the kingdom's understanding of power.

This chapter brings together a few clues about poverty, powerlessness and kingdom power by exploring

1. principles for responding to the powerless,
2. guidelines for preparing local practitioners to reequip the powerless,
3. areas for research for mission effectiveness, and
4. the present concept of mission among the poor—and rethinking it.

Revisiting the Powerless

Based on insights from the reflections on powerlessness, I propose the following grid to analyze power relations within poverty situation.

This grid (Figure 11-1) seeks to identify various expressions of power-lessness among the poor.

LIFE SPACE	MICRO					MACRO					GLOBAL					COSMIC				
	S	E	P	R	B	S	E	P	R	B	S	E	P	R	B	S	E	P	R	B
Relationships																				
Space																				
Time																				
Being																				
Worldview Aspects																				
Role of Principalities and Powers																				

Figure 11–1: A Grid to Identify Various Expressions of Powerlessness in Poverty Situations.

The Grid

In the grid I have brought together different aspects of poverty rela-tionships. The vertical columns represent the various domains of rela-tionship, namely, the social (S), economic (E), political (P), religious (R) and bureaucratic (B). These both influence and are influenced by forces at the micro, macro, global and cosmic levels of life space. On the left, I list the four dimensions of social reality (relationships, space, time, and being), worldview aspects and the role of principalities and powers.

Applying the Grid

This grid serves as a tool for gathering information about poverty relationships based on questions the poor ask, themes they discuss (generative themes) and stories about their experiences and their dreams. These questions, themes, stories, experiences and dreams serve as a window into their experience of powerlessness. We can use the grid to collate this information to develop a comprehensive understanding of the powerlessness of the poor.

The grid, as demonstrated and used throughout the study, attempts to capture the experience of powerlessness without reducing the poor to mere numbers. This tool allows for human and relational dimensions as well as impersonal forces to be considered at the micro, macro, global and cosmic levels in a poverty situation. It also brings up issues of worldview and the role of principalities and powers for analysis. This grid could also be used to highlight interaction among different forces within poverty situations at micro, macro, global and cosmic levels.

Responding to the Powerless

Reflections on the kingdom and the kingdom's understanding of power suggest seven major themes to consider in developing a kingdom-based paradigm for responding to the powerlessness of the poor. As mentioned in the Introduction, this study is directed toward constructing this paradigm. The following recommendations are not meant to serve as an action plan for grassroots practitioners. Instead, they serve as themes for grassroots practitioners to consider as *they* construct an action plan for their response to the powerlessness of the poor. A kingdom-based response

1. reverses the process of disempowerment,
2. confronts the god-complexes,
3. heals persons in poverty relationships,

4. addresses inadequacies in worldview,
5. challenges principalities and powers,
6. establishes truth and righteousness, and,
7. proclaims that all power belongs to God.

Kingdom-Based Response Reverses the Process of Disempowerment

If powerlessness is the result of systematic socioeconomic, political, bureaucratic and religious processes that disempower the poor, the church and grassroots practitioners are called to deal with this time-related, multifaceted process in poverty relationships. Poverty is no simple static phenomenon in the experience of the poor. It is the complex experience of a people.

Responding to the Powerless

A kingdom-based paradigm will deal with relational dimensions by building covenant-quality communities that are inclusive. It will challenge the dividing lines. It will make the lines that divide a religious issue in which the God of history is interested. In Josiprasda this would mean challenging the legal lines that allow landlords to cultivate wasteland while the landless are taken to court for the same "offense." In terms of programs this would mean evaluating popular community organization efforts that exploit issues and numbers. Kingdom-based response calls for building a covenant-quality community that points to the coming kingdom of God.

A kingdom-based response will deal with forces at micro, macro, global and cosmic levels. It will imply involvement at the micro level that influences macro and global dimensions, with a cosmic agenda. This should result in the church in Mogalliwakkam addressing the Madras Metropolitan Development Authorities about the landless in Mogalliwakkam being alienated from their "workplace."

A kingdom-based response will include the time dimension in considering the process of disempowerment. It will reread history from God's perspective. It will provide a prophetic alternative to distortions that "winners" perpetuate. It will infuse hope by equipping the poor to imagine the future anew. Kingdom-based response will challenge the captivity of the poor to the belief that they cannot change their present reality or the future.

Alternative Definitions

A kingdom response to the process of disempowerment calls for new understanding of mission frameworks such as sustainability, empowerment and transformation. Definitions of sustainability should consider issues of time, relationships, persons and space. Sustainability measurements must consider specifically the ability of the poor to reread history, the presence of hope, the creation of covenant-quality communities, and the expression of inclusive intent in relationships. Definitions of sustainability of impact must also consider the impact of micro-level involvement on macro, global and cosmic forces.

Empowerment strategies need to empower the poor with skills to deal with forces at each level of the life space in poverty relationships. Empowerment must address the issue of hopelessness and people's ability to reread history, with God's involvement as a crucial point of reference.

In the final analysis, transformation should mean reversing the process of disempowerment that keeps the poor powerless.

Kingdom-Based Response Confronts the God-Complexes

If the powerlessness of the poor is the result of their captivity within many god-complexes in poverty situations, then these god-complexes must be confronted and dismantled. God-complexes operate through various relationships and at different levels of the life space in poverty situations; they result from of the interplay among structures, systems, people and "spiritual interiorities." The worldview of a people also reinforces these god-complexes with divine sanctions, forbidding the poor to challenge the god-complexes. Principalities and powers seeking to destroy God's reign perpetuate these god-complexes. In the lives of the poor, these god-complexes are real, relative powers that seek to absolutize themselves and play "god."

Responding to the Powerless

Establishment of the kingdom of God is the most appropriate response to god-complexes. Mission among the poor should involve proclaiming the kingdom of God in all its glory and establishing it. This kingdom is theocentric, relational and political; it reverses the status quo, seeks response, focuses on the inner, and is redemptively biased toward captives of these god-complexes.

For the church's mission among the poor the kingdom of God must be the hub and context of all involvement. This calls for conscious acknowledgment and communication of the rule of God in all affairs of the church and the poor. This challenges all relative powers seeking to absolutize themselves. This also challenges worldviews that reinforce idolatries within poverty situations. Finally, this challenges principalities and powers and their efforts to sustain god-complexes.

Together, these reflections suggest that proclaiming the kingdom of God is no mere option. It is *the* most appropriate response to the powerlessness of the poor. When god-complexes perpetuate the powerlessness of the poor, the kingdom of God is the only viable alternative spelling true and complete liberation for the powerless poor.

Alternative Definitions

This understanding of kingdom-based response to god-complexes in poverty relationships further challenges the traditional frameworks such as sustainability, empowerment and transformation. Sustainability in missional involvement among the poor can and should be measured in terms of its impact on the many god-complexes in poverty situations.

Empowerment needs to include confronting structures, systems, people and spiritual interiorities that shape god-complexes. And transformation should be defined with the kingdom of God as foundational—a kingdom that opposes all other kingdoms.

Kingdom-Based Response Heals Persons in Poverty Relationships

Powerlessness is essentially a human phenomenon. Powerlessness involves lack of love and compassion, insecurity and hurt, exclusion and breakdown of traditional securities, and exploitation of health, mind, will, habits and curses by principalities and powers. This mars the identity of the poor.

Responding to the Powerless

Evangelical responses and historical models of ministry teach that any kingdom-based response to the powerless must consider compassion, security, healing of hurt relationships and such personal dimensions as integral missional response to the poor. This emphasis is appropriate to the experiences of the powerless and will serve to correct the impersonality in traditional cause-analysis of poverty situations.

An essential part of kingdom-based response is the healing it brings by clarifying the identity of the poor. Along with the kingdom's redemptive bias toward the poor, reflections on kingdom power suggest that God goes beyond issues of justice and dignity to deal with the underlying marring of identity inherent in injustice and disempowerment.

Another implication of this call to clarify the identity of the poor is that this clarification of identity is a prerequisite for equipping the poor to be agents of transformation in their world. Kingdom-based response goes beyond traditional approaches to the poor, moving from a project approach toward initiating movements among the poor that cause many ripples of transformation.

Alternative Definitions

Once again, this understanding of kingdom-based response calls on the mission community to review traditional understanding of concepts such as sustainability, empowerment and transformation. Sustainability of impact must be measured in terms of the identity of the poor and the healing provided for the pain that the poor suffer in poverty relationships.

Empowerment strategies must move beyond issues of justice and dignity. Kingdom power urges that empowerment clarify identity. This is not dependent on demonization and sacralization. Instead, identity clarification occurs on the basis of the image of God, the role of fellowship in community and the work of the Trinitarian God as reference points. Transformation in mission must clarify identity and heal broken relationships, particularly among the poor whose relationships and beliefs constantly mar their identity.

Kingdom-based Response Addresses Inadequacies in Worldview

Worldview perpetuates powerlessness among the poor by shaping their understanding of person-group relationships, causes of poverty, time and space. Worldview provides religious sanctions for oppressive relationships, the wealth of the rich, and the low income and occupational status of the poor, while forbidding the poor to desire change.

Responding to the Powerless

Responding to the role of worldview in relation to powerlessness, a kingdom-based response must go beyond cultural sensitivity concerns.

It must challenge the "divine sanctions" that contribute to the power-lessness of the poor. The kingdom of God regards those lines that divide people as an issue in which God is deeply interested.

Kingdom-based response raises questions of meaning, challenging the meanings assigned by a people's worldview to various life events in poverty situations. By going beyond the question of sensitivity to addressing roots of poverty hidden within the worldview and religion of a people, we imply that kingdom-based response is essentially an encounter of worldview and religion, with the Bible as our basic frame of reference.

Alternative Definitions

Sustainability definitions must consider worldview issues and changes at worldview level. Mission methods, strategies and programs must be directed to creating worldview-level change.

There cannot be any empowerment without addressing worldview inadequacies. Because principalities and powers exploit the worldview of a people to perpetuate deception, true transformation will address inadequacies in the worldview of a people.

Kingdom-Based Response Challenges Principalities and Powers

Given that most analyses of poverty situations follow the Enlightenment-oriented perception of reality and ignore the middle tier of reality as it is experienced and understood by the poor, a kingdom alternative will address this gap.

Responding to the Powerless

First, since principalities and powers are deeply involved in poverty relationships, kingdom mission among the poor must involve prayer and fasting as important tools for social action. While some in the church suggest that prayer and fasting are private disciplines, the Bible proposes that we guard against making prayer and fasting into tools that address only personal or selfish needs. We may yet rediscover the potential of prayer and fasting to move mountains and cause the devil and his forces to fall from heavenly places (Luke 10:18).

Second, if mission among the poor involves battle with principalities and powers, then grassroots practitioners should be equipped with the "whole armor of God" (Eph. 6:10–12). This implies that grassroots practitioners be constantly equipped with spiritual discipline as a necessary part of kingdom response to the powerless poor.

Finally, if kingdom-based response to the powerless involves confronting principalities and powers, then we should affirm that spiritual gifts are development skills required for responding to the powerless poor.

Kingdom-based response to the powerless is essentially a battle with cosmic powers who perpetuate powerlessness. Any confrontation of powerlessness is an engagement with principalities and powers. Kingdom-based response to principalities and powers must consciously address this cosmic agenda through involvement at micro, macro and global levels of life.

Alternative Definitions

Sustainability of impact needs to consider impact on the work of the cosmic powers. Empowerment strategies need to consider equipping the church among the poor with the spiritual disciplines necessary for dealing with the rule of the Evil One. Transformation in work among the poor must be redefined to include battle dimensions in challenging the principalities and powers active in poverty situations.

Kingdom-Based Response Establishes Truth and Righteousness

If powerlessness of the poor is captivity in a "web of lies," this web has several "spiders." They include the non-poor and the poor, with their worldviews, the principalities and powers and spiritual interiorities within structures and systems. Consequently, social analysis in poverty situations must exegete the lies that perpetuate powerlessness.

Responding to the Powerless

The most authentic response to the "web of lies" is establishing and proclaiming truth and righteousness. This Truth will radically reorder relationships, seeking to establish Truth—with a capital T—about self, in public and private life, and about power. This will restore faith within poverty relationships.

Truth also challenges inadequacies within the worldview of a people. Kingdom-based response will not examine culture and worldview merely for formulating relevant communication strategies; instead, it must go beyond, exploring the worldview and culture of a people to exhume the roots of powerlessness and poverty.

Finally, kingdom power, based on continuous study of the Word of God and armed with the Word of God, challenges deceptions that principalities and powers perpetuate. Kingdom response to the poor is more than charity; it is essentially the spiritual task of establishing truth and righteousness within poverty relationships.

Alternative Definitions

Sustainability of impact involves the integration of truth in the various spheres of life, including the worldview of a people. It ought to measure the effort to establish the Truth—with a capital T—about self, about power, and in the private and public spheres of life.

Empowerment strategies must be founded on truth at all levels. Empowerment should involve equipping the poor to establish truth in private and public life. Finally, transformation must be redefined using Truth as its framework.

Kingdom-Based Response Proclaims That All Power Belongs to God

While most responses to the powerlessness of the poor affirm the slogan "power to the people," kingdom power constantly affirms that power always belongs to God. Our understanding of power, the tendency to absolutize power, and the erosion of faith in public and private life, require more than a rearrangement of power relations.

Responding to the Powerless

Clues about the kingdom suggest a different understanding of power. Power in the kingdom belongs to God. This power can be availed of only if the Holy Spirit is the empowerer.

By proclaiming that power belongs to God, kingdom response affirms the theocentricity of the kingdom of God and also suggests that in the theocentric kingdom, even power issues are penultimate. The focus in the kingdom is on God and God's reign.

Power can never belong to the poor or the non-poor. Power always belongs to God. Therefore, kingdom-based response constantly affirms in and through all its empowerment and transformational strategies that power belongs to God and God alone.

Alternative Definitions

This understanding of the nature of power calls on grassroots practitioners to redefine issues. Empowerment definitions and strategies that affirm power to the poor, sustainability that measures mere transfer of power, and transformation that does not challenge the very meaning of power will be woefully inadequate. Sustainability measurements must go beyond mere transfer of power to the transformation of power itself.

The conflict between power and powerlessness must ultimately rest its case at the foot of the throne of the slain Lamb. In the final analysis, when the end of time comes, we will all lay our crowns before the throne and sing a new song proclaiming,

> You are worthy, our Lord and God,
> to receive glory and honor and power,
> for you created all things,
> and by your will they existed and were created.
> (Rev. 4:11)

Reequipping Grassroots Practitioners

The alternative paradigm emerging from our reflections suggests a fundamental shift in the role of practitioners on the front lines of mission. Application of this kingdom-based response calls for a radical reequipping of grassroots practitioners among the poor.

First, kingdom-based response to the powerless poor must be an authentic expression of the "inner being" of grassroots practitioners. Just as powerlessness is a human and relational phenomenon, and the kingdom of God is also relational, kingdom-based response must also focus on persons and relationships. Response cannot be reduced to a mere program of action. This understanding of kingdom-based response implies that the personal pilgrimage of grassroots practitioners cannot be dichotomized from outward expressions of their response. This will mean continuous clarification of the identity of grassroots practitioners on the basis of the Bible and in the context of the community.

Next, kingdom-based response demands that covenant-quality inclusive relationships be modeled within the community of grassroots practitioners, based on truth. An integral part of training grassroots practitioners will be enabling them to become a hermeneutical community that constantly shapes and reshapes its paradigms and models of mission.

Third, kingdom-based response to the powerless poor is a battle with the principalities and powers. This implies that grassroots practitioners must be a Spirit-led community who wear the whole armor of God (Eph. 6:13–18). Training of grassroots practitioners must affirm the role of the Holy Spirit in mission and plan for intentional spiritual formation.

Fourth, because situations of powerlessness involve principalities and powers, recognition and use of spiritual gifts must be an integral part of mission that seeks to confront powerlessness of the poor. Therefore, reequipping grassroots practitioners will include encouraging them to discern and use their spiritual gifts in missional involvement.

Fifth, kingdom-based response follows God's initiative in history. Grassroots practitioners require skill to read God's working among the poor. This reading has to be from within the context, be community-based and based on the Bible, tracing "patterns" in God's movement among the poor.

Sixth, because the roots of poverty are entangled in a people's worldview and religious systems, grassroots practitioners need reequipping with skills to analyze the worldview of a people as a necessary part of poverty analysis.

Seventh, since kingdom-based response among the poor involves establishing truth and righteousness, the task of equipping grassroots practitioners will also be shaped by this undertaking in mission. Truth must be a major determinant in relationships within the community of grassroots practitioners. The community of grassroots practitioners must be equipped to become "grief articulators," with the knowledge and ability to speak the truth about poverty relationships.

Next, grassroots practitioners need to be equipped to address macro and global issues with a cosmic agenda while they are involved in micro communities. Traditional involvement among the poor tends to be tied down to the micro level. Focus is on projects and activities. However, inquiry into the nature of powerlessness shows that poverty is affected by forces at the micro, macro, global and cosmic levels. Efforts to implement a kingdom-based response without addressing these forces at all levels in the life space of the poor will be inadequate.

By affirming inclusion, kingdom power seeks to cause ripples of transformation. Kingdom-based response equips the poor to be agents of transformation and thus initiate movements. The community of grassroots practitioners needs skill to equip the poor with right understanding of kingdom power so they may initiate ripples of transformation in their world. Grassroots practitioners must be equipped to go beyond projects and position the church among the poor to initiate movements among the poor.

Finally, kingdom-based response affirms that power belongs to God. This implies that grassroots practitioners who seek to implement a kingdom-based response among the poor must live out this affirmation. Local practitioners must be dependent on the God of the kingdom. This will enable the poor to perceive the link between power as expressed in a kingdom-based response and dependence of the community of practitioners on Jesus Christ, to whom all power and glory belongs.

Research for Mission Effectiveness

Further study for enhancing the quality of mission involvement among the poor should consider five areas:

1. There is a need to develop a theology of power from within the context of the poor. This theology of power must also deal with time and spatial dimensions related to poverty, power and powerlessness.
2. Two methodological concerns need further study. First, we need a rigorous methodology for a distinctly evangelical hermeneutic utilizing the potential of story and narratives as a hermeneutical tool need. Second, we need tools to exegete paradigms at the grassroots. Often paradigmatic inquiries have focused on "written paradigms." However, paradigms are often verbal at the grassroots level.
3. There is a need to study the relationship between the local church's understanding of the kingdom of God and kingdom power and the effectiveness of the church among the poor.
4. The role of the Holy Spirit and spirituality in missional involvement among the poor demands further reflection. Powerlessness and poverty involve the spiritual interiorities within structures and systems, the religious systems and the worldview of a people, and the role of principalities and powers. Power belongs to God, and the Holy Spirit is the final empowerer. More studies are needed to

bring these strands of thought together, exploring the encounter of conflicting spiritualities within poverty situations and the role of the Holy Spirit.

5. Identity in relation to the powerlessness of the poor and a kingdom-based response should be developed further. The role of history, the world's understanding of power, worldview and the role of principalities and powers in relation to the marred identity of the poor should also be studied.

Rethinking Mission

The reflections in this chapter suggested that kingdom-based response can reverse the process of disempowerment, confront the god complexes, heal persons in poverty relationships, set right inadequacies in the worldview of a people, challenge principalities and powers, establish truth and righteousness, and proclaim that all power belongs to God.

Finally, mission among the poor is a prophetic kingdom-based presence that critiques the world's understanding of power that keeps the poor powerless. Mission is a response in which the kingdom community's involvement at the micro level influences macro-global dimensions at cosmic levels. It is a kingdom-based response that seeks to establish truth and righteousness within poverty relationships and to heal persons in poverty relationships. In the final analysis, mission among the powerless poor will seek to participate authentically in God's answer to the prayers of the poor, as they pray

> Thy kingdom come,
> Thy will be done on earth as it is in Heaven.
> (Matt. 6:10, RSV)

Bibliography

Abercrombie, Nicholas, Stephen Hill, and Bryan S. Turner. *Dictionary of Sociology*. London: Penguin Books, 1984.

Ackoff, Russell L. "On the Nature of Development and Planning." In *People Centered Development: Contributions Toward Theory and Planning Frameworks*, edited by David C. Korten and Rudi Klauss. West Hartford, Conn.: Kumarian Press, 1984.

Adeyemo, Tokunboh. "A Critical Evaluation of Contemporary Perspectives." In *In Word and Deed: Evangelism and Social Responsibility*, edited by Bruce Nicholls. Grand Rapids, Mich.: Eerdmans, 1985.

Adishesiah, Malcom S. "Gandhi and the Indian Economy Today." *Southern Economist* 30, no. 20 (1992): 26.

Ahluwalia, Montek. *Rural Poverty in India, 1956-57 to 1973-74*. Washington, D.C.: World Bank, 1977.

Ahmed, A. *The Anatomy of Rural Poverty in Assam: A Case Study of Dibrugarh Sub-Division*. Delhi: Mittal Publishers, 1987.

Ahmed, Farzand. "The Mushars: The Rat-eaters of Bihar." *India Today* 17, no. 19 (1992):59.

Alexander, K. C. "Strategies for Rural Development in Third World Countries." In *Strategies for Third World Development*, edited by John S. Augustine. New Delhi: SAGE Publication, 1989.

All India Congress on Missions and Evangelism. "The Devlali Letter." In *Go Forth and Tell: Report on the All India Congress on Missions and Evangelism*. Devlali, 1977.

Anderson, Ray. *On Being Human: Essays in Theological Anthropology*. Pasadena, Calif.: Fuller Seminary Press, 1982.

Arias, Mortimer. *Announcing the Reign of God: Evangelization and the Subversive Memory of Jesus*. Philadelphia: Fortress Press, 1984.

Arnold, Clinton E. *Ephesians: Power and Magic: The Concept of Power in Ephesians in the Light of Its Historical Setting*. Grand Rapids, Mich.: Baker House, 1989.

———. *Powers of Darkness: Principalities and Powers in Paul's Letters*. Downers Grove, Ill.: InterVersity Press, 1992.

Asia Theological Association and Evangelical Fellowship of India Theological Commission. "The Declaration on Caste and the Church." *Transformation* 2, no. 2 (1985): 1.

Awaz. *The Kingdom of God in India: Mission of Awaz*. Orissa: Awaz, 1985.

———. *From the Field of Raipur: Report and Account*. Raipur: Awaz, 1987.

Azariah, M. "Doing Theology in India Today." In *A Reader in Dalit Theology*, edited by Arvind P. Nirmal. Madras, India: Gurukal Lutheran Theological College and Research Institute, 1991.

Bajaj. *Rural Poverty: Issues and Options*. Lucknow, India: Print House, 1985.

Berger, Peter. *Pyramids of Sacrifice: Political Ethics and Social Change*. New York: Basic Books, 1974.

Berkhof, H. *Christ and the Powers*. Scottdale, Pa.: Herald Press, 1962.

Boff, Leonardo. *Jesus Christ Liberator: A Critical Christology for Our Time*. Maryknoll, N.Y.: Orbis Books, 1978.

———. *Church Charism and Power: Liberation Theology and the Institutional Church*. New York: Crossroad, 1981.

———. *When Theology Listens to the Poor*. San Francisco: Harper & Row, 1988.

———. "The Originality of the Theology of Liberation." In *The Future of Liberation Theology: Essays in Honor of Gustavo Gutiérrez*, edited by Marc H. Ellis and Otto Maduro. Maryknoll, N.Y.: Orbis Books, 1989.

———. "The Contributions of Liberation Theology." In *Paradigm Change in Theology: A Symposium for the Future*, edited by Hans Kung and David Tracy. New York: Crossroad, 1991.

Boff, Leonardo, and Clodovis Boff. *Introducing Liberation Theology*. Maryknoll, N.Y.: Orbis Books, 1990.

Bosch, David J. "Vision for Mission." *International Review of Mission* 76, no. 301 (1987): 8-15.

———. "Mission in Jesus' Way: A Perspective from Luke's Gospel." *Missionalia* 17, no. 1 (1989): 3-21.

———. *Transforming Mission: Paradigm Shifts in Theology of Mission*. Maryknoll, N.Y.: Orbis Books, 1991.

Boulding, Kenneth E. "The Economics of the Coming Spaceship Earth." In *People Centered Development: Contributions Toward Theory and Planning Frameworks*, edited by David C. Korten and Rudi Klauss. West Hartford, Conn.: Kumarian Press, 1984.

Bradshaw, Bruce. *Bridging the Gap: Evangelism, Development and Shalom*. Monrovia, Calif.: MARC, 1994.

Bright, John. *The Kingdom of God: The Biblical Concept and Its Meaning for the Church*. Nashville, Tenn.: Abington Press, 1953.

Bromiley, Geoffrey W, ed. *The International Standard Bible Encyclopedia*. Grand Rapids, Mich.: Eerdmans, 1986.

Brown, Colin, ed. *New International Dictionary of New Testament Theology*. Grand Rapids, Mich.: Zondervan Publishing House, 1976.

Brown, Dennis E. "Introduction." In *WorldView and WorldView Change: A Reader*. Unpublished manuscript. Pasadena, Calif.: Fuller Theological Seminary, School of World Mission, 1991.

Brueggemann, Walter. *The Prophetic Imagination*. Philadelphia: Fortress Press, 1978.

Burns, James MacGregor. *Leadership*. New York: Harper & Row, 1978.

Carr, Dyanchand. *The Meaning in the Struggle for a Just Community*. Bangalore, India: Student Christian Movement in India, 1991.

Carr, Wesley. *Angels and Principalities: The Background, Meaning and Development of the Pauline Phrase* hai archai kai hai exousiai. SNTSMS 42. Cambridge: Cambridge University Press, 1981.

Cassell, Philip. *The Giddens*. Stanford, Calif.: Stanford University Press, 1993.

Castro, Emilio. *Your Kingdom Come: A Missionary Perspective*. Geneva, Switzerland: World Council of Churches, 1980.

Chambers, Robert. *Rural Development: Putting the Last First*. Essex, UK: Longman Scientific and Technical, 1983.

———. *Poverty in India: Concepts, Research and Reality*. Sussex, UK: Institute of Development Studies, 1988.

———. "In Search of Professionalism, Bureaucracy and Sustainable Livelihoods for the Twenty-first Century." *IDS Bulletin* 22, no. 4 (1991): 5-11.

Chambers, Robert, Richard Longhurst, David Bradely, and Richard Feacheim. "The Seasons of Poverty." In *People Centred Development: Contributions Toward Theory and Planning Frameworks*, edited by David C. Korten and Rudi Klauss. Hartford, Conn.: Kumarian Press, 1984.

Chester, Charles E. Timothy. *Awakening to a World of Need: The Recovery of Evangelical Social Concern*. Leicester, England: InterVarsity Press, 1993.

Christian, Jayakumar. *Powerlessness of the Poor: Toward an Alternative Kingdom of God–Based Paradigm for Response*. Ph.D. diss. Pasadena, Calif.: Fuller Theological Seminary, 1994.

Clouse, Robert, ed. *The Meaning of the Millenniums: Four Views*. Downers Grove, Ill.: InterVarsity Press, 1977.

Comblin, Jose. *The Holy Spirit and Liberation*. Maryknoll, N.Y.: Orbis Books, 1989.

Cone, James H. *God of the Oppressed*. New York: Seabury Press, 1975; Maryknoll, N.Y.: Orbis Books, 1997.

Conn, Harvie M. "Theologies of Liberation: An Overview." In *Tensions in Contemporary Theology*, edited by Stanley N. Gundry and Alan F. Johnson. Chicago, Ill.: Moody Press, 1976.

Corbridge, Stuart. "Post-Marxism and Development Studies: Beyond the Impasse." *World Development* 18, no. 5 (1990)): 623-29.

Costas, Orlando E. *Christ Outside the Gate: Mission Beyond Christendom*. Maryknoll, N.Y.: Orbis Books, 1982.

Crocker, David A. "Toward Development Ethics." *World Development*. 19, no. 5 (1991): 458.

Cullman, Oscar. *Christ and Time*. Philadelphia: Westminster Press, 1950; New York: Gordon Press, 1977.

Curtis, Michael, ed. *The Great Political Theories*. Volume 2. New York: Avon Books, 1981.

Cyrus, P. A. "Principles for Awaz." Unpublished manuscript. Personal files of author, 1992.

Dandekar, V. B., and Nilankath Rath. *Poverty in India*. Pune: Gokhale Institute of Politics and Economics, 1971.

Davids, Peter H. "Sickness and Suffering in the New Testament." In *Wrestling with Dark Angels: Toward a Deeper Understanding of the Supernatural Forces in Spiritual Warfare*, edited by C. Peter Wagner and F. Douglas Pennoyer. Ventura, Calif.: Regal Books, 1990.

Dayton, Ed. "The Cutting Edge: Beyond the Bird and the Scissors." Personal files of author, c1982.

Desrochers, John, and George Joseph. *India Today*. Bangalore, India: Center for Social Action, 1988.

De Soto, Hernando. *Other Path: The Invisible Revolution in the Third World*. New York: Harper & Row, 1989.

Devasahayam, V. "Polution, Poverty and Powerlessness: A Dalit Perspective." In *A Reader in Dalit Theology*, edited by Arvind P. Nirmal. Madras: Gurukal Lutheran Theological College and Research Institute, 1991.

Dhanraj, Sathya Singh. "The ECI Model." In *Mission Update*, edited by Ezra Sargunam. Madras, India: Mission India 2000 (Evangelical Churches of India), 1992.

Domhoff, G. William. "The American Power Structure." In *Power in Modern Societies*. Boulder, Colo.: Westview Press, 1993.

Douglas, J. D. "The Lausanne Covenant." In *Let the Earth Hear His Voice: International Congress on World Evangelization, Lausanne Switzerland*. Minneapolis: Worldwide Publications, 1975.

Doyal, Len, and Ian Gough. *Theory of Human Need*. New York: The Guilford Press, 1991.

Duncan, Michael. *A Journey in Development*. The Bridge series. Melbourne, Australia: World Vision, 1990.

Dussel, Enrique. "The Ethnic, Peasant and Popular." In *The Future of Liberation Theology: Essays in Honor of Gustavo Gutiérrez*, edited by Marc H. Ellis and Otto Maduro. Maryknoll, N.Y.: Orbis Books, 1989.

Dyrness, William A. *Let the Earth Rejoice: A Biblical Theology of Holistic Mission*. Pasadena, Calif.: Fuller Seminary Press. 1983.

———. *Learning About Theology from the Third World*. Grand Rapids, Mich.: Zondervan Publishing House, 1990.

Elizondo, Virgilio. *Galilean Journey: The Mexican-American Promise*. Maryknoll, N.Y.: Orbis Books, 1983.

Elliott, Charles. *Praying the Kingdom*. Mahwah, N.Y.: Paulist Press, 1985.

———. *Comfortable Compassion*. Mahwah, N.Y.: Paulist Press, 1987.

Elliston, Edgar J. *Christian Relief and Development: Developing Workers for Effective Ministry*. Dallas, Tex.: Word Publishing, 1989.

Ellul, Jacques. *Jesus and Marx: From Gospel to Ideology*. Grand Rapids, Mich.: Eerdmans, 1988.

———. *The Presence of the Kingdom*. Colorado: Helmers and Howard, 1989.

Escobar, Samuel. "The Significance of Popular Protestantism in Latin America: Conflict of Interpretations." Unpublished manuscript. Philadelphia: Eastern Baptist Seminary, 1992.

Etzioni, Amitai. "Power as Societal Force." In *Power in Modern Societies*, edited by Marvin E. Olson and Martin N. Marger. Boulder Colo.: Westview Press, 1993.

Evangelical Foreign Mission Association and Interdenominational Foreign Mission Association. "Wheaton Declaration." Study papers (Congress on the Church's Worldwide Mission). Wheaton, Ill.: The Congress on the Church's Worldwide Mission, 1966.

Fernandes, Walter. "Introduction." *Social Action* 38, no. 1 (1988).

Fletcher, Garth Baker. "Unquenchable Fire: A Hermeneutic of Trust and Respect." *Encounter* 53, no. 2 (1992): 182-92.

Foster, Richard J. *Freedom of Simplicity*. New York: Harper Collins Publishers, 1981.

Freire, Paulo. *Pedagogy of the Oppressed*. New York: Continuum, 1990.

———. *Pedagogy of the City*. New York: Continuum, 1993.

———. *Pedagogy of Hope*. New York: Continuum, 1994.

Friedmann, John. "Agropolitan Development: A Territorial Approach to Meeting Basic Needs." In *People Centered Development: Contributions Toward Theory and Planning Frameworks*, edited by David D. Korten and Rudi Klauss. West Hartford, Conn.: Kumarian Press, 1984.

———. "The End of the Third World." Unpublished manuscript. Los Angeles: University of California, 1991.

———. *Empowerment: The Politics of Alternative Development*. Cambridge, Mass.: Blackwell, 1992.

Galbraith, Kenneth. *The Nature of Mass Poverty*. Cambridge, Mass.: Harvard University Press, 1979.

———. *The Anatomy of Power*. Boston: Houghton Mifflin Company, 1983.

Giri, Ananta. "Social Development as a Global Challenge." *Social Action* 42, no. 3 (1992).

Glasser, Arthur. *The Kingdom and Mission*. Unpublished manuscript. Pasadena, Calif.: Fuller Theological Seminary, 1991.

Gore, Al. *Earth in the Balance: Ecology and the Human Spirit*. Boston: Houghton Mifflin Company, 1992.

Goulet, Dennis. *The Uncertain Promise: Value Conflicts in Technology Transfer*. New York: New Horizons Press, 1989.

Grist, Walter R. *Evangelism in India*. D.Min dissertation, Bethel Seminary, St. Paul, Minn., 1979.

Gupta, Ranjit. "The Poverty Trap: Lessons from Dharampur." In *Bureaucracy and the Poor: Closing the Gap*, edited by David C. Korten and Felipe B. Alfonso. West Hartford, Conn.: Kumarian Press, 1983.

Gupta, S. P. *Structural Dimensions of Poverty in India*. New Delhi: Mittal Publications, 1987.

Gutiérrez, Gustavo. *The Power of the Poor in History*. Maryknoll, N.Y.: Orbis Books, 1983.

———. *We Drink from Our Own Wells: The Spiritual Journey of a People*. Maryknoll, N.Y.: Orbis Books, 1984.

———. *A Theology of Liberation: History, Politics and Salvation*. Maryknoll, N.Y.: Orbis Books, 1988.

Hadjor, Kofi Buenor. *Dictionary of Third World Terms*. London: Penguin Books, 1992.

Harrison, David. *The Sociology of Modernization and Development*. London: Unwin Hyman, 1988.

Hathaway, Brian. "The Kingdom Manifesto." *Transformation* 7, no. 3 (1990), 6–11.

Hawthorne, Gerald F., and Ralph P. Martin, eds. *Dictionary of Paul and His Letters*. Downers Grove, Ill.: InterVarsity Press, 1993.

Henry, Carl F. "Reflections on the Kingdom of God." *Jets* 35, no. 1 (1992): 39-49.

Hersey, Paul, and Kenneth Blanchard. *Management of Organisational Behavior: Utilizing Human Resources*. 5th edition. Englewood Cliffs, N.J.: Prentice-Hall, 1988.

Hiebert, Paul. "The Flaw of the Excluded Middle." *Missiology: An International Review* 10, no. 1 (1982).

———. "Spiritual Warfare: Biblical Perspectives." *Mission Focus* 20 no. 3 (1992): 41-46.

Hoeven, Ralph van der. *Planning for Basic Needs: A Soft Option or a Solid Policy?: A Basic Needs Simulation Model Applied to Kenya*. Brookfield: Gower, 1988.

Horsley, Richard A. *Jesus and the Spiral of Violence: Popular Jewish Resistance in Roman Palestine*. Philadelphia: Fortress Press, 1993.

Jain, T. L. *Poverty in India: An Economic Analysis*. New Delhi: Ess Ess Publications, 1987.

Jefferey, Mary Pauline. *Dr. Ida Scudder: India (The Life Story of Ida S. Scudder)*. Tarrytown, N.Y.: Fleming H. Revell Company, 1945.

Jones, E. Stanley. *Christ of the Indian Road*. Nashville, Tenn.: Abingdon Cokesbury Press, 1925.

———. *Christ and Human Suffering*. Nashville, Tenn.: Abingdon Cokesbury Press, 1933.

———. *Chist's Alternative to Communism*. Nashville, Tenn.: Abingdon Press, 1935.

———. *Is the Kingdom of God Realism?* Nashville, Tenn.: Abingdon Press, 1940.

———. "The Sat Tal Ashram." *Transformation: Celebrating the One Hundredth Anniversary of the Birth of Eli Stanley Jones* 18, no. 4 (1983):10.

Kadekodi, Gopal K. "Paradigms of Sustainable Development." *Development* 3, no. 72 (1992).

Kamaleson, Samuel. Personal conversation, September 8, 1993.

Kearney, Michael. *Worldview*. Novato, Calif.: Chandler and Sharp Publishers, 1984.

Khan, Akhter Hameed. *Ten Decades of Rural Development: Lessons from India*. East Lansing, Mich.: Michigan State University, 1978.

Korten, David C. *Getting Toward the Twenty-first Century: Voluntary Action and the Global Agenda*. West Hartford, Conn.: Kumarian Press. 1990.

Korten, David C., and Rudi Klauss, eds. *People Centred Development: Contributions Toward Theory and Planning Frameworks*. West Hartford, Conn.: Kumarian Press, 1984.

Korten, David C., and Felipe B. Alfonso, eds. *Bureaucracy and the Poor: Closing the Gap*. West Hartford, Conn.: Kumarian Press, 1983.

Korten, Frances, "Community Participation: A Management Perspective on Obstacles and Options." In *Bureaucracy and the Poor: Closing the Gap*, edited by David C. Korten and Felipe B. Alfonso. West Hartford, Conn.: Kumarian Press, 1983.

Kraft, Charles H. *Christianity with Power*. Ann Arbor, Mich.: Servant Publications, 1989.

———. "Response to 'In Dark Dungeons of Collective Captivity by Pennoyer.'" In *Wrestling with Dark Angels*, edited by C. Peter Wagner and F Douglas Pennoyer. Ventura, Calif.: Regal Books, 1990.

———. "Anthropology for Christian Witness." Unpublished manuscript. Pasadena, Calif.: Fuller Theological Seminary, 1992a.

———. *Defeating the Dark Angels: Breaking Demonic Oppression in the Believer's Life*. Ann Arbor, Mich.: Servant Publications, 1992b.

Kraybill, Donald B. *The Upside Down Kingdom*. Scottdale, Pa.: Herald Press, 1990.

Kummel, George. *Promise and Fulfillment*. Naperville, Ill.: Alenson, 1957.

Kuhn, Thomas S. *The Structure of Scientific Revolutions*. Second edition. Enlarged. Chicago: The University of Chicago Press, 1970.

Küng, Hans. *The Church*. Garden City, N.Y.: Image Books, 1967.

Kurien, C. T. *Poverty, Planning and Social Transformation: Alternatives in Development Planning*. New Delhi: Allied Publishers, 1978.

Ladd, George Eldon. *A Theology of the New Testament*. Grand Rapids, Mich.: Eerdmans, 1974.

Latin American Episcopal Council (CELAM). "Medellín Document on Peace." In *Third World Liberation Theologies: A Reader*, edited by Deane William Ferm. Maryknoll, N.Y.: Orbis Books, 1986.

LCWE (Lausanne Committee for World Evangelization). *Lausanne Occasional Papers: Christian Witness to the Urban Poor*. No. 22. Thailand Report. Wheaton, Ill.: Lausanne Committee for World Evangelization, 1980.

———. *Evangelism and Social Responsibility: An Evangelical Commitment*. Exeter: The Paternoster Press, 1982.

———. "The Manila Manifesto: Calling the Whole Church to Take the Whole Gospel to the Whole World." *International Bulletin of Missionary Research* 13 (1989).

LeMasters, Philip. "Christian Social Ethics and Gutiérrez' 'The God of Life.'" *Encounter* 54, no. 3 (1993): 237.

Lewis, John P., ed. *Strengthening the Poor: What Have We Learned?* New Brunswick, N.J.: Transaction Books, 1988.

Lewis, Oscar. *Five Families: Mexican Case Studies in the Culture of Poverty.* New York: Basic Books, 1959.

Lewis, Paul. "New U.N. Index Measures Wealth as Quality of Life." *The New York Times International* 23, no. 6 (1993).

Liddle, R. William. "The Politics of Development Policy." *World Development* 20, no. 6 (1992).

Linthicum, Robert C. *Empowering the Poor: Community Organizing Among the City's "Rag, Tag and Bob Tail."* Monrovia, Calif.: MARC Publications, 1991.

Lipton, Michael. "Urban Bias in World Development." In *People Centered Development: Contributions Toward Theory and Planning Frameworks*, edited by David C. Korten and Rudi Klauss. West Hartford, Conn.: Kumarian Press, 1984.

Lipton, Michael, and John Toye. *Does Aid Work in India? A Country Study of the Impact of Official Development Assistance.* London: Routledge, 1990.

Llosa, Mario Vargas. "Foreword." In *The Other Path: The Invisible Revolution in the Third World*, edited by Hernando De Soto. New York: Harper & Row, 1989.

McAlpine, Thomas H. *Facing the Powers: What Are the Options?* Monrovia, Calif.: MARC, 1991.

McGavran, Donald Anderson. "Social Justice and Evangelism." Reprint. *World Vision* 3 (1965).

———. "Salvation Today." In *The Evangelical Response to Bangkok*. Pasadena, Calif.: William Carey Library, 1973.

McGovern, Arthur F. "Dependence Theory, Marxist Analysis, and Liberation Theology." In *The Future of Liberation Theology: Essays in Honor of Gustavo Gutiérrez*, edited by Marc H. Ellis and Otto Maduro. Maryknoll, N.Y.: Orbis Books, 1989.

McHale, John, and Magda Cordell McHale. *Basic Human Needs: A Framework for Action.* New Brunswick. N.J.: Transaction Books, 1977.

MacNicol, Nicol. *India in the Dark Wood.* London: Edinburgh Press, 1930.

Marcella, Hoest. "The Kingdom: Preferential Option for the Poor." *Missiology: An International Review* 10, no. 1 (1982): 57-68.

Martin, David. *Tongues of Fire: The Explosion of Protestantism in Latin America.* Cambridge, Mass.: Blackwell, 1990.

Mathews, Eunice Jones, and James K. Mathews. *Selections from E. Stanley Jones: Christ and Human Need.* New York: Abingdon Press, 1944.

Max-Neff, Manfred, Antonio Elizalde, and Martin Hopnhayn. "Human Scale Development: An Option for the Future." *Development Dialogue* 1 (1989): 5-25.

Messer, Donald E. *Contemporary Images of Christian Ministry*. Nashville, Tenn.: Abingdon Press, 1989.

Miles, Matthew B., and A. Michael Huberman. *Qualitative Data Analysis: A Source of New Methods*. Thousand Oaks, Calif.: SAGE Publications, 1984.

Mills, Wright C. *The Power Elite*. New York: Oxford University Press, 1959.

Miranda, Jose. *Marx and the Bible: A Critique of the Philosophy of Oppression*. Maryknoll, N.Y.: Orbis Books, 1974.

Mitra, K. Subrata. *Power, Protest and Participation: Local Elite and the Politics of Development in India*. London: Routledge, 1992.

Moberg, David. *The Great Reversal: Evangelism and Social Concern*. Revised edition. Philadelphia: J. B. LippinCott Company, 1977.

Moltmann, Jürgen. *Theology of Hope: On the Grounds and the Implications of a Christian Eschatology*, New York: Harper & Row, 1967.

———. *The Crucified God*. New York: Harper & Row, 1974.

———. *The Trinity and the Kingdom: The Doctrine of God*. San Francisco, Calif.: Harper & Row, 1981.

———. "Thine Is the Kingdom, Power and the Glory." *The Reformed Word* 37 nos. 3, 4 (1982): 3-10.

———. *The Power of the Powerless*. San Francisco, Calif.: Harper & Row, 1983.

———. *The Way of Jesus Christ*. Philadelphia: Fortress Press, 1993.

Mooneyham, Stanley, and Carl Henry, eds. *One Race, One Gospel, One Task*. Minneapolis, Minn.: Worldwide Publications, 1967.

Morris, Leon. *The Revelation of St. John: An Introductory Commentary*. Grand Rapids, Mich.: Eerdmans, 1969.

Morris, Leon. *Revelation of St. John: Tyndale New Testament Commentaries*. Revised edition. Leicester, England: InterVarsity Press, 1987.

Mouw, Richard J. *Politics and the Biblical Drama*. Grand Rapids, Mich.: Eerdmans, 1976.

Myers, Allen C., ed. *The Eerdmans Bible Dictoinary*. Grand Rapids, Mich.: Eerdmans, 1987.

Myers, Bryant. "The Excluded Middle." *MARC Newsletter* 91, no. 2 (1991): 3.

Myrdal, Gunnar. *Asian Drama: An Inquiry into the Poverty of Nations*. Volume 2. New York: The Twentieth Century Fund, 1968.

Murickan, J. *Religion and Power Structure in Rural India*. Rawat II, S. Asia, 1991.

National Seminar on Dalit Theology. *Toward a Common Dalit Ideology*. Madras, India: Gurukal Lutheran Theological College and Research Institute, 1989.

Neill, Stephen. *Builders of the Indian Church*. London: Edinburgh House Press, 1934.

Newbigin, Lesslie. *Honest Religion for Secular Man*. Philadelphia: Westminster Press, 1966.

———. *The Open Secret*. Grand Rapids, Mich.: Eerdmans, 1978.

———. *Sign of the Kingdom*. Grand Rapids, Mich.: Eerdmans, 1980.

Ng, Sik Hung. *The Social Psychology of Power*. London: Academic Press, 1980.

Nicholls, Bruce. "Strategy Paper: The Relationship of Proclamation to Service." In *Go Forth and Tell: Report on the All India Congress on Missions and Evangelism*. Devlali, India: AICOME, 1977.

Nicholls, Bruce J., ed. *In Word and Deed: Evangelism and Social Responsibility*. Grand Rapids, Mich.: Eerdmans, 1985.

Nirmal, Arvind P. *A Reader in Dalit Theology*. Madras, India: Gurukal Lutheran Theological College and Research Institute, 1991.

Nisbet, Robert. *History of the Idea of Progress*. New York: Basic Books, 1980.

Nolan, Albert. *Jesus Before Christianity*. Maryknoll, N.Y.: Orbis Books, 1976.

O'Gorman, Frances. *Transformation*. Notes on lecture at World Vision Australia, 1991.

———. *Charity and Change: From Bandaid to Beacon*. Melbourne, Australia: World Vision, 1992.

Olsen, Marvin E., and Martin N. Marger, eds. *Power in Modern Societies*. Boulder, Colo.: Westview Press, 1993.

Oommen, T. K. *Protest and Change: Studies in Social Movements*. New Delhi: SAGE Publications, 1990.

Orr, Edwin J. *Evangelical Awakening in India*. New Delhi: Masihi Sahitya Sanstha, 1970.

Orville, Petty A. *India-Burma: Fact Finders Report*. Volume 4. New York: Harper & Brothers, 1933.

Osthathios, Geevarghese Mar. *Theology of a Classless Society*. Madras, India: Christian Literature Society. 1980.

———. "The Reality of Sin and Class War." In *Third World Liberation Theology: A Reader*, edited by Deane William Ferm. Maryknoll, N.Y.: Orbis Books, 1986.

Padilla, Rene C. "A New Ecclesiology in Latin America." *International Bulletin* 11, no. 4 (1987): 158.

Padilla, Rene, and Chris Sugden. *How Evangelicals Endorsed Social Responsibility: Texts on Evangelical Social Ethics* 1974-83 (ii)- *A Commentary*. Bramcote, Nottingham: Grove Books Limited, 1985.

Palmer, Earl F. *1, 2, 3 John, Revelation*. Waco, Tex.: Word Book Publishers, 1982.

Pannenberg, Wolfhart. *Theology and the Kingdom of God*. Philadelphia: Westminster Press, 1968.

Parsons, Talcott, ed. *Max Weber: The Theory of Social and Economic Organization*. New York: The Free Press, 1947.

Perkins, Harvey. "Study Documents." In *Evangelism and the Poor*, edited by Vinay Samuel and Chris Sugden. Grand Rapids, Mich.: Eerdmans, 1987.

Pickett, Wascom Jarrell. *Christian Mass Movements in India*. Lucknow, India: Lucknow Publishing House, 1933.

Powell, Cyril H. *The Biblical Concept of Power*. London: Epworth Press, 1963.

Prabhu, Pandharinath H. *Hindu Social Organization: A Study in Socio-Psychological and Ideological Foundations*. Bombay, India: Popular Prakashan, 1940.

Pratap, Anita. "In Disaster's Wake." *Time* 137, no. 20 (1991).

Prewitt, Kenneth, and Alan Stone. "The Ruling Elite." In *Power in Modern Socities*, edited by Marvin E. Olsen and Martin Marger, Boulder, Colo.: Westview Press, 1993.

Prior, David. *Jesus and Power*. Downers Grove, Ill.: InterVarsity Press, 1987.

Puthanangady, Paul sbd, ed. *Toward an Indian Theology of Liberation*. Bangalore, India: Indian Theological Association, 1985.

Rai, Saritha. "Turning a New Leaf: A Village Steeped in Prostitution Finds a New Life." *India Today* 17, no. 6 (1992): 10.

Rappaport, Julian. "Terms of Empowerment/Exemplars of Prevention: Toward a Theory for Community Psychology." *American Journal of Community Psychology* 15, no. 2 (1987): 121-48.

Rees, Paul. "Evangelism and Social Concern." In *One Race, One Gospel, One Task*, edited by Stanley Mooneyham and Carl Henry. Minneapolis, Minn.: Worldwide Publications, 1967.

———. "E. Stanley Jones: Christ-Intoxicated." *Transformation: Celebrating the One Hundredth Anniversary of the Birth of Eli Stanley Jones* 18, no. 4 (1983): 24.

Remenyi, Joe. *Where Credit Is Due: Income-Generating Programmes for the Poor in Developing Countries*. Southampton Row, London: Intermediate Technology Publications, 1991.

Richter, Julius. *A History of Mission in India*. Tarrytown, N.Y.: Fleming H. Revell Company, 1908.

Ridderbos, Herman. *The Coming of the Kingdom*. Philadelphia: The Presbyterian and Reformed Publishing Company, 1962.

Robb, John. "Satan's Tactics in Building and Maintaining His Kingdom of Darkness." *International Journal of Frontier Mission* 10, no. 4 (October 1993).

Robinson, Gnana. *Siding with the Poor*. Madras, India: The Christian Literature Society, 1990.

Rogers, Everett M., and Floyd E. Shoemaker. *Communication of Innovations: A Cross-Cultural Approach*. Second edition. New York: The Free Press, 1971.

Sahoo, Basudeb. "India's Economic Crisis, New Dispensations and the Poor." *Social Action* 42, no. 1 (January 1992): 64-67.

Samuel, Vinay, and Chris Sugden, eds. *The Church in Response to Human Need*. Grand Rapids, Mich.: Eerdmans, 1987.

Sargunam, Ezra M. *Multiplying Churches in Modern India*. Madras, India: Federation of Evangelical Churches in India, 1974.

Schlier, Hienrich. *Principalities and Powers in the New Testament*. Edinburgh, London: Nelson, 1961.

Schmidt, William S. "Power as a Theological Problem." *The Journal of Pastoral Care* 46, no. 1 (1992): 71–77.

Sewell, John. "Foreword." In *Strengthening the Poor: What Have We Learned?* edited by John P. Lewis. New Brunswick, N.J.: Transaction Books, 1988.

Shenk, Wilbert R. "The Whole Is Greater Than the Sum of the Part: Moving Beyond the Word and Deed." *Missiology: An International Review* 20, no. 1 (1993): 65-75.

Sherman, Amy. *Preferential Option: A Christian and Neo-liberal Stategy for Latin America's Poor.* Grand Rapids, Mich.: Eerdmans, 1992.

Sider, Ronald J. "The Commitment." In *Lifestyle in the Eighties: An Evangelical Commitment to Simple Lifestyle,* edited by Ronald J. Sider. Exeter: The Paternoster Press, 1980.

———. "Jesus' Resurrection and the Search for Peace and Justice." *The Christian Century* 99, no. 34 (1982): 1103-8.

———. *Nonviolence: The Invincible Weapon?* Dallas, Tex.: Word Publishing, 1989.

———. *One Sided Christianity.* Grand Rapids, Mich.: Zondervan Publishing House, 1993.

———, ed. *Evangelicals and Development: Toward a Theology of Social Change.* Philadelphia: Westminster Press, 1981.

Sinclair, Maurice. "Development and Eschatology." In *The Church in Response to Human Need,* edited by Vinay Samuel and Christopher Sugden. Grand Rapids, Mich.: Eerdmans, 1987.

Sine, Tom. "Development: Its Secular Past and Its Uncertain Future." In *Evangelicals and Development: Toward a Theology of Social Change,* edited by Ronald J. Sider. Philadelphia: Westminster Press, 1981.

Singh, Manmohan. Quoted in *Los Angeles Times* 113, no. 92 (1984): 2.

Smith, Adam. *Select Chapters and Passages from 'The Wealth of Nations' of Adam Smith 1776.* New York: Macmillan. 1894.

Smith, Linda. *An Awakening of Conscience.* Washington, D.C.: American University, 1989.

Smith, Mont W. *What the Bible Says About Covenant.* Joplin, Mo.: College Press Publishing Co, 1981.

Stott, John. *The Lausanne Covenant: An Exposition and Commentary.* Minneapolis, Minn.: Worldwide Publications, 1975.

———. *The Cross of Christ.* Downers Grove, Ill.: InterVarsity Press, 1986.

Stott, John, and Robert T. Coote. "Willowbank Report." In *Gospel and Culture.* Wheaton, Ill.: Lausanne Committee for World Evangelization, 1978.

Study Encounter. "The Concept of Power in the Christian Tradition." *Study Encounter (SE/85)* 11, no. 3 (1975):1-15.

Sugden, Chris. *Radical Discipleship.* London: Marshall Morgan & Scott, 1981.

Tamez, Elsa. *Bible of the Oppressed.* Maryknoll, N.Y.: Orbis Books, 1982.

Tannehill, Robert C. *The Narrative Unity of Luke-Acts (A Literary Interpretation).* Volume 1. Philadelphia: Fortress Press, 1969.

Taylor, Richard W. Quote from a letter written by Stanley Jones to the *Guardian.* In *The Contribution of E. Stanley Jones.* Madras, India: Christian Literature Society, 1973.

Toffler, Alvin. *Powershift: Knowledge, Wealth, and Violence at the Edge of the Twenty-first Century.* New York: Bantam Books, 1990.

Tracy, David. *Blessed Rage for Order: The New Pluralism in Theology.* San Francisco: Harper & Row, 1988.

Transformation. "Words, Works and Wonders: The Power and Justice of the Kingdom of God." *Transformation* 5, no. 4 (1988): 1, 2.

_____. "The Oxford Declaration on Christian Faith and Economics." *Transformation* 7, no. 2 (1990): 2.

Van Engen, Charles. "The New Covenant." In *The Word Among Us: Contextualising Theology for Mission Today*, edited by Dean Gilliland. Dallas, Tex.: Word Publishing, 1989.

_____. "A Broadening Vision: Forty Years of Evangelical Theology of Mission, 1946-1986." In *Earthen Vessels: American Evangelical and Foreign Mission 1880-1980*, edited by Joel Carpenter and Wilbert R. Shenk. Grand Rapids, Mich.: Eerdmans, 1990.

_____. *God's Missionary People: Rethinking the Purpose of the Local Church.* Grand Rapids, Mich.: Baker Book House, 1991.

Van Engen, Charles, Dean S. Glliland, and Paul E. Pierson, eds. *The Good News of the Kingdom: Mission Theology for the Third Millennium.* Maryknoll, N.Y.: Orbis Books, 1993.

Verkuyl, Johannes. "The Kingdom of God as the Goal of Missio Dei." *International Review of Missions* 68, no. 270 (1979): 168-75.

Volf, Miroslav. "Doing and Interpreting: an Examination of the Relationship Between Theory and Practice in Latin American Liberation Theology." *Themelios* 8, no. 3 (1983).

_____. "Exclusion and Embrace: Theological Reflection in the Wake of 'Ethnic Cleansing.'" Unpublished manuscript. Fuller Theological Seminary, School of Theology, Pasadena, Calif., 1993.

Vyas, N. N. and S. N. Samadani. *Crossing the Poverty Line.* Udaipur: Himanshu Publications, 1987.

Wagner, C. Peter, and F. Douglas Pennoyer, eds. *Wrestling with Dark Angels: Toward a Deeper Understanding of the Supernatural Forces in Spiritual Warfare.* Ventura, Calif.: Regal Books, 1990.

Walsh, J. P. M. *The Mighty from Their Thrones: Power in the Biblical Traditions.* Philadelphia: Fortress Press, 1987.

Watson, Francis. "Christ, Community and the Critique of Ideology." *Netherlands Theologisch Tijdschrift* 46, no. 2 (1992):132–49.

Weber, Hans-Ruedi. *Power: Focus for a Biblical Theology.* Geneva: WCC Publications, 1989.

Webster, J. B. "Some Notes on the Theology of Power." *The Modern Churchman* 30, no. 1 (1988): 17-25.

Webster, John C. B. *The Dalit Christians: A History.* Delhi: I.S.P.C.K., 1992.

Welsh, Brian W. W., and Pavel Butorin. *Dictionary of Development: Third World Economy, Environment, Society.* New York: Garland Publishing, 1990.

West, Charles. "The Concept of Power in the Christian Traditions." *Study Encounter SE/85* 11, no. 4 (1975): 1-15.

Wilson, Dorothy Clarke. *Dr. Ida.* New York: McGraw Hill Book Company, 1959.

Wink, Walter. *Naming the Powers: The Language of Power in the New Testament.* Philadelphia: Fortress Press, 1984.

—————. *Unmasking the Powers: The Invisible Forces That Determine Human Existence.* Philadelphia: Fortress Press, 1986.

—————. *Engaging the Powers: Discernment and Resistance in a World of Domination.* Philadelphia: Fortress Press, 1992.

World Bank. *World Development.* Washington, D.C.: World Bank, 1978.

—————. *World Development.* Washington, D.C.: World Bank, 1980.

—————. *World Development.* Washington, D.C.: World Bank, 1985.

—————. *World Development.* Washington, D.C.: World Bank, 1989.

—————. *World Development.* Washington, D.C.: World Bank, 1991.

—————. *World Development.* Washington, D.C.: World Bank, 1992.

—————. *The World Bank News* 13, no. 17 (12 April 1994).

Wrong, Dennis H. *Power: Its Forms, Bases and Uses.* New York: Harper & Row, 1979.

Yoder, John Howard. *The Politics of Jesus.* Grand Rapids, Mich.: Eerdmans, 1972.

—————. "Power and the Powerless." *The Covenant Quarterly* 36, no. 4 (1978): 29-35.

Yukl, Gary A. *Leadership in Organizations.* Second edition. Englewood Cliffs, N.J.: Prentice-Hall, 1989.

World Vision

Other Titles from World Vision Publications

Walking With the Poor: Principles and Practices of Transformational Development by Bryant L. Myers.
The author says those who want to alleviate poverty need to walk with the poor, see their reality, and then look for solutions. He explores Christian views of poverty and looks at how it is experienced in different cultures. Draws on theological and biblical resources as well as secular development theory and practice to develop a theoretical framework for working alongside the poor. 288 pp. **$21.95**

Working With the Poor: New Insights and Learnings from Development Practitioners, Bryant L. Myers, editor.
Christian development practitioners explore how to express holistic transformational development. As they struggle to overcome the problem of dualism, they articulate a genuinely holistic approach to helping the poor. 192 pp. **$16.95**

Serving With the Urban Poor: Cases in Holistic Ministry,
Tetsunao Yamamori, Bryant L. Myers and Kenneth Luscombe, editors.
Case studies from around the world focus on the plight of the urban poor and show how they can come to know the hope of Christ and progress beyond their physical needs. 248 pp. **$16.95**

Serving With the Poor in Africa: Cases in Holistic Ministry,
Tetsunao Yamamori, Bryant L. Myers, Kwame Bediako and
Larry Reed, editors.
Holism in Africa means something different than it does in Latin America or elsewhere. The case studies presented here reveal the nature and complexities of effective Christian holistic ministry in various African contexts. 240 pp. **$15.95**

Toll Free in the U.S.: 1-800-777-7752

Direct: (626) 301-7720

Web: www.marcpublications.com

World Vision Publications • 800 W. Chestnut Ave. • Monrovia, CA • 91016

Ask for a complete publications catalog and free missions newsletter

---